WEAPONS OF DESPERATION

WEAPONS OF DESPERATION

German Frogmen and Midget Submarines
of the Second World War

Lawrence Paterson

Naval Institute Press
Annapolis, Maryland

This edition first published in Great Britain in 2006 by
Chatham Publishing
Lionel Leventhal Ltd,
Park House, 1 Russell Gardens,
London NW11 9NN

Published and distributed in the
United States of America and Canada by the
Naval Institute Press,
291 Wood Road, Annapolis,
Maryland 21402-5034

Library of Congress Control Number: 2006927630

ISBN 1-59114-453-1

This edition authorized for sale only in the United States of America, its territories and
possessions, and Canada

Printed and bound in Great Britain

Contents

Acknowledgements

As always this book could not have been written without the help, support and encouragement of many people. I would like to especially thank Sarah, Megz, James and Ernie of the Paterson Clan. Also special thanks to Audrey 'Mumbles' Paterson and Don 'Mr Mumbles', Ray and Phylly Paterson. My gratitude also goes to Graham 'Course I'm a Brummie' Jinks, Frank Bang, Gordon (Captain Ahab) Wadsworth, Rob Halford, Glen Tipton, Ken Downing, Ian Hill, Scott Travis, Lionel Leventhal, Rob Gardiner and all the staff at Chatham/ Greenhill, Maurice Laarman and his wonderful archive of information that he readily shared for this project, Dennis Feary and his inexhaustible supply of printed paper, Teduardo Savas, Chokehold, Jürgen Weber and the *U-Bootkameradschaft München*, Cozy Powell (RIP), Eddie Naughton, Mike, Sheila, Mitch and Claire French, Jo Lawler and Mike Hockin at the excellent Explosion! Museum of Naval Firepower, Gosport, and Maggie 'Mine's a Haggis' Bidmead and Martin 'Mine's a Sporran' Towell. Retrospectively I would also like to thank Bob Hackett and his co-authors of the excellent *http://www.combinedfleet.com/sensuikan.htm* website for their help with information regarding Japanese naval deployment and development.

From the ranks of the *Kriegsmarine* and Allied navies there are many veterans and their families that have helped with time and patience as I have tried to piece together this and other stories. Of the many people who have put up with my endless enquiries I would especially like to mention Norbert Keller, Helmut Deppmeier, Jürgen and Esther Oesten, Eugen Herold, Ludwig and Inge Stoll, Gerhard and Traudl Buske, Erich Schedler, Norman Ackroyd, Hans-Rudolf and Frau Rösing, Georg and Frau Högel, Georg and Frau Seitz, Hans-Joachim and Frau Krug, Gesa Suhren, Hanne Suhren, Herbert and

Frau Waldschmidt, Karl and Annie Waldeck, Hans-Peter and Frau Carlsen and Volkmaar König.

If there is anybody that I have not included in this list and should have, then please rest assured that it is an unintentional oversight and I hope that you will forgive me.

Glossary

Abwehr – German Military Intelligence Service.

BYMS – British Motor Minesweepers: US-built 'Yard' class Motor Minesweepers (YMS) in British service (B).

Chariot – British two-man 'human torpedo' with detachable explosive warhead.

FdS – *Führer der Schnellboote*; S-Boat commander.

FdU – *Führer der Unterseeboote*; regional U-boat commander.

Ing. – *Ingenieur*; Engineer (German). Inserted after rank, *eg Leutnant* (Ing.).

Kampfschwimmer – frogman (German).

KdK – *Kommando der Kleinkampfverbände*; German Small Battle Units Command.

Kriegsmarine – German Navy.

KvB – *Kleinkampfverbände*; German Small Battle Units.

LCG – Landing Craft Gun.

LCF – Landing Craft Flak.

LST – Landing Ship Tank.

MA – *Marine Artillerie*; German naval artillery.

MEK – *Marine Einsatz Kommando*; Marine Service Units, generally relating to frogmen.

MGB – Motor Gun Boat.

MMS – Motor Minesweeper.

MTB – Motor Torpedo Boat.

MTM – *Motoscafo da Turismo Modificato*; Italian one-man explosive motorboat.

OKM – *Oberkommando der Marine*; German Naval Command.

OKW – *Oberkommando der Wehrmacht*; German Military Forces Command.

RSHA – *Reichssicherheithaupamt*; the Reich Security Department.

S-Boat – *Schnellboot*; German motor torpedo boat.

SD – *Sicherheitdienst*; the SS Security Police.

SKL – *Seekriegsleitung*; Naval War Staff.

SLC – *Siluro a lenta corsa*; Italian 'Chariot'.

SMA – Italian two-man torpedo boats.

Stab – Staff (German).

TVA – *Torpedoversuchsansalt*; Torpedo Research Department.

Comparative Rank Table

German (Abbreviation)	British/American
Grossadmiral	Admiral of the Fleet/Fleet Admiral
Admiral	Admiral
Vizeadmiral (VA)	Vice Admiral
Konteradmiral (KA)	Rear Admiral
Kapitän zur See (Kapt.z.S.)	Captain
Fregattenkapitän (F.K.)	Commander
Korvettenkapitän (K.K.)	Commander
Kapitänleutnant (Kaptlt.)	Lieutenant Commander
Oberleutnant zur See (Oblt.z.S.)	Lieutenant
Leutnant zur See (L.z.S.)	Sub-Lieutenant/Lieutnant (jg)
Oberfähnrich	Senior Midshipman
Fähnrich	Midshipman
Stabsobersteuermann	Senior Quartermaster/ Warrant Quartermaster
Obermaschinist (Omasch)	Senior Machinist/Warrant Machinist
Bootsmann	Boatswain
Oberbootsmannsmaat	Boatswain's Mate
Bootsmannsmaat	Coxswain
-Maat (trade inserted as prefix)	Petty Officer
Maschinenobergefreiter	Leading Seaman Machinist
Funkobergefreiter	Leading Seaman Telegraphist
Matrosenobergefreiter	Leading Seaman
Maschinengefreiter	Able Seaman Machinist
Matrosengefreiter	Able Seaman

Introduction

The small glinting canopy could be clearly seen by the crew of the British ship that slowly approached. Inside, the hunched figure of a man was vaguely visible as his small craft floated on the Mediterranean swell. There was no movement from the curious craft or its occupant as it was caught and held with grappling hooks, pulled alongside the Royal Navy ship for boarding and examination. Eventually the fogged Plexiglas was separated from the craft's torpedo-like hull and the dead body of the Neger pilot removed from his cramped and cold tomb. The first of Germany's *Kleinkampfverbände* (Small Battle Units) had gone into action – the tragic corpse of this young German one of the results.

Germany's Small Battle Units combined an unusual plethora of formations and weapons, some of the latter well constructed and of superior design, others almost *ad hoc* in their creation. Inspired by Italian and British success in the use of small submersible weapons the *Kriegsmarine* was by comparison very late to develop them for their own use. Indeed they did not see action until April 1944 by which time German military fortunes were already waning dramatically. As we shall see, even the manner in which they were committed to combat differed enormously from the role assigned such units by other navies.

The *Kleinkampfverbände* provided an umbrella for operations involving human torpedoes, one and two-man midget submarines, explosive motorboats and frogman commandos. It was also the only German naval branch to include men from the Army, Navy and Waffen SS within its ranks.

Researching the story of the *Kleinkampfverbände* is a difficult task of assembling snippets of information from official documentation, personal recollections and dramatised 'true' stories by writers of naval history who opt to novelise their subject. This latter trait is by no means to be sneered at as it brings often dry statistical histories to life and allows readers to 'feel' more what the experience was like. However it can also drown the actual facts of the matter in a sea of romantic prose.

I have not dealt at length with the separate *Abwehr* and Waffen SS commando units that at times were almost composite parts of the *Kleinkampfverbände*. By focussing on the *Kriegsmarine*'s Small Battle Units I would hope to be able to achieve a greater focus than if the book were to study the myriad special forces available to the German military that embarked on maritime missions. Likewise I have not dwelt extensively on the machinery employed, least of all the many planned devices that were never built beyond the testing stage. These have been covered elsewhere in many excellent books – I thoroughly recommend Eberhard Rössler's *The U-Boat* for a detailed look at such equipment.

As always I perceive the story of the *K-Verbände* as not only a study of military tactics and rationale but also, more importantly, a story of predominantly young men caught in the maelstrom of war. I will never forget the emotion on the face of a Seehund coxswain during a meeting of the München *U-Bootkameradschaft* in December 2004. As the now aged man spoke to the assembled veterans he was expressing thanks that the Association of *Seehund Fahrer* had been officially recognised within the U-boat Veterans' organisation. The men of the *K-Verbände* – those that served in human torpedoes, explosive motorboats, midget submarines or as commando troops – deserve, in my view, greater recognition of their service. Courage is not measured by success necessarily, nor even by the national ideals that a flag may represent, but more by the individual's ability to perform his tasks under extreme pressure that, thankfully, most readers and I have not and will never experience.

On a more technical note I must inform the reader that I have used the original German terms for the names of the midget submarines and human torpedoes that follow. However, I have *not* used the correct German spelling for plurals of their correct names, instead I have used an 'Anglo-German' combination. Therefore, in the interest of clarity, I have included this brief description of the singular and plural below:

Singular	*Plural*
Neger	Negers (correct German plural – Neger)
Marder	Marders (correct German plural – Marder)
Biber	Bibers (correct German plural – Biber)

Molch	Molchs (correct German plural – Molche)
Hecht	Hechts (correct German plural – Hechte)
Seehund	Seehunds (correct German plural – Seehunde)
Linsen	Linsens (correct German plural – Linsen)

CHAPTER ONE

The Ideal Defence
German development of the
Small Battle Unit concept

The *Kriegsmarine* was a late starter in the concept of small naval battle
units. The idea of highly mobile self-contained strike forces was almost
as old as naval history itself, but during the Second World War its
potential was dramatically demonstrated on the night of 18 December
1941. During that calm and humid evening in Alexandria harbour,
three Italian SLCs (*Siluro a lenta corsa*, or, 'slow running torpedo') had
penetrated the British defensive harbour screen after launching from
the submarine *Scire*. The SLCs (known as *Maiali* or 'Pigs' to their
pilots) were the first operational 'human torpedo', each carrying two
frogmen riders and armed with a detachable nosecone containing
300kg of high explosive. Two of the three vehicles reached their targets
whereupon the four frogmen silently detached the explosive charges
and fixed them to the keels of the battleships HMS *Queen Elizabeth*
(with Admiral Cunningham aboard) and *Valiant*.

As they attempted to escape, all six frogmen were captured, the
group's commanding officer, Count Luigi de la Pene, and his co-pilot
taken for interrogation aboard *Valiant* as the fuses slowly burned
below them. Divulging no information, the two Italians were impris-
oned deep in the bowels of the battleship until de la Pene judged that
enough time had passed to prevent British interference with the
charges and notified Captain Morgan that within five minutes, his ship
would be sunk. The prisoners were taken from their cells and were on
deck when violent explosions shook the two capital ships. Badly holed
they both settled into the silt of Alexandria harbour.

Fortunately for the Royal Navy, the ships had developed no list and
with a visible show of 'business as usual' aboard, still appeared to be
active. With all six raiders captured, the Italian Navy remained igno-
rant of their sudden dominance in serviceable naval power within the
Mediterranean. It had only been five days since HMS *Ark Royal* had

1

been torpedoed and sunk by *U-81* and within a week HMS *Barham* would also fall prey to *U-331*. Coupled with the Italian success, there remained little by way of major surface units available to the Royal Navy. However, by the time the Italians grasped that success had been achieved, the opportunity to capitalise on it had passed.

The Italian *Decima Mas* (10th MTB Flotilla – M.A.S. an abbreviation for *Motoscafi Armati Siluranti* – *Motoscafi Anti Sommergibili*) were the sole perpetrators of Axis small battle unit operations within the Mediterranean between August 1940 and the Italian armistice in September 1943. Commanded by Prince Junio Valerio Borghese, the flotilla comprised units of SLCs, frogmen, explosive motorboats and midget submarines with which they mounted audacious and frequently successful commando raids against the British.[1]

Although the SLC was not the only weapon in Italy's midget arsenal, explosive motor boats also having already made their presence felt with successful attacks on British warships, it was the human torpedo that particularly captured imaginations elsewhere. Originally envisaged by the Italians for use in clandestine attacks on enemy harbours such as Alexandria, Valetta and Gibraltar, five planned operations had already failed before de la Pene's success. However, the Royal Navy were suitably impressed and formed their own group – the Under Water Working Party (UWWP) – to study the idea. In less than a year their own version of the SLC, named the 'Chariot' by the British, was in service and plans were made to attack the German battleship *Tirpitz* in Trondheimsfjord, Norway. Eventually, this operation failed as the two Chariots towed by trawler to within range of the German behemoth broke free from their host and sank before they could be deployed. However, elsewhere in Palermo and Tripoli, Italian and German shipping respectively were successfully attacked and sunk. With the capture of the 'Charioteers' their *modus operandi* was revealed to the Germans, Admiral Dönitz paying particular attention to their use. The success of the Chariots, combined with other British commando raids in North Africa and Europe, including the successful attack on Saint Nazaire in March 1942, led him to desire his own naval commando force, as related in his memoirs:

> I expressed the wish that (in February 1943) *Konteradmiral* Heye should be released from his present duties and placed at my disposal. I wanted him to become, as I put it, 'the Mountbatten of the German Navy'. In the British Navy Admiral Lord Louis Mountbatten had under him the commandos and the units and means for the execution of smaller,

individual naval enterprises. Hitherto no such forces or means had existed in the German Navy. Among them were frogmen, as they were called . . . the midget submarines, the one-man torpedoes, explosive motorboats and similar weapons, which, given the chance, could often at small cost in men and material score very considerable successes.

Thus the *Kleinkampfverbände* (*K-Verbände*) were born, although it would be a year before they were committed to action, by which time Germany had been firmly pushed onto the defensive.

To benefit from Japanese experience in the field of midget naval weaponry, staff at OKM asked for details of the Japanese two-man midget submarine, the *Ko-Hyoteki*, instructing the German Naval Attaché in Tokyo, *Konteradmiral* Wenneker, to obtain the necessary information. On 3 April Wenneker in company with the Italian Naval Attaché were allowed to visit Kure where they inspected a Type A *Ko-Hyoteki*. This type had been involved in raids on Pearl Harbor, later also attacking Sydney Harbour and Diego Suarez. Wenneker went to the meeting armed with forty-eight questions to which OKM desired responses, though many ultimately remained unanswered as the Japanese military, like that of Nazi Germany, guarded their technological secrets somewhat jealously. Wenneker reported his findings to Berlin, though nothing came of his despatch until much later in the year.

In actuality the original theoretical concept of the *K-Verbände* was more akin to the British Commando service than the naval organisation it became. Though the Germans were in the ideal position to learn from the experiences of their two major allies, Italy and Japan, in their use of midget weapons, they failed to fully capitalise on this. A genuine commando service equipped with midgets would have been presented with a plethora of targets against British anchorages in the early years of the war. Indeed, if Günther Prien could sneak a Type VIIB U-boat into Scapa Flow, then one wonders what a carefully planned midget attack along the lines of the subsequent British assault on the *Tirpitz* could have achieved.

The Germans' first operational unit was named *Einsatz-Abteilung Heiligenhafen* under the command of a resourceful and imaginative *Kriegsmarine* officer, K.K. Hans Bartels. Bartels – former commander of the minesweeper *M1* and chief of the *Vorpostenflottille* (Patrol Boat Flotillas) for Norway immediately after the country's capitulation – was already a popular and famous member of the *Wehrmacht*. In 1941 he authored a book (or at least was attributed one written by a propaganda ministry representative) titled '*Tigerflagge heiss vor*' that followed his Norwegian experience from the year before where he had won the Knight's Cross. During the 1940 invasion of Scandinavia Bartels had captured a Norwegian destroyer and an entire torpedo boat flotilla. He later designed his own minesweeper, ordering eleven to be built and then asking *Grossadmiral* Raeder to pay for them – an act that led to his transfer to the destroyer *Z34* where he was encouraged to reacquaint himself with correct naval protocol.

After his destroyer service he was transferred back to Norway where, through a combination of resourcefulness, imagination and ingenuity, he had constructed a powerful coastal defence system in a matter of months. During this period he had worked on the idea of stretching his meagre resources by using midget submarines, developing plans for prototype models. During 1942 he had submitted a memorandum on the subject, stating that Germany would probably require large numbers of such midget weapons to protect the thousands of miles of coastline that the Reich occupied. His 'early warnings' remained unheeded until Dönitz appointed *Konteradmiral* Heye to head the construction of the *K-Verbände*.

By early 1943 Bartels had been promoted to *Korvettenkapitän* and threw himself wholeheartedly into the task of creating a 'special forces unit'. The unit originally comprised two companies, Bartels heading one and the other commanded by another unusual officer, *Kapitänleutnant der Reserve* Michael Opladen a member of the *Abwehr* – the German military intelligence service. The *Abwehr* had come into being in 1921 and by 1943 it had developed into a large intelligence organisation with three distinct groups: Abteilung I, concerned with espionage and the collection of intelligence; Abteilung II, controlling special units and sabotage missions; and Abteilung III dealing with counter-espionage. Each of these sections had Army, Navy and Air-Force sub-sections and it was the Naval section of Abteilung II that would hold such relevance to the development of Heye's *K-Verbände* and Heye regarded Opladen as 'especially suitable' alongside Bartels.[2]

Bartels' and Opladen's combined unit that comprised both army and navy men never really progressed past the stage of early training, its envisioned role of commando raids along the English coast and within the Mediterranean soon dissipating as Germany's military star waned. Nevertheless, Bartels held an almost unlimited power to seek out and commandeer men for the unit, primarily those with foreign language skills. Opladen on the other hand brought his *Abwehr* knowledge and contacts into the mix, also acting as military instructor of the recruits, teaching them the methods employed by British Commandos.

Under the umbrella of *Marineoberkommando Ost*, Bartels' *Einsatz-Abteilung Heiligenhafen* continued its embryonic training until shortly being dissolved upon the expansion of Dönitz's vision of the *K-Verbände* and entrance into the story of Bartels' new commander. This man was Knight's Cross holder Hellmuth Heye, a career naval officer, though one who appears not to have been so steeped in tradition that he was prevented from seeing the value of small battle units.

> The war situation in the winter of 1943/44 compelled us to go on the defensive. I already held the view that there were better operational prospects for numbers of small ships and weapons than for large units. Moreover, there had been differences of opinion between the German Admiralty and myself as to the conduct of the war at sea.[3]

Graduated from the Class of 1914 (VIII), amongst his more recent posts he had commanded the heavy cruiser *Admiral Hipper* and held senior staff positions including that of Admiral Commanding the Black Sea region. In February 1943 when Dönitz's order arrived, he was Chief of Staff to *Marinegruppenkommando Nord* and the *Flottenkommando* itself. It was for this reason that Dönitz's personnel chief persuaded him that Heye could not as yet be spared for the task of raising the small battle units. Instead *Vizeadmiral* Eberhard Weichold, who had had practical experience of working with the Italian admiralty as liaison officer, was at first entrusted to the task of raising the units. Aged fifty-three, Weichold was a veteran naval officer having graduated from the Class of 1911 and beginning 1939 as part of the Fleet Command Staff dealing with the question of warfare against merchant shipping.

His remit was quite broad: to develop and build small submersibles for single-use missions; to develop several different kinds of small torpedo carriers, including small boats modelled on the Italian explosive motorboat; to continue to train naval commandos along the lines of British troops, capable of attacking enemy harbours in hostile territory. Thus the initial concentration on ground-based commando operations had already widened considerably, the focus clearly moving to light naval units. However, Weichold appears to have stalled at the theoretical stage and he proved relatively ineffectual in actual unit development. Thus, after the loss of the *Scharnhorst* in an ill-conceived and badly executed operation in December 1943 Dönitz decided there was now little practical work for Heye to be occupied with and he was transferred to command the fledgling *K-Verbände*, the unit given this official designation on 20 April 1944.

While the theory of developing weapons for the use of the *K-Verbände*, particularly the latter submersible units, was rapidly growing in pace, fresh inspiration had struck in the form of crippling explosions beneath the keel of the battleship *Tirpitz* on 22 September 1943. There, six British X-Craft had attacked the sheltered anchorage that hosted Germany's largest remaining battleship. Two of the X-Craft had aborted *en route*; the remaining four slipped their tows from their larger submarine transports and carried on towards Altafjord where the *Tirpitz* lay. The first that the Germans knew of the attack on their capital ship was a little after 07.30hrs when *X7* was spotted outside the defensive torpedo netting after already having laid her charges. Swiftly realising the nature of the threat posed by the attacking midgets the *Tirpitz*'s captain ordered his crew to begin pulling in her starboard cable to swing the bows away from where he correctly guessed charges had been laid. However, although this did indeed lessen the impact of both charges left by *X6* and one of those from *X7* it did nothing to diminish blast from the last successfully laid charge from *X7* that rested directly beneath the ship's engine room. When it exploded it lifted the ship's stern nearly 6ft and caused 500 tons of water to enter the flooded compartment. The main engines were disabled and the after turrets put out of action, one man killed and forty wounded. It had been a surgically precise attack that rendered the giant battleship inoperative. However, none of the X-Craft survived the mission though several crewmen were captured. The success of the raid was a devastating blow to the *Kriegsmarine* in Norway. Ultimately it led to the ship's demise as it was moved from Altafjord to Tromsø Fjord for repairs. There she lay within British bomber range and thirty-two Lancaster bombers carrying massive Tallboy bombs attacked her on 12 November 1944. Three direct hits tore open her hull and caused the hulk to roll over into the dark water, taking 971 men to their deaths.

However, before these events, the *Kriegsmarine* devoted considerable energy to recovering the lost X-Craft beneath the damaged Tirpitz. They would soon form the design basis of the first German midget submarine – the Hecht. The idea of a midget submersible that was capable of carrying a large mine as payload had taken root in German military thinking. According to the author Cajus Bekker in his colourful account of *K-Verbände* operations published less than ten years after the war, on the night of 17 January 1944 Kaptlt. Opladen summoned two of the *K-Verbände*'s original volunteers from the 3rd *Schnellbootsflottille*,

Fähnrichen Pettke and Potthast (the apparently inseparable duo known as the 'two Ps' within the *K-Verbände*) to a heavily guarded hut on the coast of Lübeck Bay. There the two young officer candidates saw their first glimpse of their future as they studied the remains of the salvaged X-Craft, soon undergoing a series of trials, the key for German technicians to unlock the secrets to the successful midget submarine design.

However a second capture by the *Kriegsmarine* provided yet further inspiration for a fresh midget submarine design. The Royal Navy had developed the Welman – a single-pilot craft capable of deploying a 560lb charge against its target, but originally envisioned for the beach reconnaissance role. Crews for the Welman were generally drawn from No2 Commando Royal Marines (Special Boat Service) until Combined Operations commander General Sir Robin Laycock, who had taken over from Mountbatten, decided that the Welman was unsuitable for their purposes and returned the craft to the Royal Navy. Admiral Sir Lionel Wells, Flag Officer commanding Orkney and Shetlands, thought they might be useful for attacks on German shipping in Norway, and so men of the 30th MTB Flotilla, Royal Norwegian Navy, launched the first attack using four Welmans (*W45–W48*) on 21 November 1943 (Operation Barbara) against the floating dock at Bergen and shipping in the area. However, the mission was an abject failure, *W46* encountering a net and being forced to the surface, where she was spotted by a German patrol craft. Its pilot was captured along with his craft. Alerted by the capture, German defences foiled the remaining three Welmans that were eventually abandoned and scuttled, their pilots managing to evade capture and in due course return to the UK after being recovered by MTB.[4] The captured pilot survived the war in a prison camp and, as we shall see later, his Welman (*W46*) provided design inspiration for a new German midget – the Biber.

With the groundwork firmly in place for the formation of the *K-Verbände*, weaponry was a high priority by the end of 1943.

> It is hardly surprising that the formation from scratch of a new force and the establishment of entirely new weapons in the fifth year of war presented extraordinary difficulties. As speed was essential, there was no question of lengthy test and trials. At my suggestion the C-in-C gave me considerable powers which enabled me to short-circuit tedious bureaucratic procedure and to have direct contact with all departments of the Naval Staff and – especially important – with industrial concerns . . . Among industrialists I found much understanding and support, since the more far-sighted of them realised the futility of continuing the existing

programme of warship construction . . . Engineers and workmen alike showed great interest in the problems, and gave me the utmost help.[5]

As early as two years previously the development of small U-boats of between 70 and 120 tons displacement were being actively championed by Dr Heinrich Dräger of Lübeck's Dräger Werke. On 1 October 1941 he presented a memorandum putting forward a series of designs using closed-cycle diesel and more standardised diesel-electric drive units. His construction techniques were ambitious, stressing the inadequacies of accepted warship construction methods and opting instead for the mass-production-line approach used in armoured vehicle and aircraft manufacture. Thus hull elements could be produced and fitted together at a later date – presaging the eventual use of this technique by Type XXI U-boat builders in the closing stages of the war. With the small sized units easily transported by rail, road or waterway he envisioned their time-consuming interior work could be continued in any available areas safe from enemy air attack, independent of the highly specialised shipbuilding yards.

Indeed his schedule allowed 14 to 20 days for pressure hull 'cell' construction, 30 days for the interior fitting and a further 30 for the welding together of the hull cells into a finished submarine. However, at that stage of the war the sectional construction of U-boats – of whatever size – did not sit well with higher echelons of the *Kriegsmarine* and their shipbuilding advisers and the idea was shelved as unworkable. But Dräger was undeterred and continued to promote the development of small 23- to 25-ton U-boats that could be carried to an operational area by other vessels as well as a 100-ton vessel for surface attacks at night – a form of submersible MTB – and a 'torpedo-shaped' U-boat with high submerged speed. Ironically, designs for both vessels were already in test with the Walter U-boat and the Engelmann High-Speed boat, but neither proved successful.

Dräger's ideas were never allowed to bear fruit, Rudolf Blohm (Councillor of State) going so far as to officially reject his design on 22 January 1942, stating that it was considered inadequate:

for operational purposes because, carrying only two torpedoes, it has minimal armament and because in adverse weather conditions, heavy seas do not allow small vessels to be used adequately in operations.[6]

But within two years the nature of Germany's war had changed irrevocably and purely defensive weapons that could be quickly manufactured in the face of increasingly severe Allied bombing of industrial plants were desperately required. The midget submarine project was accelerated under the auspices of Heye's command; even Japanese advice was finally accepted from such experts as submarine specialist Lieutenant Commander Hideo Tomonaga, inventor of the automatic depth stabiliser. This in itself illustrated some of the fresh urgency attached to the idea of *K-Verbände* weaponry as more often than not, the exchange of military and industrial ideas between Japan and Germany, supposedly guaranteed by the Axis agreement, fell victim to inherent racial prejudices and were ignored.

Upon the dissolution of Bartels' and Opladen's units and their incorporation within Heye's command, Bartels began the construction of a midget submarine service as head of the training ground *Blaukoppel* in Lübeck, future training centre for Biber pilots. His prototype Biber (Beaver), named 'Adam', was first launched at the Flender shipyard in Lübeck – where it promptly sank. Undeterred, work continued on this and other models of midgets and human torpedoes. Opladen on the other hand at first was appointed F1 (General Operations Officer) to Heye at Timmendorfer Strand. His function was to develop operational plans for the new service, utilising his *Abwehr* background to the fullest though by July 1944 Kaptlt. Thomsen, an experienced *Schnellboot* and *Torpedoboot* officer, had replaced him due to lack of naval background and practical knowledge. Opladen was moved to a sphere of operations far more suited to his talents and from July he held a pseudo-intelligence position as foreign political advisor to Heye, monitoring all overseas developments likely to impact the *K-Verbände*.

Heye fostered a strict sense of camaraderie within the *K-Verbände* with little attention paid to the stiff formality of *Kriegsmarine* regulations and traditions. Rank badges were rarely worn and there was informality throughout the service that helped imbue it with a sense of belonging to an elite unit. The organisation grew rapidly, eventually becoming a labyrinthine structure containing many respected veterans of the *Kriegsmarine*. Immediately beneath Heye in the *K-Verbände* chain of command was Knight's Cross holder Fritz Frauenheim, an ex-U-boat captain and commander of La Spezia's 29th U-Flotilla.

Encouraged by the obvious energy and vision of Heye and Frauenheim's partnership, Dönitz also appointed several notable veterans of the U-boat and minesweeping services to the posts of Group commanders for the *K-Verbände*'s submersible units. Hans Bartels was cemented in his role as head of Lehrkommando 250 responsible for Biber training. Hermann Rasch, ex-commander of the successful

U-106, was placed in command of Seehund units in Lehrkommando 300 though later, in February 1945, superseded by one of the two most highly decorated members of the *Kriegsmarine*, F.K. Albrecht Brandi. Kaptlt. Heinz Franke, ex-*U-262*, commanded the Neger, Marder and Molch units as head of Lehrkommandos 350 and 400, later superseded in this post by Kaptlt. Horst Kessler, ex-commander of *U-985*. Specialists in different fields were recruited for the *K-Verbände*'s other units. *Schnellboot* veteran Kaptlt. Ulrich Kolbe was given charge of Lehrkommando 200 and its Linsen boats, ably supported by a former destroyer and torpedo boat officer, Kaptlt. Helmut Bastian.

These veterans would provide the experience and also a sense of legitimacy to the fledgling service, though ultimately it had been decided that the U-boat arm could not spare men for the ranks of the *K-Verbände*. Instead recruits were to be drawn from volunteers originating from all branches of the *Wehrmacht* and Waffen SS. Eventually, as we shall see, events meant that the embargo placed on recruiting U-boat men was relaxed at the end of 1944. However, there remained rules that would not allow U-boat commanders to volunteer as *K-Verbände* pilots or crew.

There could be seen to be three distinct branches of the *K-Verbände*. The first would comprise explosive surface craft and assault boats of a type already operated by the Italian *Decima Mas* in the Mediterranean. The second group were *Kampfschwimmer* – frogmen capable of raiding enemy harbours and ships. This style of warfare had already been developed for use in the Second World War by the *Abwehr*, though with little success thus far. The last branch comprised the actual human torpedoes and midget submarines capable of delivering either a mine or G7e torpedo warhead into action against the enemy.

It was an engineer at the *Torpedoversuchsansalt* (TVA; Torpedo Research Department) in Eckernförde that eventually put forward the first design that suited requirements and conformed to the necessary rapid construction speed. Naval Construction Advisor Richard Mohr expounded his idea during a discussion headed by the TVA commanding officer KA Rudolf Junker on 21 December 1943. The theory was simple. A single G7e electric torpedo was to have its warhead removed and rudimentary controls fitted in a compartment barely able to fit a single pilot. Then another active torpedo was to be slung beneath the carrier, sailed to striking range and released. The carrier would approach enemy targets, line up his shot using this most basic of sighting mechanisms and release the underslung torpedo by pulling a small switch lever, which would finish the job. Once deployed, the

10

pilot could return to friendly shores where the carrier was scuttled. A single-shot weapon of very little cost and development time, its possibilities if used in large numbers against massed shipping seemed enormous and Mohr was encouraged to enthusiastically develop his proposal. In fact as Dönitz correctly summed the matter up: 'We require four years to complete a battleship . . . but only four days to prepare ten one-man torpedoes.'[7]

On 18 January 1944, Hitler approved the construction of fifty midget submarines of both mine-carrying and torpedo carrying capabilities and also the one-man torpedo designed by Mohr, which the minutes of the meeting between Dönitz and Hitler noted were 'to be used particularly as a defence weapon in case of enemy landings' due to its rather basic construction. It was indeed a rudimentary device, capable of only a modest 4 knots under power from the AEG electric motor and its 110-volt battery. Displacing 2.7 tons of water, the weapon would be capable of a range of 30 nautical miles.

Trials began at the TVA in Eckernförde under the watchful eye of Mohr and his small construction team as well as *K-Verbände* Chief of Staff Frauenheim. Oblt.z.S. Johann Otto Krieg, ex commander of *U-81*, was purloined from his post by Dönitz to undertake the testing of the first prototype despite the ban on U-boat commanders entering the *K-Verbände*. *U-81* had famously sunk HMS *Ark Royal* in 1941 while Krieg had been first officer to Oblt.z.S. Fritz Guggenberger. However, after Guggenberger's departure and Krieg's succession to captain, the veteran Type VIIC had been sunk by Allied bombing in Pola on 4 January 1944. Thus Krieg was a free agent by Dönitz's standards and on the eve of his planned marriage he was summoned by the *Grossadmiral* to Berlin and personally charged to immediately begin trials. Joining him were the two *Fähnrichen* Pettke and Potthast. The three men threw themselves eagerly into the task ahead, Krieg becoming in the process the first commander of the *K-Verbände*'s inaugural unit: 361 K-Flotilla.

The first formative barracks for the *K-Verbände* were established at Timmendorferstrand in Lübeck Bay, nestled within a spruce forest on the banks of the River Trave. The various bases that were to follow for the use of the *K-Verbände* over subsequent months were all codenamed with the suffix '*koppel*', meaning paddock or enclosure. Thus Timmendorferstrand, the headquarters of the *K-Verbände* became known as *Strandkoppel*.

It was also at this stage that the first formative MEKs (Marine-Einsatz-Kommandos, or, Special Naval Commandos) were also formed, each comprising an officer and twenty-two men, fifteen vehicles, trailers and equipment. The absorption of *Abwehr* men and units had provided this already established organisational level for the *K-Verbände* to utilise. Command of MEK60 was given to Lt Prinzhorn, MEK65 to Lt Richert and MEK71 to Lt Walters. They would become cadres for units that undertook some of the *K-Verbände*'s most difficult operations.

The human torpedo trials meanwhile had rapidly gathered pace and it was during this intensive period of testing that the one-man torpedo received its new name of Neger – literally 'nigger' and meant as a play on the inventor's name Mohr, which in turn literally meant 'Moor' (of Moorish origin). The weapon was simple; a manned torpedo with a simple joystick control. Using this the torpedo could be steered to port or starboard and have the inclination altered slightly, greater manoeuvrability afforded by extended control surfaces operated by simple external pull rods in place of the standard G7e stern fins. This would be the 'carrier weapon' and 7cm beneath it was slung another G7e electric torpedo with its 279kg warhead. Initially Krieg took the first Neger into the cold Baltic waters without any shielding dome, merely a rubberised canvas 'spray skirt' protecting him from the harsh sea and wind. This was swiftly found to be bordering on impossible and a Plexiglas dome – in fact a nose gunner dome from the Dornier aircraft factory in Friedrichshafen – was fitted. As well as protecting the pilot, along the bottom of the canopy were graduated marks with which the pilot aligned a short rod welded to the nose of his carrier torpedo to provide a rough aiming device. However, the Plexiglas in turn proved problematic for the pilot's air supply. Tests were carried out with the three pioneer pilots that showed that the available air inside the torpedo would allow seven hours at 4 knots before the pilot risked suffocation. Though this was possible, and certainly allowed trials to continue, it would be awkward in operational circumstances and potentially lethal to the pilot.

While the intensive trials continued, the first batch of forty volunteer pilots (including the two Ps) was assembling at Eckernförde (*Blaukoppel*). Drawn from all branches of the *Wehrmacht* and the Waffen SS they had already undergone gruelling commando-style training at Heiligenhafen (eastern Kiel Bay) under the command of Kaptlt. (*Sonderführer*) Michael Opladen. However, though the volunteers were physically fit and willing to join the new service, they possessed little, if any, seamanship skills. Again Opladen took charge of their instruction in basic navigation and torpedo shooting. With Krieg's initial trials completed and the rudimentary method of

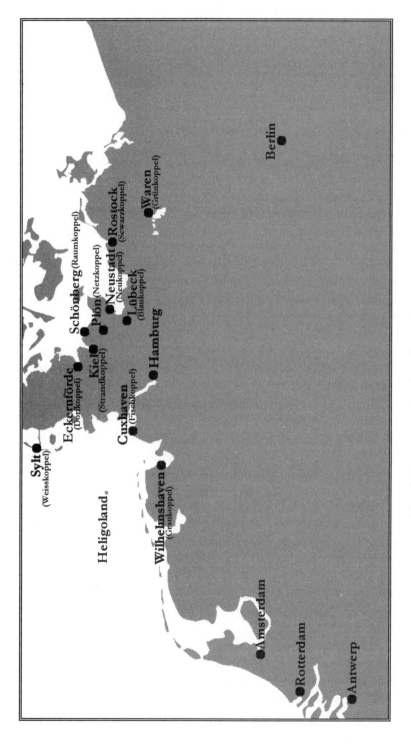

North German K-Verbände Training Centres

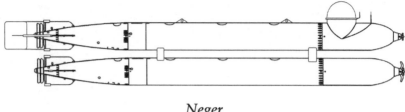

Neger

operation for the Negers fully understood by Krieg and the two mid-shipmen, the time swiftly arrived for the prospective pilots to also begin their hands-on training.

As soon as they had mastered the basics, Krieg swiftly moved them on to night operations, in which conditions they would eventually go into action. The training was not without its price. At least one man was killed when the live torpedo failed to disengage from the carrier during a practice attack on a moored ship. Unable to release the canopy from the inside the pilot was helpless as his speeding vessel grated along the ship's keel, killing him instantly.

As the training had progressed Mohr finally managed to find suitable breathing apparatus for the young pilots. Once again Mohr's team had looked to the aircraft industry and equipped Krieg with potash cartridges and breathing equipment borrowed from *Luftwaffe* fighter pilots. Though battery storage space had to be sacrificed in order to fit the equipment, it was a necessary compromise.

As the pilots increased in confidence and skill, there still remained one problem. The Neger was unable to dive and the Plexiglas dome remained above water all the time, moonlight reflecting on the shiny surface and potentially betraying the attacker. A brief attempt at fitting a diving cell that could be flooded and allow the Neger to submerge was initially unsuccessful. Not only did it and the accompanying com-pressed air tank required to blow the cell free of water take valuable battery storage room, but also the trim was impossible to maintain resulting in the torpedo burying itself nose first into the seabed. It was a persistent problem that for the moment seemed insoluble.

Three weeks had passed since Krieg had received his orders from Dönitz, by which time the Negers were ready for action. Heye visited the men of the pioneering flotilla and confirmed their readiness for action as they had been requested for urgent service. Allied troops had been inching northward along the Italian peninsula after landing on the mainland during September 1943, though their progress was slow and painful in the face of a skilful defence from *Feldmarschal* Albert

Kesselring. General Mark Clark, in overall command of the US Fifth Army, opted for a fresh assault behind the formidable defences of the Gustav Line which Kesselring's men held with such tenacity.[8] Clark reasoned that a fresh beachhead would force the German defenders to withdraw from their defensive positions and could even directly threaten Rome. Thus the attempt to bypass the Gustav Line led to another amphibious landing, this one made by the Allied VI Corps under Major General John Lucas just south of Rome at Anzio in January 1944. However, once again Kesselring managed to contain the enemy threat after Lucas hesitated at pushing his troops immediately off the beaches and towards an undefended Rome. During the six days of inactivity that followed the landing Kesselring rushed whatever forces he could throw together into the area, quickly managing to establish a virtual ring of steel around the Allied beachhead. The 1. *Fallschirmjäger Korps*, comprised of cadres from the 3. Panzer Grenadier Division and the 'Hermann Göring' Panzer Division, moved rapidly into position, gradually being joined by other formations drawn away from the already stagnant front to the south. When the Allies eventually moved they were repulsed and forced into what transpired to be four months of grinding bloody stalemate.

As Kesselring hammered Anzio with the heaviest firepower he could muster, the *Luftwaffe* began the first of several successful attacks with Henschel guided missiles against Allied shipping. In turn, Dönitz was determined to assist the effort at sea. The safety of their sea borne supply route to the Anzio beachhead was one of the main concerns of Allied planners. Beginning on 28 January, six Landing Ships Tank had begun to leave Naples each day. Their cargo totalled 1,500 tons of vital supplies distributed among fifty preloaded trucks. Once at the Anzio beachhead the trucks were driven off the huge transports and moved directly to front-line positions with ammunition, fuel, and rations for the Allied troops. These in turn were replaced aboard the LSTs by the fifty trucks that had made the voyage the previous day. Additionally, fifteen smaller vessels arrived each week, and every ten days four massive Liberty ships delivered heavier equipment. This was the potential Achilles Heel to the Allied invasion force, an artery that Dönitz hoped to sever. Traditional U-boats were proved largely ineffectual against the invasion fleet that was effectively shielded by prowling destroyers. It was the turn of the specialists – the *K-Verbände* was going into action.

CHAPTER TWO

Baptism of Fire
Anzio

Heye's visit on 16 March provided the stamp of approval for the 361 K-Flotilla to become operational. Accompanying Heye on his tour of inspection were *Marinestabsarzt* Professor Dr Orzechowski (Pharmacist for the *Marinekommando Ostsee*) and *Marinestabsarzt* Dr Arnim Wandel (Medical officer of the *Marine Einsatzabteilung Heiligenhafen*). Wandel had been present during the training of the Neger pilots, able to become fully acquainted with the stresses and demands made upon the young men.[9] The two medical officers were also on hand during Heye's visit to solve the potentially unique problems caused by long hours of solitary confinement within the cramped craft during operational use.

Their answer was the provision to the human torpedo service of a drug cocktail called DIX, tablets that were considered free of serious and adverse side effects but which would provide chemical stimulus to the men. It comprised 5mg of Eukodal, a narcotic similar to morphine and codeine, with the known adverse effects of euphoria and dysphoria, 5mg of Cocaine 5 and 3mg of Pervitin, a methamphetamine known now to cause euphoria, dysphoria, severe social disabilities, personality changes and psychosis. Five hundred tablets of DIX – containing three highly addictive substances – were provided to the human torpedo branch of the *K-Verbände*. After more extensive use it was found that following any heavy physical activity the recipient experienced euphoria, but after approximately one to three days extreme exhaustion would occur.[10]

The Negers received last-minute trim adjustment to compensate for the difference between Baltic and Tyrrhenian Sea's specific gravity of seawater. The variation in salinity would cause the Neger to either ride high or sink: in the case of the Tyrrhenian Sea there was a higher level of salinity that would cause the Neger to rise above the surface. A single machine was placed in a tank at Eckernförde to which was added store-bought salt until a rough match was considered to have been reached. The satisfactory adjustment to its trim was then undertaken on all the unit's other machines by the addition of small internal ballast weights.

By 6 April 1944, Krieg's men (designated MEK175 for this operation) were entrained along with their forty Negers concealed under heavy canvas, bound for Rigano Sull'Arno 20km southeast of Florence on the Arno River.[11] From there onwards the rail system was unworkable as a result of Allied bombing and Italian partisan operations so the roads were the only other option. After unloading in the small town there was a delay of ten days of chafing inactivity as suitable heavy vehicles and trailers were procured, the torpedoes eventually transferred for the remainder of their journey to trailers drawn by Sdkfz 9 heavy artillery tractors. On the night of 13 April Krieg's unit had arrived at their destination, concealed in a pine forest south of Rome at the small village of Pratica di Mare southwest of Pomezia and midway between the ancient Roman port of Ostia Antica and the busy fishing harbour at Anzio. Only 5km from the front line, the forest fringed a small road that led to the low scrubby coastline that was some 33km from the Allied invasion support fleet massed at Nettuno. Three of Krieg's valuable Negers had slipped from their transports and been destroyed in transit, though there still remained a formidable strike force of thirty-seven machines.

Immediately Krieg and his officers set about reconnoitring the nearby coastline for a suitable launching spot. However, this too proved to be problematic. Not only were there no suitable harbours which could be used but also the seabed off the Italian coastline generally sloped very gradually, meaning that the Negers would need to be manhandled dozens of metres offshore before there was any hope of them having sufficient depth to float free. The arduous task of launching the weapons was already a logistical nightmare for Krieg; 500 *Fallschirmjäger* of a nearby training unit soon to be attached to 4. *Fallschirmjäger* Division, would be pressed into service, providing the necessary manpower required for the task of manhandling the 5-ton Negers.

Eventually Krieg and his men decided that the coastline near Torvaianica would indeed allow a successful launch. Literally at the end of the road leading from Pratica di Mare itself to the sea, the deserted resort area of Torvaianica, which had in happier times hosted wealthy Romans during their summer holidays, now lay abandoned as the tide of war ebbed toward it. The Italian coastline that runs from Ostia to Capo d'Anzio is a sweeping expanse of gradually sloping sand, the beach itself slowly rising to low sand dunes topped with sporadic patches of often-dense scrub thickets. However, despite the slight incline above the sea, once in the water the seabed at Torvaianica shelved rapidly enough to allow room beneath the weapons at a range of only 30m from the shore. With at least 18 nautical miles from there to the Allied anchorage at Nettuno, the Neger's maximum range of 48 miles allowed distance in hand in which to manoeuvre for attack before needing to break away and head for the nearest German-held coastline. There the pilot would scuttle his carrier torpedo and abandon it before coming ashore.

The co-ordination of the attack was determined by *Kapitän zur See* Paul Friedrich Düwel, released from his position on Admiral Staff for *Nordmeer* and acting as *Einsatzleiter für 1-Mann Torpedos Nettuno*, giving the necessary rank and credentials for the groundbreaking operation. The role of the *Einsatzleiter* (director of operations) in *K-Verbände* operations was multi-faceted, responsible for: supervising mission preparation and providing support and encouragement for both flotilla commanders and crews; assisting in negotiations between the *K-Verbände* Flotilla commander and local army and air force units in regard to transport and supply requirements; liaising between Kdo-Stab and Flotilla Commander, particularly to supply the local commander with all relevant tactical information available and to exert 'a moderating influence on the very young and often inexperienced Flotilla Commander'.[12] Additionally, the *Einsatzleiter* exercised overall control of all operations in his area and could veto suggestions and plans made by flotilla commanders. Needless to say this required great strength of character and a forceful personality to accomplish these roles, often placing the *Einsatzleiter* on the 'outside' of the younger flotilla officers, who correspondingly often – though not always – held a certain degree of antipathy toward their older and more reticent seniors.

Between them Düwel and Krieg decided to mount the attack on the night of 20/21 April in the period of the new moon, the total darkness allowing complete stealth to be used by the attacking human torpedoes. In addition, the *Abwehr*'s Brandenburg commando unit planned to mount raids off the Pontine Islands using two units of its newly developed explosive motorboats. Thus there were still several days for the *K-Verbände* men to ready themselves for their impending mission, the distant sound of artillery fire from the front lines a reminder of the perils that awaited them. They moved under cover of darkness from the shelter of their pine forest to the abandoned holiday houses that actually fringed the beginning of the dunes. There the Germans found accommodation for both themselves and their torpedoes, the latter still covered with their heavy canvas shrouds.

Krieg's plan called for the thirty-seven machines to form into three attacking groups. Oblt.z.S. Leopold Koch, an ex-U-boat man and holder of the Iron Cross First Class, would lead the first. The 25-year-old Koch had served as First Watch Officer aboard *U-97* before commanding the Type VIICs *U-258* and *U-382*, handing over command of the latter in November 1943 and subsequently transferring to the fledgling *K-Verbände*.[13] Koch would lead his group of Negers around the Capo d'Anzio and into Nettuno Bay in search of targets. The second group – and largest of the three – led by L.z.S. Seibicke would harry whatever shipping could be found offshore in the Anzio roadstead while *Oberfähnrich* Karl-Heinz Potthast would take five Negers to hunt in Anzio harbour itself.

Reports were continuously updated by local *Wehrmacht* outposts as to the coming and going of Allied shipping to the Anzio beachhead and it was established that there were usually at least four freighters in harbour unloading troops and ammunition. Arrangements were made with army units holding the seaward flank of the German line to ignite a large bonfire in order to provide a reference point for the returning Negers as to the whereabouts of safe landfall – the battle at Anzio unpredictable in its position of the actual front line and the coastline virtually featureless from the sea. Also, a flak unit was ordered to fire starshells toward Nettuno every twenty minutes to illuminate possible targets for the attackers. Though the range would actually prove too great to achieve this purpose, the artillery fire provided a handy directional indicator for the Neger pilots.

As luck would have it, early on the morning of 20 April an Allied convoy was sighted approaching the beachhead and as dusk fell Krieg began his operation, though the Brandenburger's explosive motorboat sortie was cancelled at the last moment by the *Kriegsmarine* regional staff due to the small number of available boats and their crews' inexperience. The press-ganged paratroopers were assembled and the heavy Negers on their two-wheeled launching chariots prepared for sea. The pilots climbed into the tiny cockpits, their domes bolted into place and the basic handling controls tested ready for action. Each Neger was then manhandled to the water's edge down one of six pre-laid runways made of coconut matting stiffened with hemp and wire. There the sweating paratroopers eased them into the sea.

The problems began almost immediately. Though the thick matting prevented the wheels bogging down in the sand, they stopped not far below the tidemark and there several of the unwieldy burdens sank axle deep into the sand, the soldiers unable to move the Negers far enough off the beach so that the weight of the torpedoes dragged them headlong into deeper water. Attempts to move some of those that had become stranded failed and several were tipped on their side in an effort to free them from the quagmire. However, once the 5-ton machine had rolled on its side it became hopelessly stuck in the glutinous sand, the pilot having to be freed and pulled out of his useless weapon. The carefully-laid matting began to become intertwined around straining axles as men tried to heave the Negers backwards and forwards into the sea and soon several were abandoned and lying uselessly in the lapping water where they were destroyed the next morning.

In the hours that followed fourteen Negers were abandoned at the launching point and later blown up, the remaining twenty-three heading quietly into the night and their first combat patrol. Each pilot was equipped with a small wrist compass though they proved of extremely limited use. Thus their crash-course in celestial navigation guided them slowly toward their target areas, the dome of the human torpedo too low in the water to remain in anything but extremely close contact with accompanying Negers or the distant coastline. By the time the Negers had reached their target areas dawn would be lightening the Italian sky – aiding navigation but rendering them vulnerable to detection. To add to the assault, during the night *Luftwaffe* aircraft made three separate antipersonnel attacks against Allied forces ashore, continued at dawn by low-level Focke Wulf Fw190 bombing raids, all designed to distract the enemy and wear down their vigilance by constant alarms.

The Neger's commitment to action was supposed to take the Allied navies by surprise, though this was not totally the case. Warnings that the Germans had been planning midget submarine attacks had come to the British from 'Dolphin' naval Enigma decrypts during December 1943. These decrypted Enigma messages had revealed that X-Craft lost in the attack on the battleship *Tirpitz* had been salvaged and workable German midget units developed. The threat having been identified, further *Kriegsmarine* and *Luftwaffe* Enigma decrypts gave good warning of the German human torpedo attacks on 20 April. Allied naval intelligence in Naples was alerted on that day to the fact that reports had been received of 'two-man torpedoes' having arrived at Fiumicino for commitment against Anzio shipping.[14] A special state of alert was ordered (codenamed 'Wideawake') and maximum patrolling levels reached, with sporadic depth charges dropped on the peripheries of the Allied naval cordon to dissuade any potential attackers.

USS *PC591* radioed the first contact reports with the *K-Verbände* while on 'H' patrol (the 'How' patrol line listed as running from a point bearing 267° at a range of 5.4 miles to one bearing 240° at 8.7 miles). The American craft had been at General Quarters due to the almost constant *Luftwaffe* presence and reported surface radar contact 9 miles northwest of the Anzio light, though no target was identified despite the expenditure of many star shells hunting for the intruder. A brief burst of 20mm fire was directed at a suspected enemy that then turned away inside the patrol craft's turning circle. To further confound Lieutenant J L Clark and his crew, a mysterious underwater explosion rocked *PC591* from dead astern at 03.07hrs. Though its cause remained unidentified it gave rise to speculation of a foiled torpedo attack. Clark spent the rest of the night chasing shadowy radar contacts that appeared to be constantly moving across his ship's line of travel, other stationary targets occasionally transpiring to be channel marker buoys. However, the alarm had been raised and immediate reinforcement of the Allied patrol lines was ordered as the German attack began to develop.

A definite sighting was finally reported at 07.25hrs when a lookout on *PC558*, engaged on 'P' patrol, sighted a 'circling torpedo on the surface' at a range of 3,000 yards, rapidly identified as a human torpedo with the Plexiglas dome and a portion of its tail visible. Gunfire from 40mm and 20mm cannon was brought to bear on the novel enemy, combined with two depth charges as the patrol craft roared past its target. Within twenty-five minutes after the first sighting the torpedo was sunk and an unharmed *Oberfähnrich* Walter Schulz rescued.

It wasn't long before *PC558* encountered the enemy again as the Neger attack gained momentum, another American patrol vessel, *PC626* joining *PC558* as the latter made contact with its second Neger. The two Americans made bold attacks with cannon fire and depth charges, several 20mm rounds being seen to enter the Plexiglas dome. Once again the Neger disappeared beneath the disturbed sea, its pilot emerging seconds later and plucked from the water. Hans Figel, who wore no distinguishing rank insignia (later listed in Allied intelligence reports as an 'Apprentice Shipwright') was exhausted and had to be lifted aboard the American ship, where he was cared for by the crew before being handed over to senior British officers.

Lieutenant E B Harvey's *PC626* continued to patrol, frequently dropping depth charges as 'Wideawake' remained in force throughout the night and following day. At 10.03hrs the American engaged another Neger, forcing it to the surface with depth charges and sinking it and its pilot with sustained gunfire. However, their next definite sighting of a Neger pilot was not until 07.00hrs on 23 April, two days after the attack, when another German was found floating in the water. Harvey's crew pulled Georg Hoff from the sea, though this time he was less fortunate than the other rescued Neger pilots, dead as he was lifted aboard. He was buried at sea and his personal effects later turned over to the authorities in Naples.

As Harvey had been attacking his second Neger, another American patrol craft made the last of the day's confirmed sinkings, the after action report painting a vivid picture of the confused melee off Anzio.

At 0945 . . . uss *SC651* received radio instructions from Lt. Nocco, the Escort Sweeper representative aboard *LST358*, to proceed immediately to the assistance of the *PC558* who had just sunk a midget submarine or human torpedo five miles northwest of Cape d'Anzio light in position 41° 30'N and 12° 30' 30" E.

Just after passing Cape d'Anzio abeam the lookout spotted a round object in the water on our starboard bow, distance 4,000 yards.

At first glance this object had no resemblance to a submarine or torpedo, but we went to general quarters to be prepared and also to get the men topside because we were leaving the swept channel and entering a suspected minefield . . . After closing to 2,000 yards we could discern a wake trailing out behind this dome shaped

object and a rudder above the surface about 15 feet aft of the dome
. . . At this point he was about 4,000 yards from the anchorage and
was heading directly for a cluster of two Liberty ships and a hospital ship in the anchorage area.

We altered course to bring the object on our bow to clear any
possible stern tube (we were then under the impression that the
object was a small submarine). As he was extremely close to our
shipping, we decided to ram and ran up flank speed. We also
ordered all depth charges and projectors set for 50 feet.

After closing on a collision course down to 500 yards, we
decided that the object was a human torpedo and that it would be
foolish to ram . . . At 400 yards we opened fire with our 40mm and
port 20mm and when we were abeam of him at a range of about
75 feet, fired the port K-gun. The charge failed to explode and
although we thought we had scored several hits with the 20mm, the
torpedo was still proceeding to the anchorage.[15]

In his report the American captain, J W Barr, recalled that it was
while reading an *Office of Naval Intelligence Weekly* article entitled
'Italian Naval Assault Units' that he had first heard of the human
torpedo. Armed with this recollection he decided not to ram the
enemy vessel lest it detonate the warhead and destroy his own ship.
The first attack had failed to stop the Neger and *SC651* passed its
target's starboard flank, circled to starboard and ran in again with
the 40mm and starboard 20mm opening fire. Once again a depth
charge was released that failed to detonate.

The 40mm and 20mm had registered several hits on this run and
the torpedo dived abruptly. We turned hard left and began a sound
search, but soon saw an object bob up dead ahead. We assumed it
to be the torpedo and opened fire again with the 40mm. As we
closed, the object began waving its arms and we knew it was the
operator.[16]

After expending a total of twenty 40mm and ninety-five 20mm
rounds during the attack, Barr ordered fire ceased and speed
reduced as *SC651* nosed alongside the German, who was hoisted
from the water. It was a badly shocked Günther Kuschke who was
dragged from the sea, his woollen outer garments and olive-green
naval uniform peeled off and replaced by a dry blanket. Kuschke
was given coffee and cigarettes while the American Executive
Officer, Ensign H C Tee dressed a shoulder wound sustained from
the gunfire. Questions about the nature of his craft were answered

by the simple 'I don't want to talk, I am a German soldier' from the 23-year-old pilot who was shortly afterward transferred aboard the escort destroyer USS *Frederick C Davis* for more thorough interrogation.[17]

In total ten Negers reached their target areas where they claimed to have achieved at least some success. The group that reached Nettuno Bay found no targets worthy of engagement, some pilots firing their torpedoes landwards in the hope that something would be in the way. Another Neger of this group, piloted by *Matrose* Horst Berger, headed seaward eventually finding a darkened ship that was furiously weaving and turning. He later claimed to have fired his torpedo and hit the zigzagging patrol vessel or corvette, the flash of the explosion showing a gun mounted forward of the superstructure. If so, this was truly a remarkable feat as the Neger's weapons sight allowed small margin for error against a stationary target, let alone one engaged in evasive manoeuvring. A second pilot, *Oberfähnrich* Hermann Voigt, also reported a ship hit and badly damaged at a range of 400m. Three of the five Negers bound for Anzio harbour crept slowly past sentries on the concrete harbour mole and fired their torpedoes at the crowded Allied shipping, claiming to have witnessed detonation among a group of small craft clustered at the quay.

The return of the surviving German human torpedoes to friendly territory proved just as dramatic and nerve wracking as their outward journey. Thoughts inevitably turned to the limited endurance of their carrier torpedoes as they searched in vain for the burning hut that would mark the front line of friendly troops. Of the twenty-three Negers that launched the attack, ten failed to return. One of these ten, piloted by *Fähnrich* Pettke, was beached behind enemy lines though Pettke managed to evade capture and reached German positions unscathed. Of those lost, the Germans recovered a single body. The Neger had reached friendly lines but hit the bottom and became buried in the thick sand before its pilot could escape the small cockpit. He was found suffocated inside his Neger the following day by German troops.

The operation was considered a success with two ships definitely hit and possibly more from the confusion within Anzio harbour. The Allies for their part confirmed at least four attackers sunk by their patrols and another washed ashore on the beach four and a half miles to the north of Anzio, its pilot captured by American troops. Three torpedoes were also washed ashore having failed to detonate. However, the wish appeared to have become the father of fact. No hits or damage was ever confirmed by the Allies that could definitely be attributed to the Neger attack. To make matters worse for the *Kriegsmarine*, an intact Neger was later discovered by the Allies slowly circling with its pilot dead in the cockpit, overcome by lack of oxygen, the Neger's motor not yet having exhausted its battery. The capture displayed the primitive new weapon and removed whatever element of surprise the Germans could have hoped to maintain. The *K-Verbände* had at last seen action, but results were, at best, disappointing.

There were new Negers and the improved diveable Marder ready for operational deployment in Germany after the end of Krieg's maiden mission, but the decision was made to return MEK175 to the Fatherland as their secrecy had already been compromised by the capture of the intact vessel and in order to pass on their experience to the next batch of recruits. As it transpired, it would not be long before they would be needed again to counter an invasion the scale of which had never before been seen.

CHAPTER THREE

The *K-Verbände* in Italy

Linsens and Storm Boats

Though the Neger attack against Anzio–Nettuno could rightly be considered the first operation mounted by the *K-Verbände*, there had been German involvement already in the use of Italian explosive motorboats since September 1943.

For three years beginning in August 1940, Axis naval small battle unit operations within the Mediterranean had remained the uninterrupted domain of the Italian *Decima Mas* flotilla. On 8 September 1943 Italy signed an unconditional surrender with the Allies, the fascist leader Benito Mussolini arrested and incarcerated in an alpine hotel at Gran Sasso that, somewhat ironically, had been ordered built as part of Mussolini's desire to raise the physical fitness of his nation. There then followed the spectacular rescue mission by SS commando Otto Skorzeny and a select group of paratroopers of the deposed dictator Mussolini. Freed from his exile, the dictator – a mere shadow of his former self and more a puppet for Hitler's ambitions than ever before – formed the fascist *Repubblica Sociala Italiana* (RSI) for those of his people that remained loyal. The RSI's small navy would have little effect on the remaining years of the Second World War and by German order the only naval vessels allowed to carry the Italian fascist flag were those of the *Decima Mas* which in actuality comprised the bulk of the Italian fascist navy anyway.

At the surrender of the Italian government Prince Borghese's *Decima Mas* was barely operational though still situated both at its training grounds at Sesto Calende on Lake Maggiore and the front-line bases of La Spezia and Livorno. By the time of Italy's capitulation the unit had accounted for forty-eight enemy ships sunk or badly damaged (totalling 450,596 tons) in raids using the variety of weapons at its disposal, the fact that these ships had been within the heavily defended harbours of Suda Bay, Gibraltar, Alexandria and Algiers making the Italians' achievements even more spectacular. The majority of Borghese's men opted to remain loyal to the Axis cause, only a small number deserting to join pro-Allied partisan units. The morning following the Armistice, Borghese gathered all those naval personnel loyal to him and the RSI within La Spezia's *Decima Mas* barracks whereupon he communicated his allegiance to the German forces before travelling further throughout Italy recruiting soldiers.[18]

On 19 September Kaptlt. Mantey, the *Kriegsmarine* liaison to the *Decima Mas*, was given instructions to restore the unit to operational readiness, in particular its cadre of two-man torpedo boats and one-man explosive motorboats as the Allied landings at Salerno had found only a skeletal *Kriegsmarine* presence to oppose it. Mantey's major concern were the two-man assault boats (MTSMA – *Motoscafo da Turismo Silurante Modificato Allargato*, or, 'Modified and Enlarged Tourism Torpedo Motorboat') that the Italian formation used, armed with one 45cm torpedo, two 70kg depth charges and small arms for the crew. There was another craft, the MTM (*Motoscafo da Turismo Modificato*) that more closely resembled the Linsen, a single pilot steering his craft toward enemy shipping and abandoning it at a range of 300m to leap to safety with a small inflatable raft. There was no remote control capability, though the warhead detonation worked on the same principle of sinking alongside the target vessel and activated by a time fuse.

The concept of the *Sprengboot* (explosive motorboat) was not limited to the Second World War. Both Italian and German forces had used them during the First World War with varying degrees of success. During the next war, where Germany and Italy this time found themselves allied, the Italians again led the way. They used explosive motorboats in action within the Mediterranean, the cruiser HMS *York* being severely damaged in Crete's Suda Bay by an attack by one such unit in March 1941.

Mantey's rebuilding of the *Decima Mas* from September 1943 onward proceeded very slowly, due in large part to some disaffection within the *Decima Mas* and also industrial unrest in the centres that provided the assault boats and their necessary equipment. It was not until December 1943 that the first assault boats became ready for use. Nevertheless, due to the fragile state of the *Decima Mas*'s morale, the *Marineoberkommando Italien* recommended that a separate German unit be formed to utilise the few

available assault boats, as well as a German cadre being incorporated into the Italian flotilla.

During December 1943 this mixed unit of Italian and German
crewed assault boats launched its first raid at sea against Allied
MTBs and submarines off the Ligurian Coast, but with no success.
Mussolini's order for the arrest of Prince Borghese on 16 January
1944, threatened the flotilla's very existence of the *Decima Mas* as
its men demonstrated their allegiance to their nominal commander
and refused to obey orders. Swift German intervention resulted in
Borghese's reinstatement, the reasons for his initial arrest deemed
trivial by the *Kriegsmarine*. Further patrols were launched – again
with no success – and on 22 January when Allied troops landed at
Anzio three serviceable assault boats sortied, though without
achieving any definite results despite tangling with enemy gunboats
and destroyers.

This uneasy Italian-German concord continued through sporadic engagements against enemy shipping, with decidedly mixed
results. With greater pressure from Berlin to bring *Decima Mas*
to heel, 1,765 German personnel were transferred to the flotilla
which was reorganised into three distinct units: assault boats and
Maiale SLCs, S-boats, and saboteur units (still controlled by the
Abwehr at this stage). Furthermore, Admiral Heye, who was
rapidly building the *K-Verbände* by this stage, requested that 75
per cent of assault boat deliveries from April onwards be allocated to German use and that Italian trainees should be withdrawn from the school at Sesto Calende to make room for his
men. Needless to say, the Italians were insulted by this proposal
and there followed numerous squabbles over the division of available assault boats between the Axis partners. In one instance
Italians seized an entire shipment of boats, the Germans enlisting
the aid of police, security forces and the military to recover their
share of them.

On the German side of the Axis alliance, the pioneering unit of
explosive motorboats was in fact not a part of the *Kriegsmarine*.
The *Abwehr* intelligence service had developed the idea of a small
vessel for sabotage diver delivery in river operations. In time the
Brandenburg Regiment, the *Wehrmacht*'s special forces unit that
combined *Abwehr* elements with more standard military personnel,
established the first formation of such craft which were also provided with the dual capability of explosive warheads within the
boat itself closely modelled on the Italian concept.

The nucleus of the Brandenburg Regiment's *Kustenjäger Abteilung* began to form in Spring 1942, with an eye to predominantly river-based operations. Men of the Regiment's Light Pioneer Company underwent basic naval training in Swinemünde, the first elements of the *Küstenjäger Abteilung* seeing service in small unit actions with the *Afrika Korps* during 1942, others in the Crimea and other areas of the southern USSR.

It was under the leadership of *Oberleutnant* Kuhlmann that the unit's First Company began to experiment with explosive motorboats at the end of 1942. They assisted in the design and construction of the craft and began training on the calm surface of Lake Constance, the unit based at Langenargen. Ironically it was this very training that would render them almost immediately ineffective when committed to action. The small Linsens entrained from Germany for Italy on 24 March 1944, first due to be committed by the Brandenburgers into action at Anzio in support of the Neger attack launched in April 1944, though this deployment was cancelled. They were finally used on 1 July when they were launched from La Spezia into the Gulf di Genova where they were found to be almost useless in the rougher conditions found at sea as opposed to an inland lake. The light spruce hulls made them virtually beyond the handling capabilities of the inexperienced pilots and the brief sortie rapidly became a fiasco without even meeting the enemy. Heye, not unjustifiably, demanded that naval operations be left to the *Kriegsmarine* and appealed to OKW to back his view. Ultimately they did just that, and the Brandenburg men were given a choice to make, as illustrated by the recollection of Ernst Ertel's of his service in the Linsens.

> I myself began my successful service on 19 December 1944 in the Scheldt, later in the legendary Linsen Flotilla under Kaptlt. Bastian, serving as *Rottenführer* . . . until 18/19 April 1945 and the last explosive boat operation in the Thames.
>
> In 1942 I . . . went to Swinemünde and the sailing ship *Gorch Fock* as part of the seaman detachment of the Brandenburgers. The Light Pioneer Company was raised, with me in it, under *Hauptmann* Kriegsheim, and sent to the Black Sea . . . With 50 Caucasian comrades we returned to Langenargen/Bodensee, where under our unforgettable commander Rittmstr. Konrad ('Conny') von Liepzig the KJA (*Küstenjäger-Abteilung* 800) was formed.
>
> Our 4th (Heavy) Company was established with small 'torpedo carrier', codenamed Linsen . . . The tactical plan was for these

boats to be used in the framework of coastal operations against military obstacles such as bridges etc.

The inventor of this boat was our Major Golbach (later a *Kriegsmarine Korvettenkapitän*) who had already experimented with remote-control methods during the First World War.

The first operation in April 1944 against Anzio/Nettuno we hoped would be very successful as defence against the invasion. But it wasn't. The *Kriegsmarine*, under Admiral Heye, considered themselves to be in command of all naval operations and that such operations were only allowed with their permission! Thus it later came to a unique choice, that we little '*Küstenjäger*-Lords' could choose to return to the *Küstenjäger Abteilung* with our admirable 'Conny' or go with Admiral Heye and his *Kommando der Kleinkampfverbände* and head for service on the invasion front in the boats. I had been with the Linsens of the 1.*Sprengboot* unit during construction, testing on the Bodensee and wanted now to also take a shot, so I decided to remain with the boats as a pilot.

Thus we became part of the existing frogmen, human torpedoes, midget submarines of the existing *K-Verbände* as an integrated explosive motorboat flotilla . . . One often heard at that time the expression 'Suicide Squad' given to our service, I find this title unjustified. We had these hard assignments but no more and no less than comrades in other services!

The *K-Verbände* training unit Lehrkommando 200 developed from the skeleton of the former *Küstenjäger Abteilung* Linsen element. The *Kriegsmarine* took a major portion of the Brandenburg detachment, part of its training staff – who subsequently were transferred to the *Kriegsmarine* – and at least a dozen Linsen explosive boats and their crews. The boats were tested in Lübeck Bay where their deficiencies were soon highlighted. Nevertheless, the need for them at the frontline in Normandy had become desperate by this stage and it was not long before they were again sent to the front line after having had larger fuel tanks fitted as part of a general overhaul.

The absorption of this Linsen unit was not the first surface craft formation of the *K-Verbände*. Admiral Heye had despatched Kaptlt. Heinz Schomburg (ex-*U-561* and Heye's head of naval recruitment) to the Mediterranean in February 1944. There, Heye charged Schomburg with surveying the existing Italian light naval forces and building a German training organisation based upon similar lines. Schomburg reached Italy on 22 February 1944 accompanied by *Oberleutnant* Härting as Administrative Officer.

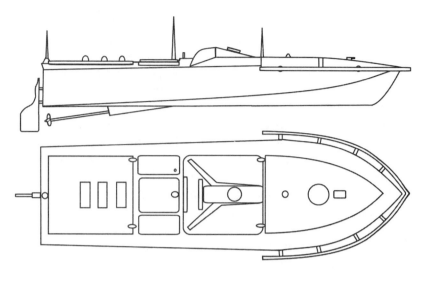

Linsen

Almost immediately they established in the town of Castelletto the first headquarters of *K-Verbände Kommando Stab Süd*, though it was known as *Einsatz und Ausbildungs Stab Süd* (Service and Training Staff South) at that point. Simultaneously the Germans established a school that was later redesignated Lehrkommando 600 at Sesto Calende on the same premises that were used by *Decima Mas*, the German contingent commanded by L.z.S. Bloomenkamp. The separate headquarters and training aspects of this base were quantified by the former retaining the title Lehrkommando 600, the latter being renumbered 601. During May Oblt.z.S. Frenzmeyer replaced Bloomenkamp who moved on to command a second training centre that Schomburg established at Stresa, this in turn named Lehrkommando 602.

Transport for *Einsatz und Ausbildungs Stab Süd* was provided in May 1944 when an established motorised column, designated *Kraftfahreinsatzzug Süd*, was placed under its command. The column comprised requisitioned Italian vehicles, including about sixty Fiat and Lancia trucks ranging from 2.5 to 6 tons, eighty trailers, twelve private cars and an unspecified number of motorcycles. Its commander, *Leutnant* Brüggemann, occupied a headquarters at Sesto Calende and was also responsible for all maintenance for units of *Einsatz und Ausbildungs Stab Süd*, a task that would later mean catering for the transport requirements for four assault boat flotillas, Lehrkommando 700 and a German *Maiale* group. The remaining units that later served beneath the umbrella of *Einsatz und Ausbildungs Stab Süd* were already motorised and considered self-sufficient. In addition to operational movement Brüggemann's transport column also collected new explosive motorboats from factories and delivered them to Lake Maggiore for testing, before moving them onward to the flotilla to which they were allocated. In October 1944, Brüggemann's unit was combined with the *Abnahmekommando* at Sesto Calende, this new body renamed *Gruppe Nachschub* and working under the direction of the newly-renamed *Kommando Stab Süd*. Brüggemann remained in command until March 1945 when K.K.(Ing) Herbert Burckhardt of the *K-Verbände*'s Quartermaster Staff replaced him.

By the beginning of August 1944 the *Decima Mas* was in a state of complete disarray and the mixed German and Italian assault boats missions that had been carried out during the preceding months had met with little success. On 23 May the flotilla had come completely under German operational control and shortly afterward Borghese resigned his command of the unit. This signalled a complete collapse of morale and on 2 August the available Italian boats split into factions, several going over to the Italian partisans. Following Heye's urging and the agreement of the Italian fascist hierarchy, the few remaining active and reliable factions were incorporated completely into the *K-Verbände* and Heye's dominance over Mediterranean special forces was complete.

On 9 August, with fierce battles raging off Normandy, Heye ordered every available *K-Verbände* unit to be used in France and so the assault boat units in Italy were made ready to entrain. However, Allied landings in southern France forestalled the redirection of this fighting strength and fresh orders for the use of the *K-Verbände* in the Mediterranean were soon issued. German-manned S-boats were moved towards the new battlefront and the assault boat headquarters relocated to Monaco where they awaited their new German commander.

At the end of August K.K. Haun arrived from Germany to take charge of the first detachment of SMA and MTM boats strictly for the use of the *K-Verbände*, his formation named *Einsatzstab Haun*. The unit's genesis was on 22 August 1944 at Sesto Calende when Haun and approximately 100 German personnel from Lehrkommando 600 began training alongside fifty Italians. Half of the twenty available MTM boats, of which only two or three were of the SMA type, were used by the Italian element, the remainder handled by the Germans who constituted *Einsatzstab Haun*. On 22 August 1944 the combined German and Italian flotilla moved to Villefranche using trucks of Brüggemann's transport column.

From there the flotilla undertook four missions against shipping in the area of Nice. On the night of 25 August an SMA commanded by *Sottotenente Siccola* of the Italian component claimed a cruiser sunk, while the *K-Verbände* man L.z.S. Kind sank an Allied gunboat. Two nights later an explosive MTM piloted by *Bootsmaat* Grunwald claimed to have sunk what he described as a small naval auxiliary. There are no Allied records of these successes. The sole recorded German casualty during these missions was the loss of L.z.S. Bloomenkamp – the ex-commander of Lehrkommando 601 – who died of wounds received, though another man had come close to joining the casualty list during an engagement on the night of 27/28 August. The last of eight assault boats despatched to attack enemy MGBs, the young German pilot of the two-man boat had engaged an enemy vessel at too close a range to use a torpedo, opting instead to fire a Panzerfaust. He had been about to use the small rocket against his twisting target when the weapon misfired. His co-pilot, seeing the problem, immediately snatched a grenade but, while throwing it as hard as he could, lost his balance and fell overboard. The assault boat then took heavy fire and burst into flames, the pilot extinguishing the blaze and heading back to base, his companion taking three hours to swim back to Villefranche. By German reckoning it had been a successful deployment of the *K-Verbände* unit.

On the penultimate day of August the flotilla moved to San Remo where Kaptlt. Wilhelm Ullrich assumed command on 5 September. The unit was henceforth known as 611 K-Flotilla. Haun himself transferred to Istria where he later took charge of what was to become known as 'VI K-Division', located at Opicina and established in September 1944 under the control of Adriatic Naval Command to provide the link between themselves and regional *K-Verbände* operations. That same September, the headquarters staff of *Einsatz und Ausbildungs Stab Süd* moved to Meina on Lake Maggiore that bordered Switzerland.

As 611 K-Flotilla rested and recuperated from its first operational use, K.K. Hugo Gerdts who had previously been the Liaison Officer between Heye's *Kommando der K-Verbände* and *Decima Mas* at Genova was appointed to the post of *Einsatzleiter* of 611

K-Flotilla, later exercising the role of operations director for all *K-Verbände* units stationed along the Ligurian Coast. Somewhat strangely, Gerdts also exercised direct control over four large MAS boats at Imperia though they were considered inoperative due to their high petrol consumption.

On 1 September 1944 Kaptlt. Ullrich visited Dresden with eight members of his 611 K-Flotilla. There they attended a mass demonstration of the Hitler *Jugend*, attended by Dönitz who praised the work of the *Kriegsmarine* to the eager field of potential recruits. *Reichsjugendleiter* Artur Axmann, head of the Nazi youth organisation, then bestowed the title 'Hitler *Jugend*' on Ullrich's flotilla in the name of the *Führer*. From that moment onward the membership of the flotilla was to be drawn, theoretically, solely from the fertile recruiting-ground of the Hitler *Jugend*, an armband similar to that worn by men of the 12th SS Panzer Division inscribed with the title being issued to all of its members, though ironically for security reasons they were never worn.

CHAPTER FOUR

Battles off Normandy
Attacks against D-Day shipping

The long awaited Allied hammer-blow fell on Normandy's sweeping coastline on 6 June 1944. There the 'second front' – a somewhat ironic term considering the bloody battles in Italy that had been raging since 1943 – was opened against the Atlantic Wall and Germany's days as master of Europe were numbered.

All of the *K-Verbände* units to be deployed to France came under the jurisdiction of K.z.S. Friedrich Böhme who had been designated as Chief of *Kommando Stab West* during June. Böhme had had an interesting career, volunteering for the navy in 1916 and holding the appointment of instructor of heavy anti-aircraft weaponry at the *Kriegsmarine* artillery school in Swinemünde when war with Poland broke out on 1 September 1939. Given command of the destroyer *Anton Schmidt* that same month, he took part in the invasion of Norway in April 1940. In the course of the battle for Narvik his destroyer was torpedoed and sunk and Böhme, like hundreds of his comrades, found themselves ashore taking part in the fierce battle on land, Böhme acting as supply officer. After the German triumph in the Arctic port he was appointed *Seekommandant* Narvik, before reverting to command of the destroyer Z23 in August 1940. In May 1942 he served a year as naval liaison to *Luftflotte 5* in Oslo, then transferring back to Swinemünde as commander of the artillery school at which he had been during 1939.

On 2 June 1944 Böhme was posted to Timmendorfer Strand to join the *K-Verbände*, appointed director of operations for 361, 362 and 363 K-Flotillas. As such he became operational commander of the *K-Verbände* in the Seine Bay, his headquarters situated in Villers-sur-Mer, 10km west of Trouville. The first units of the *K-Verbände* began arriving on the French Channel coast during the latter half of June as fighting raged amongst the bocage of Normandy. Attempted intervention by conventional U-boats of the Allied invasion fleet had resulted in spectacular failure as the near-obsolete Type VIICs succumbed to the saturating effect of Allied naval and air power. With his S-boats, torpedo boats and destroyers similarly doomed Dönitz turned to the only other weapons in his dwindling arsenal that may be able to have an effect, though he appeared to not have the same dubious faith that his commander in chief possessed:

'Admiral Dönitz mentioned . . . difficulties when reporting to Hitler on 29 June 1944. At that time the Negers . . . were due shortly to begin operations on the invasion front.

'We shall be able to start operations with the first explosive motor-boats soon as well,' Dönitz said. 'But all these weapons are naturally very dependent on the weather.'

Hitler was obviously unperturbed by this reservation. His hopes were high. 'Of course,' he declared, 'the enemy warships – particularly the battleships – must be attacked, just as the merchant ships are. Just imagine it: if England were to lose six to eight battleships in the Seine estuary, the strategic consequences would be enormous.'

Dönitz looked at Hitler, aghast. Did he really believe you could sink *battleships* with one-man torpedoes? And six or eight of them![19]

The arrival in Normandy of the sixty Negers that comprised 361 K-Flotilla was accomplished by transport on an increasingly beleaguered railway system. With frequent targeting by Allied bombers much of the journey was made by road in ninety-two trucks from Rudolstadt in Thüringen, via Paris, and finally reaching Normandy where the first thirty Negers arrived at Trouville on the early afternoon of 28 June. From there they were moved to their operational base at Villers, the cumbersome trailers and their cargo hidden amidst the trees of Favrol Wood while the pilots were accommodated in a nearby Norman chateau. During transit by road the trailers and trucks had their naval licence plates blacked out, the carried equipment covered and camouflaged. Any identifying flotilla emblems were removed and the *Kriegsmarine* men exchanged their uniforms for standard *Wehrmacht* army uniforms.

A second batch of Negers arrived at the forest on 6 July after reaching their temporary base at Pont l'Eveque the previous day. However, their journey – like their predecessors' – had been frequently disrupted by Allied fighter-bombers who exercised almost complete dominance of the skies over France. Little movement could be attempted by daylight lest the swarms of sharp-eyed pilots discovered them and strafed the convoy below. It was during one such attack on 30 June that Krieg himself was seriously wounded, his place taken as flotilla leader by *Fähnrich* Potthast who compensated for his lack of rank with experience aboard the Negers. Twelve Waffen SS volunteers also augmented the unit; men from Otto Skorzeny's newly formed SS-*Jagdverbände* of hardened adventurers.[20]

Indeed the *K-Verbände* remains the only *Kriegsmarine* unit to have admitted SS members knowingly into its ranks. However, this knowledge was not open to all. In June 1944 Böhme discovered this for the first time as is evidenced in his POW interrogation after the war's end:

> The presence of SS men amongst the fighting personnel of *K-Verbände* units first came to light in June 1944 when Böhme accompanied a party of eight men to Berlin to receive decorations. During the proceedings Skorzeny appeared and admitted that four of the men were members of the SS.
>
> Böhme was subsequently informed by Admiral Heye that an arrangement had been made between himself and Skorzeny in May 1944 whereby *K-Verbände* would absorb SS men under sentence who would be willing to undertake suicidal actions (*Totaleinsatz*) on a voluntary basis as a form of probation.
>
> The flotillas in KdK subsequently received a number of SS men from the Lehrkommandos without knowing their real origin.[21]

It is unclear how many SS men served in the *K-Verbände* and to which units they were definitely attached. At least twelve Waffen SS men are known to have joined 361 K-Flotilla, eight each in 362 and 363, six in 611, eight in MEK 80 and ten in Lehrkommando 700. Whether the SS volunteers were truly of a probationary nature or rather motivated by the high *esprit de corps* that marked Skorzeny's unit can only be surmised, certainly the above text suggests the former, while knowledge of the SS commando unit's actions during the war reflects the latter.

However, the Neger was not the only part of the *K-Verbände* to be deployed. A single Biber had also been shipped from Kiel via Aachen, Paris and Rouen for an attack against British-held bridges on the Caen Canal and Orne River. As we shall see later the proposed mission was aborted before the Biber could be deployed. As in Italy, it was the Linsen that would be first deployed in action.

After the absorption of the Brandenburg Regiment's *Küstenjäger* battalion into the *Kriegsmarine* following their disappointing performance in explosive motorboats off Anzio, the initial cadre of the *K-Verbände*'s Lehrkommando 200 had been established in June 1944 on the south bank of the River Trave between Lübeck and Travemünde. Named '*Blaukoppel*' the base hosted Kaptlt. Kolbe who commanded the training unit for the prospective Linsen pilots and crew. Among the fifty permanent staff of the Lehrkommando (at least twenty of them ex-Brandenburgers) was Oblt. Taddey, a wireless expert, his experience crucial for the operation of the remote-controlled explosive Linsen. A small ancillary Linsen training centre was also established on Lake Müritz, named '*Grünkoppel*' and comprising around 100 men and six Linsens.

While the initial batch of Linsens used by the *K-Verbände* was of Brandenburger origin, the *Kriegsmarine* had swiftly set about designing and constructing their own boats in a crash-building programme. The theory behind the units' structure and operation was simple. Each Linsen combat unit (called a *Rotte*) would comprise a control vessel and two explosive craft (the group controlled by the group leader, or *Rottenführer*). The control boat carried three men, a pilot and two radiomen, one each to control the remotely-operated explosive boats. These carried a single pilot who would bail out of the craft when it was set on the correct path and be (hopefully) picked up by the control boat afterward.

The Linsens built for the *K-Verbände* measured 5.75m in length (25cm longer than the Brandenburg design) with a beam of 1.75m (5cm slimmer). The height of the craft measured only 80cm making it a small radar profile at best. The total displacement was a maximum of 1.85 tons. Beneath the engine cover amidships was a 3.6-litre, 95-horsepower Ford V8 'Otto' engine that could push the boat at a speed up to a maximum rated 33 knots, though the 100 nautical mile radius of action was calculated for 15 knots. Two 5-litre containers held enough fluid to lay a smokescreen in action as the explosive boats hurtled towards their enemy carrying a charge of 300–400kg of explosives in the stern. Fitted around the bow of each explosive boat was a metal framework that was held 15cm away from the gunwale by spiral springs. If a pressure exceeding 80kg was exerted on these springs the metal framework would be forced against the gunwale closing a circuit that ignited a small charge in the bow. Blowing the bow off, this would enable the craft to sink while also starting a delay fuse to the main charge in the stern that was preset to between two and seven seconds. In theory this allowed the remains of the boat to sink beside the target ship where its subsequent detonation would cause the maximum damage.

In practice the three-boat unit would approach the enemy using stealth, until the explosive boats were close enough to begin their attack run. At the appropriate moment the two explosive boats would be accelerated to maximum speed and begin their attack. The pilots would make whatever adjustments were necessary before turning on two navigation lights visible only from astern, switching the controls to radio-control and throwing themselves overboard. In the control boat the radio operator used a small box that he cradled on his knee to control the now-pilotless explosive craft. There were six settings for the lever: starboard, port, stop engine, start engine, slow ahead and accelerate. The final control was a firing switch. The radio control equipment was much the same as that which had been developed by the Army for use in the 'Goliath' remote-control demolition charge carrier. By keeping the two navigation lights – one green towards the bow and a red stern light – in a vertical column, the operator knew that the boat was heading in a straight line towards the intended target. Production of the improved Linsen began at the end of May 1944 in Königsberg's Empacher & Kalisch boat builders, soon farmed out to firms throughout Germany.

Kaptlt. Ulrich Kolbe's Lehrkommando 200 despatched Linsens of Oblt. Helmut Plikat's 211 K-Flotilla from Germany on the day of the invasion, the unit arriving at Bolbec east of Le Havre on 19 June accompanied on their maiden posting by Kolbe himself. The entire flotilla numbered around 250 men, including the support staff commanded by flotilla engineer Lt (Ing.) Max Becker. The pilots were quartered in a luxurious villa that belonged to the Rothschild family at Molitor. The cutting edge of the unit numbered twenty-four Linsens, though the accompanying communications, armaments, transport and other logistical units (including a small flak detachment) considerably swelled its ranks. From Molitor they moved during the ensuing two days forward to Honfleur, which would be their operational base and from where they initiated operations.

The German *K-Verbände* faced a well-prepared and dauntingly massive enemy that was ready to face the novel German weapons all across the invasion front, as evidenced in this US Navy appreciation of Allied naval dispositions and the foe they faced:

Enemy naval forces within the Channel consisted of an indeterminate number of human torpedoes, self-exploding pilotless surface craft, sea mines to be laid by aircraft, and . . . 195 miscellaneous vessels.

To repel these enemy forces, the Task Force Commanders established an area screen . . . Manning the area screen required a careful phasing in the use of vessels. Until Allied forces arrived in the assault area, there was no screen. On arrival, a proportion of the escorts and patrol vessels took up screening patrols. Still later, other vessels, which had completed their initial tasks of boat control, close fire support, or some other job, took over patrol duties, while a proportion of the escorts returned to the UK in company with the convoys.

B. Eastern Task Force . . . [that bore the brunt of K-Verbände attacks]. The system of defence employed in the eastern area was the following: constant patrols to seaward by corvettes, trawlers and sometimes destroyers were carried out.

Every 24 hours one division of four destroyers was detailed as duty division for the entire area while two other destroyers were detailed as guard for areas O and J. By day, these destroyers performed such other tasks as were assigned, but they were subject to call in case an attack threatened. By night they were posted as directed by Captain (Patrols). In neither case did they actively patrol up and down the defence line. The plan was that Captain Patrols would vector them against enemy forces, whose presence was discovered by radar or other means.

During the hours of darkness or low visibility, this defence was augmented by a line of minesweepers anchored 5 cables apart along a defence line parallel to the shore and six miles to seaward.

This defence line was continued down the eastern flank by a line called the 'Trout' line, composed of LCGs and LCFs, anchored 1 cable apart. The duty of the minesweepers and Landing Craft on this defence line was to prevent all enemy ships and craft from entering the British Assault Area, to illuminate the outer areas when ordered and to counter attack any submarine detected.

Two or three divisions of MTBs were stationed, stopped but under way, to the Northeastward of the N.E. portion of the defence line; two or three sub-divisions of destroyers were stationed on patrol, to the north of the western half of the area, and sometimes to the northward of the MTBs; other light forces were stationed close inside the defence line, to act as reinforcements or as 'pouncers'. BYMS and MMS were anchored as mine spotters, originally in the approach channels, but later in the lateral swept channel established within the area.

These defences were augmented by a smoke screen laid by specially fitted craft at dawn, dusk, and as required.

The enemy's day activity was limited to one long-range torpedo attack, by torpedo boats from Le Havre, at 04.50 on D-Day . . . By night the enemy's attack was more determined. On four occasions he operated torpedo boats, and on eight occasions E and R-boats, in the eastern Task Force area. On every occasion except one these forces were intercepted and forced to retire. In no case was any success obtained by enemy. The line LCG and LCF, anchored on the eastern flank took a heavy toll of the human torpedoes which attacked in July . . .[22]

The Allies had also gained a huge advantage over the *K-Verbände* when during May 1944 they had penetrated the Enigma code net in use by Heye's service. Named *Eichendorff*, and codenamed 'Bonito' by the Allies, the Enigma net had been instigated in March 1944 and was used until the end of the war. Though first broken by the Allies during May it was not until July 1944 that it was considered mastered by Allied cryptanalysts. The sole saving grace for Heye was that he and his commanders rarely mentioned specific areas or timings in their reports. Nonetheless it was a severe handicap, though one of which they were oblivious.

On the evening of 25 June the Linsens were readied for their first mission. Eight control and nine explosive boats were towed to sea by R-Boote of the 4. R-Flotilla (2. *Sicherungsdivision*). These motor minesweepers had been based in Boulogne-sur-Mer since the fall of France in 1940, their strength gradually eroded by years of insidious mine warfare and the sudden onslaught of Allied power in the prelude to D-Day. However, the remaining captains and crew were familiar with the local waters and several were pressed into service as towing vessels for the small Linsens. Unfortunately for German plans, the pilots of the explosive boats were not so skilled and as *R46* eased from port with its tow, bad handling by the Linsen operator caused the little craft to veer wildly while running alongside the minesweeper, nudging the large craft's hull with enough force to close the detonation circuit and explode it. Both were lost in the blast as well as a further two control Linsens and one explosive Linsen. As the explosions buffeted the remainder many fouled their towlines and in the increasing confusion the operation was scrubbed, the *R-Boote* and their charges returning to Honfleur the following morning. Two further attempted attacks were launched during June though they too ended in confused failure. Accidental rammings by the inexperienced Linsen operators – resulting in several sinkings and much damage, as well as defective weaponry saw both attempts turn into fiascos until on 30 June Böhme reported to Dönitz that the remaining Linsens of 211 K-Flotilla were no longer serviceable. Their planned deployment was postponed and instead the human torpedoes brought forward into action.

This time there was to be no repeat of the problematic launching suffered at Anzio. Two companies of *Wehrmacht* pioneers were commandeered and they prepared the landing site by first of all clearing a wide strip of the tangled coastal defences erected by the Germans and clearing a track along two sandspits that were almost completely dry at low water. From these promontories two wooden slipways were also prepared to provide a firm base on which to wheel the human torpedoes into the water. To avoid the unwelcome attention of the RAF the runways were covered in camouflage netting.

The German radio listening service (B-Dienst) had detected news of Allied convoys headed to Sword Beach, protected by the so-called 'Trout Line' of modified landing craft on 5 July and the Neger pilots launched their weapons into the English Channel for the first time that night, twenty-six of them were wheeled along the prepared tracks and into the cold water of the English Channel under Böhme's watchful eye. Conditions were ideal after days of squalls; the night was clear and an ebb tide took the Negers out to sea heading into Seine Bay in search of targets, while hours later the flood tide should aid their return. Though two of the torpedoes aborted their mission due to trouble with their motors the remaining Negers pressed home their attack, resulting in wildly enthusiastic success reports. Walter Gerhold – a former clerk – was among the wave of attacking Negers.

I saw the first ship shortly before two and I made it out to be a destroyer. So I estimated it at 1,200 to 1,500 metres away. As I went past I saw the second destroyer. Then I went past five destroyers on the port side. We had received a command to shoot between 4 and 5 o'clock and I was in quite a favourable position. I launched the torpedo. It jumped about two or three times out of the water. You had to measure the time with a stopwatch so that you could work out the running time. I was sweating loads and was quite nervous when the explosion came. So then I set off on my way back. I saw three destroyers following me. I cleared the windscreen and looked back at them with a pocket mirror. I thought to myself, 'Ah . . . now he's listening' so I switched off my motor. Then he came up to my port side and stopped and I lay still also. Then they got the searchlights out and searched the sea. But we all had a towel on board so I put the towel over my head and made myself as small as possible inside. I put my trust in God and said to myself – 'you'll make it'.

I've tormented myself for years. In the small hours of the morning I've thought about how many people must have gone down with that ship; how many mothers had lost their sons, how many wives had lost their husbands and how many children their fathers . . . it really bothered me and I've thought about it a lot. It moves me still today. I lost my own father as well in that war.[23]

At 03.04hrs Gerhold fired his torpedo at the tempting target. After forty seconds he registered a powerful detonation as his torpedo struck home. Dodging the ensuing storm of enemy ships racing to the scene Gerhold eventually made landfall near Honfleur where he was pulled from the water by *Wehrmacht* troops after scuttling his carrier torpedo. The Allies captured two other pilots when their Negers were detected and sunk. In fact it had been the British destroyer HMS *Trollope* that Gerhold had hit. The destroyer had been loaned from the US Navy (who had designated it DE566) on 10 January 1944 as part of the Lend-Lease Agreement. Generally attributed to an S-boat attack, *Trollope* was damaged so severely that she was written off as a total loss, towed away and later broken up in Scotland.

Potthast himself, leading the attack, suffered catastrophic failure in his underslung torpedo when it developed a leak that added so much weight to the weapon that it threatened to pull his carrier torpedo underwater. Jettisoning the useless torpedo his carrier was also damaged and began to leak, forcing him to abandon his Neger. Eventually he pulled himself ashore west of the Orne estuary and was taken back to the flotilla's base by local German troops.

Observers deployed by Böhme along the coastline reported a number of large explosions to sea and much gunfire and by next morning ten Negers had been lost. However, between the remaining pilots they claimed to have sunk an *Aurora* class cruiser (Gerhold's target HMS *Trollope*), two destroyers, one merchant ship of approximately 7,000 tons and two LSTs (one of them claimed by *Matrosengefreiter* Horst Berger who had also claimed a patrol boat sunk off Anzio) totalling 2,000 tons. They also claimed damage inflicted on another cruiser, destroyer, two LSTs and a pair of steamers. The results appeared to have more than justified the human torpedoes' deployment.

However, the reality was slightly less overwhelming. Three ships had indeed been destroyed, HMS *Trollope* and the British minesweepers HMS *Cato* and *Magic*. Of the two minesweepers HMS *Magic* was the first to be hit as she lay 10 miles from Ouistreham. Many of the crew were sleeping when at 03.55hrs (British time) the torpedo exploded against the hull and the minesweeper rapidly sank with twenty-five men still aboard. A little less than an hour later HMS *Cato* suffered the same fate, also sinking rapidly and taking one officer and twenty-five seamen to the seabed with her. Mercifully for the Allied shipping clustered off the British beachhead, they were the only confirmed successes for the *K-Verbände* pilots.

Nonetheless the *Wehrmacht*'s propaganda machine went into overdrive at the image of an ex-clerk destroying what was believed by the *Seekriegsleitung* (SKL; Naval War Staff) to have been a cruiser using such a rudimentary weapon. Dönitz concurred and Gerhold became the first *K-Verbände* man to be awarded the Knight's Cross on 6 July. Two days later his flotilla commander was similarly rewarded, his Knight's Cross bestowed for his role as chief of the 361 K-Flotilla.

A second attack was rapidly planned for the following night when twenty-one Negers were launched against enemy shipping in the same area. From this desperate raid no German human torpedoes returned, several reportedly attacked by Allied aircraft, prompting Hitler to enquire of the *Luftwaffe* on 9 July whether they could aid returning Neger pilots by laying smokescreens. However, Potthast lived to later recount his tale in Cajus Bekker's book *K-Men*:

I was one of the last to be launched and I remember the 'ground crew' coming up and tapping on the dome of my Neger to wish me good luck. The launching went perfectly; soon I was heading for the enemy ships. At about 3am I sighted the first line of patrol vessels, which passed me not more than three hundred yards away, but I had no intention of wasting my torpedo on them. Half an hour later I heard the first depth-charge explosions and some gunfire. Perhaps a fellow Neger had been spotted in the moonlight, for the British were on the alert. The depth charges were too distant to affect me, but I stopped my motor for fifteen minutes to await developments. A convoy of merchant ships was passing to port of me, too distant for an attack; anyhow I was determined to bag a warship.

I went on and towards 4am sighted a 'Hunt' class destroyer, but she turned away when no more than five hundred yards distant. The sea was freshening slightly; I was thankful that the five hours already spent in the Neger had not exhausted me. Soon I sighted several warships crossing my course. They appeared to be in quarter line formation, and I steered to attack the rear ship, which seemed larger than the others and had evidently slowed down to permit redeployment of her escorts. Was rapidly closing in on this ship; when the range was a bare three hundred yards I pulled the firing lever, then turned the Neger hard around. It seemed ages before an explosion rent the air, and in that moment my Neger was almost hurled out of the water. A sheet of flame shot upwards from the stricken ship. Almost at once I was enveloped in thick smoke and I lost all sense of direction.[24]

Interceptions of garbled enemy radio traffic led the Germans to claim a single unidentified cruiser sunk. In actuality Potthast had hit and fatally damaged the Polish cruiser ORP *Dragon*, while at least two other Negers had sunk minesweeper HMS *Pylades*.

Following the enormous blast that devastated the Polish cruiser an elated Potthast was unable to navigate his small machine with any certainty. There were no stars to guide him and his inexact compass was of little use in the darkness of the Neger cockpit. After nearly an hour he noticed the sun dawning behind him so he reversed his course, realising that he had been sailing further away from his home port. He successfully eluded several enemy warships, though fatigue was taking its toll.

> I must have been dozing when a sharp metallic blow brought me to my senses. Turning my head I saw a corvette [*sic*] not a hundred yards off. Instinctively I tried to duck as the bullets rained on the Neger, shattering the dome and bringing the motor to a stop. Blood was pouring down my arm and I collapsed.[25]

Acting more on instinct than anything else Potthast managed to free himself from his stricken Neger, which plunged to the bottom. Floating barely conscious in the water Potthast was caught by a British boathook from the deck of his attacker, the minesweeper HMS *Orestes*, and he was hauled from the water and his injuries treated. He soon learnt that another single Neger pilot, a severely-wounded *Obergefreiter*, had been rescued by the enemy – though he did not realise that they two were the only survivors of the second Normandy attack by the *K-Verbände*.

Potthast's target, the 'D' class cruiser *Dragon*, had seen meritorious service since commissioning in August 1918. Briefly seeing action in the First World War as part of the 5th Light Cruiser Squadron, *Dragon* served during the inter-war period in American, Chinese, Mediterranean and Caribbean waters before reducing to reserve on 16 July 1937. In September 1939 the ship was with Home Fleet's 7th Cruiser Squadron, transferred first to the Mediterranean and then to South Atlantic Command, where she captured the Vichy French merchantman *Touareg* off the Congo in August 1940. During the Dakar operation of September 1940 she had been unsuccessfully attacked by the Vichy French submarine *Persée* and was stationed at Singapore on escort duties, serving with the China Force from the beginning of 1942 until February of that year and the fall of the British bastion. After carrying out strikes from Batavia at the end of February, *Dragon* sailed for Colombo on 28 February and joined the Eastern Fleet, where she was attached to the Slow Division. After her return to the Home Fleet in Britain she joined the 10th Cruiser Squadron until paid off in December 1942. It was then, while sitting in the Cammell-Laird dockyard that *Dragon* was transferred to the Polish Navy who took control of the ship on 15 January 1943. Despite her new Polish masters the ship's name remained unchanged. Their wish to rename her *Lwów* was politically embarrassing to the British whose Russian ally occupied the Polish city, thus she continued to sail as ORP *Dragon*. Brief service in Russian convoy duties was followed by attachment to 2nd Cruiser Squadron for part of the D-Day support off Sword Beach (Force B) in June 1944. *Dragon* shelled batteries at Calleville-sur-Orne, Trouville, Houlgate and Caen as well as German armoured formations during the invasion until the early hours of 8 June when Potthast's torpedo struck amidships, abreast of Q magazine. The impact caused a sympathetic detonation of the stored ammunition. Though many casualties were suffered during the explosions and resulting fires, the ship remained afloat. She was soon declared a constructive total loss, however, and was subsequently towed to and beached at the Gooseberry harbour as part of the breakwater that sheltered the fragile beachhead.

While it can be ascertained with certainty that Potthast had been responsible for the sinking of the cruiser, the second successful torpedoing that night has only recently been confirmed as sunk by human torpedo. HMS *Pylades* had been in almost constant service off the Normandy coast since the initial landings on 6 June 1944. The battle against German minelaying continued as German sea and air units periodically replenished already thick fields. Two explosions relatively close together shook *Pylades* in the early hours of 8 July, the minesweeper sinking in minutes. Her commander listed the cause of the explosions as having struck a pair of German mines, but debate has long continued as to whether they were in fact caused by the Neger attack. During 2004 a BBC film crew filmed French diver Yves Marchaland and an English television presenter as they dived the wreck of the *Pylades* which now lies almost upside-down in 34m of water. Conditions were less than favourable and eventually an ROV took over the task of filming the wreck in order to deduce the cause of her demise. Though the stern section of *Pylades* had been mangled by the force of the blasts, Ministry of Defence damage assessment expert David Manley was able to compare the difference in damage patterns caused by mines and torpedo strikes. Influence mines such as the type deployed by the *Wehrmacht* off Normandy leave a characteristic crimping pattern on the hull of target ships after exploding beneath them. The explosion of a torpedo did not give this signature and the *Pylades* bore no such distortion on her ruptured and corroding hull. Indeed she had been the victim of two torpedo strikes, the first struck the ship and incapacitated her, the second hitting and blowing a large hole in the hull, sending the minesweeper under and leaving dozens of shocked British sailors floundering in the Normandy swell. Both Neger pilots remain anonymous to this day, lost in the course of events.

For Böhme it had seemed a costly exercise. Though he was aware that a cruiser may have been sunk, not a single Neger returned. Five pilots had been captured by the British, the remainder destroyed by surface gunnery and aircraft of the RAF and Free French. A single undamaged Neger had also washed ashore to be recovered by the enemy. Nonetheless the Neger pilots' exploits, in particular that of Walter Gerhold, perhaps served to encourage men to enter the ranks of the *K-Verbände*, though not necessarily into the human torpedoes. Werner Schulz, a Seehund engineer, recalled a conversation amongst new *K-Verbände* personnel in 1944 that showed that propaganda could not disguise the perilous nature of the human torpedoes despite the lure of glory:

> 'I have heard' an *Obermaschinist* told us – he introduced himself later as Kurt Keil from Uelzen – 'that in the English Channel one-man torpedoes have grounded a Polish steamer and sunk an English destroyer. One pilot, an *Oberfähnrich*, has even won the Knight's Cross. It was announced in a *Wehrmacht* report.'
>
> 'That makes sense' confirmed *Oberfunkmaat* Papke. 'I heard it on the wireless.'
>
> 'The one-man torpedoes are nevertheless pure suicide squads. They are not even proper sailors. There every Tom, Dick and Harry arrives, sits down inside the Eel [torpedo], presses on a button and bang, either they hit or they don't.'[26]

Nonetheless a further assault was planned for the night of 20 July pending reinforcement for the flotilla from Germany. This time the sole success was the destruction of the destroyer HMS *Isis* seven miles north of Arromanches, often incorrectly attributed to German mines. The 1,370-ton ship was hit amidships on the starboard side, this explosion swiftly followed by two more on the port side, blowing such a large hole that she heeled violently to port and sank in minutes.

Though now treated as little more than a footnote in history, the loss of *Isis* left only twenty survivors. A glimpse of their experience in the cold Channel waters can be gleaned from the following account written by one of the twenty, Ken Davies:

> I came aboard *Isis* some nine or ten days before she was mined [*sic*] and not only witnessed the bombarding of German shore positions but also took part in the excitement of depth-charging a suspected U-boat. I remember nothing of either event. It appears that the sights and sounds of the mine explosion and its aftermath induced some sort of mental block. I nevertheless stand by my recollections of the mining [*sic*] itself and of my time on the Carley Float and subsequent rescue by the American Coast Guard cutter.
>
> I was on deck when the ship hit the mine. Shortly after this explosion there was a second, which I assumed was that of the boiler. On both occasions I was thrown to the deck. On seeing the for'ard hatch falling away, I began to release one of the Carley Floats. There must have been a dozen or more men just standing by the port rail obviously in shock and doing nothing to help themselves. They only came to life when the float hit the water. Naturally they were the first on.
>
> The emotional strain of our situation was soon demonstrated. On my raft one young fellow's mind went – he kept talking to his mother whilst refusing to give up the paddle he was clutching. Another was wearing a Duffel coat and a polo-necked jumper. He was asked to give up his coat to cover a fellow who was wearing only a singlet and appeared to be badly scalded or burnt. Duffel coat refused. Someone suggested taking the coat off him but wiser heads said that a struggle would have us all in the water and if that happened some would not make it back to the float.
>
> I remember the speed with which men died. The fellow next to me said he was feeling warm at last. This I knew was a sign of hypothermia. I tried to keep him awake by talking to him, but failed. It seemed no time at all before he was as stiff as a board and we tipped him over the side.
>
> Just as the sun was about to disappear, we saw the silhouettes of two ships. They wouldn't have been much more than a mile away. Duffel coat stood up to shout and wave. Whether he stumbled or was given a nudge, I don't know, but he ended up in the water. I don't know if he got back on board or not, but then I didn't look for him; it was at this time that a man I was told was the ship's R.P.C. and I were fixing lifebelt lights onto a paddle.
>
> Eventually the American Coast Guard cutter spotted us and nosed between our float and another, not realising that the two were roped

together. This had the effect of turning our float onto its starboard side. We had to quickly jump across to the cutter. I was second to jump and was terrified I would mistime my jump and end up in the water. In the event all went well and I was taken below and put in a bunk with white sheets![27]

In Germany the shortcomings of the Neger human torpedo were becoming immediately obvious. Thus an improved and slightly larger model was designed and manufactured as a replacement. This new model – named the Marder – incorporated a pressure chamber immediately behind the pilot's seat, carrying 200kgs of compressed air and a 30-litre flooding tank in the nose that added 65cm to the length of the weapon, which now measured 8.3m. The increased size raised the displacement of the Marder to $3m^3$ as opposed to the $2.7m^3$ of the Neger. With 10kgs of compressed air used in theory for every surfacing, the Marder could thus submerge up to twenty times before exhausting the air supply. A further oxygen supply was also fitted to the Marder, 200kgs of oxygen mixture connected to the pilot via a rubber tube. Released by a valve, it passed over a purifying agent while impure air was ejected by means of a small jet. Like the Neger pilots' main breathing equipment, the fighter pilot's mask and air bottles were also still carried for backup use.

Other refinements included the ability to secure the hinged Plexiglas dome from inside the Marder, an iron traversable ring fixed inside the manhole, which could be turned in a spiral motion by use of a special key. Once turned the ring pressed firmly against another ring fastened to the bottom of the cupola, squashing a rubber joint between them and ensuring water-tightness. This was considered vastly preferable to the Neger's design in which the dome was removed completely, and which could only be done from the outside. A small depth gauge marked off to 30m was provided, as well as a spirit level on the left hand side of the cockpit graduated from $+15°$ to $-15°$ to provide guidance for the pilot in the featureless surroundings of green seawater. In practice the pilots were trained to dive and surface at an angle around 7 to 8°. Gauges indicating the pressure inside the pressure chamber, oxygen container and cockpit were also included in the tiny cockpit. Interestingly, many Marders incorporated Italian parts, at least the stern motor compartment being manufactured in Italy and supplied complete with Italian engraved markings for the adjustment screws. Of course, these adjustments were redundant as the pilot exercised complete control over the navigation and attitude of the weapon.

There were reinforcements already *en route* to France by the time of the loss of the 361 K-Flotilla Negers. Sister unit 363 K-Flotilla had completed three weeks of training during the early part of July before travelling to Saalburg near Rudolstadt and drawing sixty human torpedoes from the *Torpedoarsenal Mitte*. This arsenal was the central issuing depot for the human torpedoes, their batteries and pressure chambers fully charged there before despatch. All necessary equipment for the pilots was also stored and issued from there. The young pilots enjoyed a short recreational stay in Paris before they arrived at Villers at the beginning of August. There they also joined the newly-arrived men of 362 K-Flotilla whose experience thus far mirrored their own.

After already suffering heavy losses, of whom many had been taken prisoner, a fresh directive was given to the new Neger crews that comprised a simple code to be used in the event of capture. By this method the *Kriegsmarine* could be notified of the results of their mission. In a letter written from the POW camp and delivered via the Red Cross the pilot was to use the first letter of the third line to indicate the target attacked: K would mean cruiser (*Kreuzer*); Z a destroyer (*Zerstörer*); B an escort ship (*Bewacher*); S an MTB (*Schnellboot*); L a landing craft (*Landungsboot*); T a transport (*Transportschiff*) and N would denote no target at all (*Nichts*). The first letter on the fifth line would then specify the result of the attack: V meaning sunk (*versenkt*); T denoted torpedoed (*torpediert*) and B indicating that the target had been damaged (*beschädigt*).

It was 362 K-Flotilla's Marders that first took their place immediately in the front line, transferred to their jumping-off area at Villers-sur-Mer on 2 August and launching their attack that same night. They comprised a portion of a larger attacking force, joining the Negers of 361 K-Flotilla, fifty-eight human torpedoes deployed in total. In conjunction with them, sixteen control and twenty-eight explosive Linsens from Houlgate's 211 K-Flotilla were also earmarked for the operation. As well as these forces the Germans intended to divert attention from the *K-Verbände* by use of a *Luftwaffe* attack and S-Boat sortie from Le Havre by units of 2. *S-Bootflottille* as well as the planned deployment of the Dackel (Dachshund) torpedo for the first time.

The Dackel (TIIId) torpedo had been developed as a coastal-defence weapon, improvised from the standard G7e electric torpedo. It was designed to give an exceptionally long range for use against targets such as concentrated invasion shipping where weapon speed was not important. Equipped with the *Lage unabhängiger Torpedo* (LUT) pattern-running apparatus that allowed a torpedo to be fired from any angle and run a desired course, the Dackel was able to cover 57km at 9 knots while carrying its 620lb warhead into action. The LUT gear installed had been slightly modified to allow a straight run of 34,600m before embarking on the first of what could be a maximum of 2,650 long pattern legs. Enlarged to 36ft by the addition of an empty battery chamber immediately behind the warhead, into which was fitted compressed air bottles that could provide enough air for the operation of depth gear and steerage during over three hours of travel, the weapon could be fired from S-Boats or rafts thus negating the costly and time-consuming exercise of constructing launch bunkers. It was estimated that if Dackels were fired from the entrance to Le Havre they could reach the Allied disembarkation area off the Orne River and their bombardment station off Courseulles, 29km and 37km distant respectively. Allowed to run their patterns under cover of darkness, *Marinegruppenkommando* West expected great results despite protestations from *Schnellbootführer* that with the low profile provided by S-boats, any possible targets at 29km distance would be beyond the visible horizon. He also correctly pointed out that original plans to launch at twilight – giving the entire night in which to run – were untenable due to Allied fighter-bombers. The S-boats would be forced to depart at night under cover of darkness. He further reckoned that the only possible method of firing was thus by compass bearing, using two waypoints to triangulate and obtain a true bearing of possible targets, transmitting this information to the S-boats by radio. He also feared that inaccurate firing data, faulty running and the effect of strong tidal movement on the slow running torpedoes might wash one ashore thereby revealing the LUT gear to the Allies. He was, however, overruled. As events transpired, the new weapon was never destined to play its part in the operation of 2/3 August. In the wake of heavy bombing the necessary loading gear was put out of action and the torpedoes remained ashore.

On schedule, the diversionary force of S-boats from Le Havre slipped from harbour. Several times that night they skirmished with what they took to be three British MTBs, *S167* being damaged in a collision and *S168* and *S181* hit by enemy fire. All the remaining boats reported splinter and machine gun damage, though there were no serious losses. The *Luftwaffe* was scheduled to operate over the clustered shipping off Sword Beach between midnight and 02.00hrs on 3rd August. An hour later the *K-Verbände* would begin their attack. However, as the operation was launched there were severe delays in taking to the water, particularly with the human torpedoes, while four control Linsens and eight explosive boats never put to sea at all. Of those that sailed, only seventeen Negers and ten control Linsens returned, claiming a substantial total of enemy shipping sunk after suffering heavy defensive fire and constant harassment from the air from Spitfires of 132 Squadron as dawn broke. The human torpedoes claimed two destroyers, two corvettes, one 10,000-ton cruiser or troop transport and one merchant ship estimated at 3,000 tons sunk. Like his comrade Gerhold, 24-year-old *Oberfernschreibmeister* Herbert Berrer of 361 K-Flotilla was awarded the Knight's Cross on 5 August for what was recorded as his part in the sinking of a 10,000-ton freighter and previously sinking another enemy ship during the attack at Anzio. With two Knight's Crosses awarded and requiring urgent replenishment of their depleted ranks, the Neger pilots of 361 K-Flotilla were returned to Germany, headed to Suhrendorf/ Eckernförde ('*Dorfkoppel*') where they were issued with the improved Marder and later transferred onward to Denmark on 30 September.

The nature of the human torpedo as an effective weapon has often led to them being characterised as a suicide weapon, akin to the Japanese 'Kaiten' which truly was a human torpedo with no separate warhead capable of detachment. Though we have already mentioned the small number of SS men for whom assignment to the *K-Verbände* appeared to have been of a probationary and perhaps even suicidal nature, in general usage it was clearly untrue of the Neger and Marder. However, the fighting ardour of the young volunteers also hints at a near suicidal attitude, as evidenced in the SKL Diary entry regarding this operation.

> Three officers of the Marder Flotilla as well as one cadet officer, one NCO and five men announced shortly before the start that they would make contact with the enemy and completely destroy any worthwhile targets, regardless of their radius of action and question of getting back. These men did not return from the operation.[28]

In turn the Linsens, who had lost one officer and eight men, claimed one transport, one freighter with a 'lattice mast' and an LCT sunk. This optimistic appraisal of results once more caused a storm of enthusiasm amongst the units that reached all the way to Berlin. However, seven of the returning control Linsens (*Kommandolinsen*) also reported having to discharge one *Ladungslinse* each during the run in to the target, the explosive boats lost as a result of 'technical failure'.[29] Between them, the Linsens and Negers reckoned to have destroyed between 40,000 and 50,000 tons of enemy shipping, their attack leading onshore observers to report:

'Seven explosions some of them with high jets of flame and large mush-rooms of smoke and another succession of loud explosions . . . during the hours 02.30 and 06.00.'[30]

In fact they had definitely sunk only three ships. The first of the sinkings, the 'Hunt' class destroyer HMS *Quorn*, had had an event-ful career thus far during the war, striking mines twice and being one of five destroyers that intercepted the German raider *Komet* in the English Channel during 1942. In June 1944 *Quorn* was an escort for personnel convoys during Operation Neptune until hit and sunk during the *K-Verbände* attack, the violence of the explo-sion almost rending the hull in two. Four officers and 126 ratings were lost.

> Already having been torpedoed twice while serving in the Mediterranean earlier in the war, Christopher Yorston . . . was up in the gunnery tower when *Quorn* was hit.
>
> 'Within seconds I was in the water, looking up at the ship split in half,' he said. 'If I had been in a cruiser, where the gun turret is com-pletely sealed, I'd have been a goner. I grabbed hold of the first thing in the water, a lump of wood, and a converted trawler picked me up. It's the luck of the draw.'[31]

Norman Ackroyd was another survivor from HMS *Quorn*. Part of the No. 3 gun crew on the quarterdeck, he remembers no mention of the Small German Battle Units that eventually destroyed his ship:

> No, we were not warned before about explosive motorboats or the human torpedo but if we had I doubt at the time if it would have caused much more than passing interest, after all we were using weapons of a similar nature.
>
> One unusual event before we sailed that night was that we were warned that it was a punishable offence not to wear a lifebelt at sea (very few of us did). We were also ordered to check our lifebelts and if it was found to be faulty to draw a new one from the stores. I found that mine would not inflate and drew a new one but it must have been damaged when I left the ship, as it would not inflate when I was in the water. Thinking about this afterwards it must have been considered at the time that we would be taking part in a very dangerous mission the following morning.
>
> The ship had been part of the beachhead defence force for some nights before, on the night of August 3rd we sailed as normal just before dusk . . . accompanied by an American radar ship and we were

informed over the tannoy that at dawn we were going in close to Le Havre in order to bombard the E-boat pens. The American ship was to control the shelling. Just before midnight however there was a massive explosion amidships and I understand she had been hit in the boiler rooms, broke in two, and sank in a few minutes. I personally was blown overboard by the blast and found myself in the water fully dressed. A large number of my shipmates must have gone down with the ship but there were quite a lot of us in the water. The American ship left the scene at full speed which caused a lot of resentment at the time but it was explained to us later that if she had stayed she would possibly have sustained the same fate as *Quorn*.

I personally did not see the American ship depart at speed but I was told of this by others when we survivors wondered why we had not been picked out of the water by them. Just after *Quorn* was sunk there was quite a lot of us in the water but by morning when we were picked up only a few were left. 130 lads lost their lives that night out of a crew of just under 150. We were informed after that the ship had been sunk by a German human torpedo . . . and that the German pilot had been picked up by another of our destroyers of the defence force. We were also told that we had run into a number of these torpedoes which were being carried into the beachhead by the tide but as a result of the *Quorn* being sunk the alarm had been raised and the other torpedoes had been dealt with.[32]

The two other confirmed sinkings were that of the 545-ton 'Isles' class minesweeping trawler HMT *Gairsay* engaged in clearing the dense German minefields, hit by a Linsen, and *LCG764* rammed by two Linsens simultaneously. The LCG (Landing Craft Gun) was an example of the 'Mark 4 Landing Craft Tank' that had been converted to provide close inshore fire support during amphibious landings. Carrying a crew of around fifty, including a sizeable Royal Marine detachment, these craft carried two 4.7in guns mounted facing forward with one superimposed to fire over the other on a reinforced deck over the tank well, with large quantities of ammunition above the waterline as well as three 20mm cannons.

Further to these three ships, three others had been so severely damaged that they were eventually written off. The transport SS *Fort Lac la Rouge* on bareboat charter to Britain's Ministry of Transport from the US Maritime Commission and the Liberty ship SS *Samlong* were both considered structural losses. *Fort Lac la Rouge* had been one of the vessels constructed in an accelerated building programme instigated due to the heavy losses suffered by the Allied Merchant

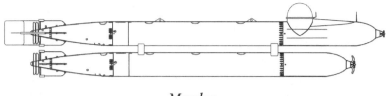

Marder

service in the war's early months. Ships were commissioned from Canada and the United States for management by British Shipping Companies, the names of those built in Canada all prefixed 'Fort' along with their sister ships the 'Parks' and the U.S. built 'Oceans'. Hit and badly damaged, *Fort Lac la Rouge* was beached at Ouistreham, after which her cargo was discharged. Towed to Cardiff and then Newport for survey, the freighter was eventually moved to the River Torridge where she was laid up until broken up in 1949. Likewise SS *Samlong* was so badly damaged that it was towed to Blackwater River and laid up as a structural loss. The last of this unfortunate trio was another warship, the ageing cruiser HMS *Durban*. The largest warship victim of the *K-Verbände* attack, this cruiser had served in the Royal Navy since 1921, one of its most notable assignments alongside the destroyers HMS *Jupiter* and *Stronghold* when they had provided the escort for the last convoy of evacuees from Singapore bound for Batavia before the bastion fell to the Japanese in 1942.

As the *K-Verbände* retired to lick their wounds and prepare for another attack, the delayed Dackel were put into action in the early morning hours of 6 and 7 August, launched by S-boats from the Le Havre approach buoy: six boats (*S 174, S 176, S 177* of 2 S-Flotilla, *S 97, S 132* and *S 135* of 6 S-Flotilla) firing between 01.36hrs and 02.34hrs on the first night, three boats between 02.26hrs and 02.50hrs on the second.

The Linsens sortied once more on the night of 9 August, twelve control and sixteen explosive boats departing the Dives estuary in three separate groups to attack shipping off Sword Beach. Four of the control boats failed to return from the attack, which was timed to coincide with Dackel torpedoes launched between 03.59hrs and 04.20hrs by three S-boats. The survivors claimed one destroyer, one escort vessel, one LST and six merchant ships hit. Again, the results were enthusiastically greeted by German naval command and on 12 August Ltn (V) Alfred Vettner, Group leader of 211 K-Flotilla was also awarded the Knight's Cross.

Our group [4 *Rotten*] went with Ltn Alfred Vettner . . . from Trouville for service against the Allied invasion fleet.

The Linsens, with the pilots in them, were pushed over the beach on their carriages and into the sea where they floated free and formed up. The course was laid in and the journey begun. First the command boat then explosive boats number one and number two. The sea was quiet and the moon shone in the sky. . . . After a short time the enemy shone searchlights high over our heads in our direction. I was the command boat leader and behind me sat both remote controls for the explosive boats. We remained lying quietly after disengaging the engines until the enemy fired star shells and then we increased speed. After we acquired the target we gave the pilot of number one boat the signal to go faster and the Linsen sprang forward in the water. We sped behind the explosive boats also at full speed. The remote control took over steering only on the final shot at the target. I, as pilot of the command boat, had the task of picking the other pilots up out of the water. It wasn't long before I sighted him and pulled him, with his help, onto our forward deck. I noticed by a sudden flash at the Linsen, that the enemy had been hit. But now I had to concentrate completely on my task and save my comrades. An enormous explosion told us of our success.

Then it was the turn of target number two, but this time our luck ran out. The escorts shot at us with every barrel and the second boat was sunk. Also it took some time to search for the second Linsen pilot in the water, but we did find him and dragged him on deck too.

We had success with nearly every one of the explosive boats. But on the return we were attacked by Allied fighter-bombers and lost a command boat with all of its passengers.[33]

The seas off Normandy remained perilous for the Allied fleet as Dackel were deployed again on the nights of 10 August (three S-boats launching ten torpedoes) and 14 August (two S-boats launching eight torpedoes). During this period the cruiser HMS *Frobisher*, the freighter *Iddesleigh*, the *Algerine* class minesweeper HMS *Vestal* as well as the minesweeper repair ship HMS *Albatros* (a 4,800-ton ex-seaplane carrier) were all damaged. *Albatros* was hit forward, over 100 casualties suffered in the blast and declared a write-off, though later placed in reserve and recommissioned as a minesweeper hulk.[34]

HMS *Frobisher* had been part of Bombarding Force D covering landings on Sword Beach during D-Day, before being damaged by a bomb hit and later assigned as depot ship for the Mulberry Harbour B at Arromanches. Leslie Finlay remembered the *Frobisher* being hit in an article published in *The Newcastle Evening Chronicle* 60 years later.

I was below and it was 7.30 in the morning and I had just made the tea, it was D-Day+9 or 10, so I'd just made the tea and there was such a bang. And one of the first things you do is you want to get to the top. I think I was the only one hurt, because the teapot fell on my foot. Out of 800 I was the only one hurt.[35]

However, the value of the Dackel in combat appeared to be minimal, even to optimistic German naval staff. The *Führer der Schnellboote* (FdS) raised serious doubts with SKL as to the reliability of reported sinkings, presenting the following on 16 August:

'. . . [a] survey of the Dackel employment sector from the 4th to the 11th August, which enclosed six operations off Le Havre with a total of 76 torpedoes.

FdS believes only the sight and detector sets of two specially equipped direction finder stations to be reliable as far as observations were possible during night and in the twilight, when judging the observations of effect. The same applies to the observation post of Operational Staff Böhme. In return observations of the naval and army coastal batteries were regarded as unreliable and expelled, just so, observation from the *Luftwaffe* stations. Also flying reconnaissance is not reliable as they very often take firing ships' artillery for detonations.

The FdS, without pronouncing a final sentence to the value of Dackel operations, is therefore sceptical to the majority of reported observed successes, as real observations from the sinking of ships were not at hand and especially as the radio monitoring up to now made no reports about torpedoing, averages, sinkings, etc.[36]

Once again the remaining Neger pilots were sent into action on the night of 15 August. Their target was the concentration of Allied shipping off the Dives estuary and fifty-three Negers from 363 K-Flotilla were earmarked for the attack (six had become unserviceable due to damage in transit from Germany). However, atrocious weather conditions of thunderstorms and heavy rain – combined with inexperienced launching parties – virtually foiled the attack before it had begun. Only eleven craft were launched, seven of these returning prematurely due to the bad conditions. The remaining four valiantly stuck to their plan and claimed a munitions ship hit and sunk. Five of the Negers were lost at the launching site.

The last roll of the dice for the Neger crews of 363 K-Flotilla came the following night when forty-two set sail from Villers-sur-Mer. Their deployment was to be matched by other *Kriegsmarine* units involved in torpedo operations in the south of the Seine Bay, committed to the waters off Dungeness and also mining the sea off North Foreland. Only sixteen Negers would return, the remainder falling victim to depth charges, surface defensive fire and air attack. *Matrosengefreiter* Wolfgang Hoffmann was one of the fortunate few to survive.

He had patrolled the Seine estuary in search of targets until nearly full light the following day. Finding nothing, Hoffmann was about to fire his torpedo at a barge to which was tethered a barrage balloon when he sighted an Allied speedboat heading across his path at high speed. Attempting what was a doubtful shot at best, Hoffmann released his torpedo but, unsurprisingly, missed the speeding craft. He then headed for home; hugging the coastline until at about 10.00hrs he was sighted by Allied fighters and attacked. Hoffmann quickly cut the power on his Neger and the torpedo sank by the stern so that it was nearly vertical, the young pilot hoping that it would either resemble a buoy or look like it was already sinking. Not fooled by his sub-terfuge, the fighters continued to attack, one bullet hitting the Plexiglas cupola, splintering it and allowing some water to enter. Hoffmann restarted the motor and regained horizontal trim, firing a distress flare through the shattered canopy, after which the aircraft stopped their attack and banked away from him. It had been a lucky escape and some two hours later Hoffmann was able to stagger ashore once again on the German-held coastline.

Seven Neger pilots were captured during the mission, another mor-tally wounded and taken with an intact machine by the support craft *LCS251* as he sat dying at the controls. The Neger was soon returned to Portsmouth for investigation. The German pilots claimed to have sunk one destroyer and one freighter as well as the probable destruction of another destroyer. In actuality a single small landing craft, *LCF11*, and the small 757-ton barrage balloon vessel HMS *Fratton* were sunk, the latter with twenty-nine of its crew. Two torpedoes also impacted against the ancient French battleship *Courbet*, though this had already been deliberately sunk as a Gooseberry blockship. A hit was also regis-tered on the 5,205-ton transport ship *Iddesleigh* though this too had already been beached following damage sustained from a Dackel hit six nights previously. The return course of the surviving Negers revealed the dire situation of the German frontline in Normandy: they were ordered to make for Le Havre as the position at Villers was no longer tenable. Böhme and his staff would also relocate to Le Havre on 18 August, shortly afterward moving onwards to Amiens.

It was the end of the Neger's deployment in western France. The original concept of the midget service weaponry had been to use a rotating selection of weapon types; once the Allies had learnt to counter one, a new type could be despatched. However, the Neger was clearly no secret to the Allies and obviously vulnerable due to their inability to dive. Thus their tenure in the frontline could no longer be justified and they were soon withdrawn entirely from combat, replaced by the Marder. The Linsens too were no longer novel to the enemy, consequently on 18 August both 363 and 211 K-Flotillas were also withdrawn from the coast.

The Negers of 363 K-Flotilla relocated to St Armand Tournai in Belgium and the Linsens to Strasbourg in preparation for shipment to the south of France where a fresh Allied invasion, 'Operation Dragoon', had begun on 15 August. The last Negers passed over the Seine on 20 August as a fresh batch of sixty Marder human torpedoes – Oblt.z.S. Peter Berger's 364 K-Flotilla – arrived in Le Havre from Reims in Germany. They too were directed to Tournai to await possible redeployment to the south of France though naval planners were acutely aware that they faced severe transportation problems between Belgium and the French Mediterranean coast.[37] Shortly thereafter OKM ordered the transfer of both 363 and 364 K-Flotillas to the Mediterranean. There they would pass from Böhme's command into the localised control of *Kommando Stab Italien* and be made ready for action against the Allied forces of Operation Dragoon.

However, before their relocation the mauled remains of both 362 and 363 K-Flotillas returned to Suhrendorf via Amiens, Tournai and then Lübeck, to take charge of the improved Marder design, even this movement order proving to be problematic in an increasingly hostile occupied country. As well as the omnipresent threat of air attack, other forces had risen against the *Wehrmacht* troops, *Mechanikermaat* Dienemann being killed by French partisans during the road journey.

The now veteran pilots of the *K-Verbände* flotillas had by this time adopted a tradition of the U-boat service. Men of 362 K-Flotilla now sported silver seahorses on their caps as a flotilla emblem, the pilots of 363 wearing a small silver shark, its tail adorned with a red stripe for each successful mission. Between them they had amassed considerable awards for valour, the *K-Verbände* no longer labouring under the image of an untried service, but now revelling in the brief flare of propaganda attention. Once in Germany, 363 K-Flotilla's commander L.z.S. Wetterich, who had been wounded in action off the Normandy coast, was invalided out of active service and remained at Suhrendorf to oversee future training, replaced by L.z.S. Münch as nominal flotilla chief while Wetterich retained his title as Senior Officer. The flotilla received sixty Marders, these split into six groups of ten for the purposes of training, each group commanded by a man of at least *Fähnrich* rank. As established in the Neger units, the flotilla would total approximately 110 men, though many of the logistical branches were only attached during combat and were shared with other human torpedo units. The flotilla composition comprised sixty pilots, sixty truck drivers to haul the Marders into position from the nearest railhead where they had been taken by railroad flat car, plus fifteen to twenty engineers and up to thirty-five headquarters staff and administrative personnel.

Tournai became the new concentration point for *K-Verbände* forces with the despatch of 261 K-Flotilla's twenty-five Biber one-man submarines from Germany for the Belgian town on 21 August. A flotilla of Molchs was also due to arrive there from the Fatherland eight days later, but last minute appreciation of the lack of possible launch sites for this latter submarine diverted them to the south of France and Mediterranean operations.

The Biber and Molch designs were the first of what could be rightfully called midget submarines to be committed to the front line by OKW. The Biber (Beaver) was the brainchild of K.K. Hans Bartels, developed by Lübeck's Flenderwerke and modelled closely on the British Welman craft that had been captured at Bergen on 22 November 1943. The progress on delivering a working submersible was remarkably rapid given that negotiations between the builders and Bartels began on 4 February 1944 and within six weeks they had a prototype ready for testing – the so-called 'Bunteboot', named after Flenderwerke Director Bunte, though known more widely as 'Adam'. Visibly different to the eventual finished Biber design, Adam measured 7m long with a beam and draught of 96cm each. Displacing three tons of water the small boat could dive to 25m, running for two and a quarter hours at six knots. This speed almost matched her surface capability of 7 knots, though the craft's endurance was rated at 91 nautical miles for surface travel using a petrol engine.

Following the unexpected sinking during the first attempted 'Adam' trial, further tests undertaken in the Trave River on 29 May proved highly successful and an immediate series of twenty-four craft were ordered, with several slight refinements that led to the final Biber model. The submarine was not without its faults though, the most prominent being the use of petrol engine power rather than diesel for surface travel. Heye expressed extreme misgivings about the use of petrol and its subsequent risk of carbon-monoxide poisoning of the operator and explosion from an accumulation of highly-combustible fumes from the engine. However, the designers and officers of *Marinegruppenkommando Nord* responsible for the trials expressed no such misgivings. Their rationale was that while there was an acute shortage of suitably-sized diesel engines, there were an almost unlimited supply of petrol engines that could fit the submarine's purpose and they were almost silent into the bargain. Heye's fears were overruled and the Biber went into immediate production at both Flenderwerke and the Italian Ansaldo-Werke, further labour on the hulls later farmed out to Ulm's Klöckner-Humboldt-Deutz and other manufacturing companies. Thus the three sections were built in three distinct geographic locations and later assembled, almost as envisioned by Dräger years before. The specially constructed trailers used to transport the finished submarines were made by a firm in Halle and it was this asset of transportability that the *K-Verbände* rated highly. It was even suggested to use this portability to its most extreme by transporting a Biber by Bv222 flying boat to Egypt. There the aircraft would land either on the Great Bitter Lakes or the Suez Canal and the Biber released to find and torpedo a ship so as to block the strategically vital waterway. Fortunately for the pilot of this submarine, the far-fetched plan was abandoned as unworkable.

Costing 29,000 Reichsmarks each to produce, the final Biber model displaced 3.645 tons of water, the length having been increased to 9.035m, the beam to 1.57m with torpedoes and the draught remained the same as 'Adam's'. Two torpedoes of near zero specific gravity comprised the Biber's usual armament, the torpedoes having to have neutral buoyancy lest they swamp the small parent craft with their weight and also obliterate any chance of keeping trim on discharge. This reduction of weight was achieved by the removal of half the battery from the weapon, accepting the loss of speed that this reduction would incur. Thus the TIIIb (Marder torpedoes) and TIIIc (Biber, Seehund and other midget submarine torpedoes) were capable of only 5,000m at 17.5 knots. The Biber's two weapons were slung from an overhead rail, one on either side of the boat at the top of a scalloped cavity. They were launched with compressed air stored at 200 Bar in five steel bottles, the high-pressure air also being used for blowing ballast tanks.

As well as the torpedo, the Biber was capable of carrying mines on its twin racks. Generally the mines used were the *Magnet-Akustisch-Druck* (MAD) combined magnetic-acoustic-pressure triggered weapon. This was smaller than the standard midget torpedo, measuring between 5 and 5.5m in length, though having the same diameter. Set to explode by a ship of over 6,000 tons displacement passing overhead, the trigger relied on all three mechanisms to explode the warhead. The mines were heavier than torpedoes, therefore the two hemispherical ends of the weapon comprised of float chambers to offset this negative buoyancy. Correspondingly Bibers were subjected to a slight heeling to one side if a torpedo was carried on the opposite rail. When the mine was released, a spring-loaded lever held in place on either end of the mounting rail was also released, springing upward and piercing the float chambers though on discharge the mine had the disturbing habit of rising to the surface due to the slightly positive buoyancy, generally remaining there for about three minutes until enough water had flooded the holed compartments to make it sink once again. Perhaps more alarmingly the Biber also had a tendency to surface after releasing the mine, the weapon's centre of gravity lying slightly to stern of the Biber's, causing the boat to be in turn slightly bow heavy when loaded. Upon release, unless the operator was exceptionally skilled, the general counterbalancing action of the freed submarine would lift the bow too rapidly to be stopped.

Nevertheless, this was not necessarily a fatal design flaw. The Biber's true Achilles Heel remained, as Heye had feared, its petrol engine and the resultant accumulation within the small craft of toxic and highly flammable fumes. A 2.5-litre, 32hp Opel-Blitz petrol truck engine provided this main propulsion, the 225 litres of petrol carried in the small craft's tank giving a surfaced range of 100 nautical miles at 6.5 knots. Exhaust from the engine was vented outboard via a pipe that ran from the engine compartment to a small enclosure aft of the conning tower. For submerged travel the Biber was provided with three battery troughs (Type 13 T210) carrying four batteries in total (two of twenty-six cells and two of twelve cells) and a 13hp electric torpedo motor turned the 47cm diameter propeller, providing 8.6 nautical miles at 5.3 knots plus a further 8 nautical miles at 2.5 knots. The diving depth had been slightly decreased to 20m because the balance of size and weight had meant a corresponding use of 3mm sheet steel for the pressure hull. Internally, the three-sectioned hull (bolted together with rubber flanges between the joins) was strengthened by flat bar frame ribs spaced about 25cm apart. The flanges themselves were sometimes prone to leaking and Biber pilots were instructed to dive their boats for two hours to check the seals before they would be released for combat duty. One Biber veteran, Heinz Hubeler, later recounted that he had made many such dives, dropping to the seabed and reading a book until an alarm clock that he had taken for the purpose indicated that his two hours were over.[38]

The relative weakness of this segmented hull was exacerbated by the twin-scalloped indentations that allowed streamlined stowage of the torpedoes but lessened depth charge resistance. Two heavy-duty lifting lugs were fitted to the upper hull fore and aft to enable moving by crane. Another lug was welded to the stern for towing something behind the small submarine, while yet another was fitted forward to enable the vessel to be towed to its operational area. However, experiments at using Linsens to tow the Biber resulted in failure as the small motorboats could not develop sufficient power, while S-boats were also unsuitable as they created too much wake for the Biber. Thus this task would fall to the overworked minesweepers of the R-Flotillas stationed in the combat zone. These were by no means ideal, especially those highly manoeuvrable craft fitted with the directional Voigt-Schneider propellers, but they were the best that could be provided for the *K-Verbände*.

The small conning tower in which the pilot's head naturally was positioned was made of aluminium alloy casting bolted onto an oval aperture in the hull. Six rectangular ports – one aft, one forward and two others each side – provided armoured-glass windows for the operator to view his world around him. A circular hinged hatchway above was held in place by a single internal clip, another window in it providing upward view for the pilot as well. Expectations were high as the first completed Bibers began to be issued for training of their prospective crew.

However, the Biber was not an easy craft to handle. Two circular wheels, one slightly smaller in diameter than the other but both turning on the same axis immediately in front of the pilot, controlled a wooden rudder and single wooden hydroplane. It was undoubtedly a complicated and highly skilled manoeuvre to handle the hydroplane and rudder simultaneously while at the same time observing the compass, depth gauge and periscope, and perhaps even using the bilge pump as well. Correspondingly the Biber moved almost entirely surfaced, a freeboard of about 60cm showing when at normal trim, submerging only when it was absolutely necessary.

Compensating and trimming tanks had been dispensed with and solid ballast was stowed during preparation for operational use. While at sea, weight and trimming changes could only be accomplished dynamically or by partial flooding of the diving tanks situated fore and aft, both tanks free flooding with small vents in the top. This in turn made it nearly impossible to remain at periscope depth meaning that torpedo attacks also had to be conducted surfaced, though the Biber was theoretically capable of submerged firing. Pilots perfected the art of lying silently on the bottom in shallow water while awaiting an opportune moment to surface and attack whatever targets were at hand, though often when tanks were blown the Biber had an uncomfortable habit of shooting rapidly to the surface rather than making a stealthy appearance.

The periscope itself represented another problem. Due to the space constraints within the tiny aluminium conning tower the periscope was only capable of being directed forward, providing vision up to 40° to the left and to the right. The windows provided in the tower frequently became iced during the winter months rendering them useless; the pilot virtually blind other than what was visible through the periscope. Distance was difficult to estimate through the periscope, though it was fitted with cross-hairs, thus the whole operation was one of 'point and shoot', the torpedoes running at a little over 3m below the surface. If the forward windows were able to be used, a ring and cross hair sight was fitted near the tower that could be lined up with a bead fixed to the bow for surface firing.

Navigation was aided by a projector compass, the magnets for which were housed at the top of a sealed bronze alloy tube some 75cm in length, rigidly fixed to the forward end of the conning tower immediately in front of the periscope, passing through the tower ceiling to extend some 45cm above the craft. Behind the periscope was the boat's air intake. Originally only 30cm above the conning tower, this was increased to a metre, all three masts joined together by metal bracing. Like the subsequent Seehund design, air was drawn in and circulated through the pilot compartment before reaching the engine, therefore acting as a source of fresh air for both the machinery and crewman. Once closed down for action the pilot was left a single oxygen bottle for breathing from, approximately thirty-six hours of air available.

Instruction for the Biber crews was undertaken at *Blaukoppel* near Schlutup opposite Lübeck's Flenderwerft shipyard where the boats' segments were primarily assembled. The camp of wooden huts was relatively isolated, three-quarters of a mile from the nearest tramline. Reckoned to require eight weeks of training, the first batch of pilots were rushed through in three, ready to follow Bartels into their first operational assignment. During their schooling the prospective pilots were often brought in to familiarise themselves with Bibers still in repair or construction in the shipyard workshops – almost a microcosm of the *Baubelrung* undertaken by U-boat crews. The men were next despatched to the depot ship *Deneb* that lay in Lübeck Bay, the Bibers in use resting either nearby in the water or housed in barges off Travemünde. Those who swiftly displayed a flair for the small submarines were tasked with instructing their flotilla mates while Bartels remained supervisor at *Blaukoppel* as Senior Officer, assisted by his small staff that comprised an Adjutant, Oblt.dR Mitbauer, Senior Engineering Officer, Oblt. (Ing) Endler, Staff Officer, LdR Steputtat, Torpedo Officer, Lt(Ing) Preussner, and Chief Instructors, Oblt.z.S. Bollmeier, L.z.S. Bollmann, L.z.S. Kirschner, L.z.S. Dose and *Oberfähnrich* Breske.

The first three Bibers were delivered to *Blaukoppel* in May 1944, and were taken over by the eager recruits of 261 K-Flotilla. The following month saw six more completed, the number eventually rising to a production high of 117 Bibers completed in September.[39] Each of the eventual ten planned Biber flotillas were supposed to consist of thirty boats and their pilots apiece, supported by an ancillary staff of nearly 200 men. As an example of the organisation of these combat units, the headquarters staff for 261 K-Flotilla as it headed for operations in France comprised:

> Senior Officer: Kaptlt. (MA) Wolters (replacing Bartels who remained in Lübeck)
> Engineering Officer: L.(Ing.) Schwendler
> Torpedo Officer: Oblt. (T) Dobat
> C.P.O. (Navigation): Obersteur. Kramer
> Medical Officer: *Oberassistentarzst* Borcher

An unnamed mine specialist officer and shore personnel numbering nearly 100 were under the command of *Stabsoberfeldwebel* Schmidt.

After being put onto an operational footing in August, Kaptlt. Wolters' flotilla of Bibers faced a daunting journey from *Blaukoppel* to the front-line base allocated in France. As they neared the enemy the large trucks towing the canvas-draped Bibers on their trailers came under increasing pressure from air harassment as well as becoming aware of the proximity of several enemy armoured formations as the *Wehrmacht*'s western front crumbled rapidly.

Days after the Bibers departed Germany, a fresh Linsen flotilla was also despatched, bound for Fécamp. However, the military situation on the ground had so changed by 30 August that the Linsen unit was halted in Brussels while OKM debated the wisdom of deploying them against British convoy traffic off Boulogne or Calais. As the situation worsened, they were eventually completely withdrawn and sent via Ghent to München-Gladbach in the Rhineland before possible transfer to the south of France. Their luck had deserted them though as they clashed with British armoured units at the start of their new road journey, taking heavy casualties and losing several Linsens. The mauled remains were transferred back to Lübeck for refitting before planned redeployment to the south of France. As events transpired it was to Groningen – west of the German border in The Netherlands – that the flotilla would eventually be sent on 23 October.

Wolters' Biber unit at Tournai had in the meantime been transferred to Fécamp harbour on 29 August having also suffered losses on the way – this time to enemy aircraft. They were to be immediately launched against Allied shipping in the Seine Bay, but difficulties in getting them into the sea caused a postponement of 24 hours. By the night of 30 August, twenty-two of them had been placed in the water but due to the destruction of port facilities, damage to several Bibers and the loss of many personnel through the persistent air attacks only fourteen were able to actually sail between 21.30 and 23.30hrs. After nearly nine hours of strong winds and heavy seas twelve returned without reaching their target area, the remaining two, piloted by L.z.S. Dose and *Funkmaat* Bösch, claiming to have sunk a Liberty Ship and a large merchant ship between them before they too successfully returned to harbour.

In action the Biber pilots were subjected to the same trying conditions that the pilots of the human torpedoes had been. As most Biber sorties would last from one to two days – and subsequent Seehund sorties sometimes as many as ten days – German midget crewmen received a special, low-bulk or 'klinker-free' diet. Once under way they were instructed that during the first 24 hours they must use food tablets and thereafter energy tablets – including the DIX amphetamine cocktail – which would keep them going for another 24 hours. If they were reluctant to use DIX, which many men were once the side effects became known, many ate '*Schoka-Kola*' a type of chocolate that comprised 52.5 per cent cocoa, 0.2 per cent caffeine and the balance sugar. To compound their discomfort many Biber pilots suffered from sea-sickness and owing to the inherent danger of water entering when the hatch was opened, vomited instead into the bilge. This in itself was unpleasant enough, though it was also something that had to be carefully monitored by the pilots, as one of the initial symptoms of carbon monoxide poisoning is nausea and vomiting.

After this single costly exercise the Bibers at Fécamp were withdrawn to München-Gladbach. Travelling by road they once again suffered heavy casualties along the way as Allied ground-attack aircraft controlled the skies by day. As the German convoys raced for safety, Allied pursuit caught traces of the *K-Verbände* units left behind on the French roads. Among them was Royal Marine Patrick Dalzel-Job, an experi-

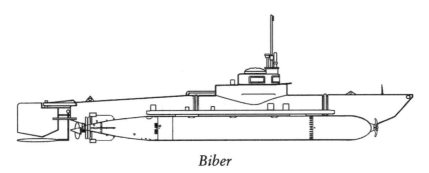

Biber

enced commando who had worked for Combined Operations since 1942 and ironically had taken part in training aboard the Welman midget submarine. In 1943 he had been transferred to 30 Assault Unit – a specialised group of Marines and naval officers that raced alongside more orthodox combat units at the front-line, tasked with finding men and equipment from Germany's naval secret weapons programme, gathering all available intelligence regarding the *Kriegsmarine*.

On 2 September, Patrick arrived in Fécamp to learn from liberated locals that the last eight Bibers had only recently departed on their long, low trailers concealed under canvas and towed by heavy trucks. Patrick and his men managed to trace the submarines to Abbeville, and eventually discovered one on the Amiens-Bapaume road, abandoned after suffering severe damage from Allied aircraft attack:

> It was almost an anti-climax after such a long search; there it was, off the side of the road where the towing lorry must have left it – a midget submarine, itself intact, on a burnt-out trailer. It was indeed much more like a miniature of a normal submarine than were the British Welmans with which I was already familiar, and it carried two twenty-one-inch torpedoes instead of the Welman's delayed-action nose charge. Given the right circumstances and a skilful pilot, it could no doubt be a formidable weapon.[40]

The captured Biber, its interior ravaged by fire possibly ignited by the attack or in an attempt by its crew to destroy its controls, was transported back to Portsmouth where it underwent careful inspection.

In the meantime *Kommando Stab West*, K.z.S. Friedrich Böhme and his staff, had also departed for the same destination as the retreating Biber unit on 1 September, marking the end of *K-Verbände* West's presence in France.

CHAPTER FIVE

River Assault

German frogmen in action

Alongside the development of the Linsen, the emergence of *Kriegs-marine Kampfschwimmer* (frogmen) is another aspect of the *K-Verbände* development intertwined with units of the Brandenburgers. This time there was additional inter-service cross-pollination with the amalgamation of men from the Waffen SS and *Sicherheitdienst* (SD – SS Security Police) as well as *Abwehr* personnel.

Frogman delivery of explosives was an idea that the German Armed Forces first used in 1915 during the First World War. The original German frogman unit that formed at this time was the 2nd Reserve Pioneer Company of *Stettiner Pionierbattaillon 2*. Trained in the Rhine River near Mainz they first went into action on 17 August 1915 against Russian guardships near Kowno. Successfully disabling the Russian target it was also to be the last time that the Kaiser's frogmen were used during that conflict.

Once again the Italians provided fresh inspiration for German *Kampfschwimmer*, the *Decima Mas* having used them to great effect already in the Mediterranean. The *Abwehr* immediately seized on this idea and formed its own maritime sabotage troops, one of the first and the most successful of whom was Friedrich Hummel who took part in Italian raids on Gibraltar and Seville harbours. Hummel remains one of the German armed forces most colourful characters. His back-ground had involved years in the German merchant navy aboard the sailing vessel *Passat* that had visited Chile, South Africa, Japan and China amongst other destinations. He had joined the *Kriminalpolizei* in Altona, Hamburg, eventually transferring to the dreaded SD and promoted to *Hauptsturmführer* in 1942. Hummel had also been involved in *Abwehr* intelligence work in Poland on the eve of the war and in Madrid between 1942 and 1944. The *Abwehr* began to form small units, *Marine-Einsatz-Kommandos* (MEK), that would undertake tasks such as reconnaissance missions, bridge demolition, mine laying and so on. The first such MEKs to be established by the *Abwehr* were the MAREI and MARKO in Hamburg, which later served as templates for the *Kriegsmarine* when Heye's *K-Verbände* took over responsibility for the maritime commando service.

The Germans possessed a genuine advantage when developing the theory of military divers. While Jacques Cousteau, a Vichy French naval officer, is credited with the creation of the aqualung, it was noted Austrian diving pioneer Hans Hass who developed the first modern rebreather, ideal for military use as it left no tell-tale bubble exhaust. The unit originated from the Dräger firm's 1912-patented U-boat escape apparatus. The company continued to work on an evolution of this basic design until June 1942 when Dräger patented a recognisable rebreather with the air contained within a back-mounted bag. This is the device that Hans Hass used during his Aegean expedition in the summer of 1942. Hass had already excited the nautical world when he shot an underwater film '*Pirsh unter Wasser*' ('Stalking beneath the sea') in the course of a 1939 diving expedition with two friends, fellow-Austrian Alfred von Wurzian and Jörg Böhler. Their journey encompassed visits to Curaçao and Bonaire, the trio being forced to return to Vienna via the United States after the outbreak of war.

In 1942 Hass planned another expedition, though its location was constrained by wartime and thus took place in the Aegean Sea. It was there that Hass tested the new 'Dräger-Gegenlunge' oxygen rebreather. Though limited to a depth of approximately 20m due to the risk of oxygen toxicity, it was the perfect apparatus for military purposes. Hass and Alfred von Wurzian demonstrated the pioneering equipment to the *Kriegsmarine* commander of the Aegean, VA Erich Förste, and his Chief Of Staff K.K. Rothe-Roth from the mole in Piraeus Harbour on 11 July 1942. Oddly, despite the success of this breathing apparatus, the *Kriegsmarine* were slow to grasp its potential. Von Wurzian persevered, even attempting to get officers of the Army Pioneers interested in developing his frogman ideas, but to no avail. It was not until he began talking to representatives of the *Abwehr's Ausland Abteilung II*, responsible for sabotage, that he found more enthusiastic listeners though the *Abwehr* already possessed five specialists in ship sabotage – including Hummel.

Von Wurzian was also fortunate to meet a man who shared his vision of military frogmen within the Brandenburgers. *Gefreiter* Richard Reimann became his assistant, helping to develop other tools of their fledgling trade such as suitable compasses and depth gauges. In spring 1943 the two men were again asked to demonstrate the potential of the underwater fighter in Berlin, using the Olympic swimming baths before an audience of German and Italian officers. After the successful exercise Von Wurzian and Reimann found themselves invited to join the training units of the Italian *Decima Mas*, which they did the following May. Until September 1943 the two men worked alongside their Italian counterparts, training under the command of the outstanding athlete *Tenente di vascello* (Lieutenant Commander) Eugen Wolk and learning the *Decima Mas*'s techniques. Born of mixed German-Russian parentage in Cernogov in the Ukraine, Wolk had returned to Germany with his family during the Bolshevik revolution of 1917, where they found themselves less than welcome in a Germany teetering on the brink of wartime defeat. Moving onwards to Constantinople and then Rome, with his father's encouragement Wolk enrolled in the naval academy at Livorno. The academy's director, Angelo Belloni, was one of Italy's leading experts on diving and involved in training the *Decima Mas*'s divers (known as 'Gamma men') and correspondingly nurtured Wolk's enthusiasm for the subject of frogman operations.

Von Wurzian became a *de facto* member of the *Abwehr* while in Italy and eagerly began training. He and Reimann were in Rome when the unconditional surrender of Italy to the Allies was announced on 8 September, the German pair deciding to escape what they believed would be incarceration by the Italian authorities. Travelling on foot by night they reached German lines and discovered that Wolk and the bulk of the *Decima Mas* had also remained loyal to the fascist government. They would train together once more, this time in Valdagno, northeast of Verona, using the swimming pool already in existence as part of a sporting complex owned by the Manzotti textile manufacturing plant.

Wolk and Von Wurzian first arrived in the small town in the foothills of the Italian Alps on 2 January 1944, Wolk accompanied by eighty Italian frogmen and his deputy, Luigi Ferraro. Ferraro was one of a successful Italian demolition team that had sunk Allied shipping on operations from the Turkish harbours at Alexandretta (now Iskenderun) and Mersina (now Mersin). Von Wurzian in turn was accompanied by Reimann and thirty German recruits for the soon-to-be-established Lehrkommando 700. This unit provided the most complicated training structure to be seen within the *K-Verbände*, combining several different services within the German armed forces and intelligence apparatus. It was established at the end of March

1944 and remained based alongside the *Decima Mas* trainees at the swimming baths at Valdagno.

With the formation of the *K-Verbände* came the '*Einsatz und Ausbildung Süd*' under Kaptlt. Heinz Schomburg that was already involved in forming Linsen units within the Mediterranean theatre. Schomburg made a brief attempt to gain complete autonomous control of the Valdagno swimming baths for the *K-Verbände* but encountered obstructions almost immediately from both the *Abwehr* and also the SS who had become interested in the development of the *Kampfschwimmer* service. Nevertheless, the thirty German recruits that were training with Von Wurzian were subsequently transferred *en masse* to the *K-Verbände* and thus became *Kriegsmarine* personnel. In addition to these men and the *Decima Mas*, there were fifteen *Abwehr* personnel, commanded by *Hauptmann* Neitzer, and ten SS men also training alongside the *Kriegsmarine* personnel. One of the primary reasons that Wolk encouraged such wide German interest was in order to obtain a greater recognition and source of supply for his school, which was largely ignored by the existing Italian naval hierarchy. Regardless of his motivation, the results justified his efforts and three German service branches became enmeshed alongside the Italians within the training facilities. However, with Heye's ascendancy in controlling naval Special Forces came the crystallising of German service boundaries in Valdagno followed by the *K-Verbände*'s accession to overall command of the German contingent during April. Von Wurzian promptly resigned his *Abwehr* post immediately upon the formation of Lehrkommando 700 and became an official member of the *K-Verbände*.

Prior to April 1944 Wolk and Von Wurzian had trained the Germans of all three services jointly, but after the formation of the Lehrkommando, Wolk henceforth trained the Italian swimmers separately, the two nationalities being kept strictly segregated during their time spent in Valdagno. After the absorption of the school into the *K-Verbände*, Oblt.z.S. Sowa was placed in charge, displacing the *Abwehr*'s Neitzer who had acted as 'caretaker' director, though he remained on the premises to oversee Von Wurzian's continuing separate training of the fifteen *Abwehr* men. The relationship between Sowa and Neitzer soon soured and Sowa was transferred to Heiligenhafen, his place taken by the redoubtable *Hauptmann* Friedrich Hummel of the *Abwehr*, who also promptly resigned from the intelligence service and was enlisted as a *Kapitänleutnant* into the *K-Verbände*.

The Valdagno training centre covered the initial schooling of the *K-Verbände* recruits, another centre soon opened in May 1944 on the island of San Giorgio in Venice Lagoon for more advanced skills, the headquarters for Lehrkommando 700 transferring to Venice also shortly afterward. As the diving arm of the *K-Verbände* grew the subsidiary centres were renumbered: Valdagno as Lehrkommando 704 and San Giorgio Lehrkommando 701. Space had become rather limited in Valdagno by this stage and a further training centre was opened at Bavaria's Bad Tölz in the swimming baths at the SS *Junkerschule*. This new branch of the *K-Verbände* tree was named Lehrkommando 702.

The Venetian setting for Lehrkommando 701 was an ideal one in which the men could train. The isle of San Giorgio in Alga is situated within the Lower Lagoon in the proximity of the Isle of Trezze and Isle of San Angelo della Polvere. Benedictine monks had founded the first monastery and built a church consecrated to Saint George during the eleventh century on the small island, which lay in a strategic central position between dry land and the city of Venice. In 1717 fire destroyed the monastery and church, the island subsequently used first as a prison and then from 1806 a powder magazine for the Italian military. The 15,113m^2 roughly quadrangular island was surrounded by an imposing outside wall, pierced by one small harbour on its northwestern face. By the time of Lehrkommando 701's arrival the island possessed an Italian AA unit that comprised four obsolete 7.6cm Vickers Armstrong 1914 pattern guns, one 2cm Oerlikon and three 2cm Bredas commanded by a German artilleryman, *Leutnant* Kummer.

There the *K-Verbände* men trained both on land and in the water. In the Venice Lagoon they practised attacking two old ships moored for that purpose, the freighter *Tampico* and the tanker *Illiria*. Recruits were trained in the necessary tasks that would be faced by commandos including navigation, unarmed combat and stamina – the divers being dumped at sea and ordered to swim back to their island base amidst the currents that swirled around the many small islands. In fact much information had been gleaned for the Germans by captured orders for British commandos landed at Dieppe including handbook moves straight from their adversaries' training manuals. It was not long before Oblt.z.S. Fölsch had been placed in charge of Valdagno's Lehrkommando 704 and Von Wurzian was promoted to *Leutnant* and posted as Chief Instructor to San Giorgio.

The German frogmen were not adverse to playing pranks on their Italian allies as well, stealing a rowing boat from the nearby Italian arsenal and also attempting to steal a motor torpedo boat, though they were driven away by nervous sentries firing into the darkness after them. The lightness of such moments helped to disguise the deadly nature of the lessons learnt and also continued to foster the sense of elite that the *Kampfschwimmer* were imbued with. However, alongside the camaraderie, hard training and horseplay, the spectre of death that followed such dangerous work as that of the frogman saboteur claimed at least two lives. On 20 June 1944 *Verwaltungsmaat* and professional swimmer Werner Bullin was killed in a training accident, followed on 31 August 1944 by paratrooper *Obergefreiter* Herbert Klamt.

By June 1944 the divers had begun to be organised into units. The MEK MARKO that had been inherited by the *K-Verbände* from the Hamburg *Abwehr* was renamed MEK20 in April 1944 and placed initially under the command of *Sonderführer* KaptltdR Michael Opladen, later transferred to Oblt. (MA) Bröcker as Opladen retired to the *K-Verbände* Staff. MEK60 under the command of Oblt.MAdR Hans-Friedrich Prinzhorn, MEK65 under Oblt.z.S.dR Karl-Ernst Richert, MEK71 under Oblt.MAdR Horst Walters and MEK80 commanded by KaptltMA Dr Waldemar Krumhaar were also ready by June. Each unit comprised one officer and twenty-two men spread between fifteen trucks that would carry their personal and operational equipment. In action German frogmen wore a rubber suit of approximately 3mm thickness that was elasticised at the wrist and ankles and had a tight-fitting neck seal. Beneath this he wore a long thick knitted woollen suit that in turn was pulled on over an extra layer of woollen undergarments. The rubber layer comprised trousers with built-in boots and a separate jacket, pulled on and the ends of both segments rolled together and sealed with a thick rubber belt. This airtight 'dry-suit' was then covered by a canvas outer suit that acted as camouflage, pulled tight about the body by lace adjustments. A hood – and often the application of black face paint – finished the clothing. The breathing apparatus was worn on the diver's chest and he was trained to swim on his back toward the target, using his mouthpiece and nose clips only when necessary. Whatever natural buoyancy the trapped air within the suit and its woollen layers afforded was offset by the required lead weights, worn around the diver's waist.

The German frogmen were armed with several varieties of sabotage weapons for use against shipping targets. Sabotage Mine I consisted of a circular rubber float with charge and firing mechanism mounted within its centre. The float was to be inflated when positioned beneath the hull of a ship, the air holding the charge in place until detonation. Sabotage Mine II was a torpedo-shaped mine, constructed in four bolted-together sections. This was attached to a ship's keel by a simple clamp, the firing mechanism activated by water motion when the ship got underway. Sabotage Mine III was similar to the last type. Approximately 33cm long, of elliptical cross-section and with slightly convex ends, rubber buoyancy chambers could be affixed to the mine's body which again was clamped onto a ship's keel. As well as the motion detonator, a clockwork timing mechanism was contained within the fuse at the forward end. Allied reports indicated that often the clamps were booby-trapped so that the mine detonated if an attempt was made to unscrew it from the target vessel. Additionally, arming and firing mechanisms were fitted in both ends of the mine so that the weapon could be fired whether the vessel was proceeding forward or astern.

For attacks on bridges and caissons and such targets, the K-Verbände utilised cylindrical charges known as Muni Pakete and Nyr Pakete, containing respectively 600kg and 1,600kg of high explosive. Fitted with a timer based on the Italian ten-hour model, the weapon could only be defused by the keep ring being unscrewed. In addition, a modified GS Mine was used against bridge targets. Two buoyancy chambers were fitted at either end of the torpedo-shaped weapon enabling the mine to be floated down a river by divers and attached to the intended target. The timers used could be set for any length of time up to six days, though hourly settings were considered more accurate. In an attack against the Nijmegen bridge, the timer was set for four hours.[41]

The first use of K-Verbände frogmen came during June 1944 when divers were assigned the task of destroying two bridges 6km northeast of Caen; the Pont de Ranville over the Orne Canal (Canal de Caen) and Pont d'Heronville that spanned the Orne River, the two waterways running parallel with each other. Situated at the eastern extremity of the Allied Normandy landing zones, the bridges had been deemed as vital targets for the invaders in order to secure the left flank of the British Sword Beach. To the east of the river and canal is the Breville highland, which overlooked the British force's approach to the strategically important city of Caen. Therefore, Allied planners had decided that the heights must be captured, the bridges required to be left intact so that paratroopers could be supplied and reinforced once they had captured this high area. The river bridge is now famous as Pegasus Bridge, seized by an audacious British glider-borne assault in the early hours of 6 June. Though the area soon boasted bailey bridges to augment the two hard-won spans, they were considered of prime importance as targets, able to take more weight than their more makeshift counterparts.

Because of the importance of their first operation, the attacking force included Friedrich Hummel and von Wurzian – though the latter was excluded from actually entering combat and was kept in an advisory role. They and ten frogmen were despatched in three Lancia trucks from Venice to the German held area near Caen. However, on the road between Dijon and Paris one of the trucks was involved in a collision that injured four of the divers including Hummel, the wounded men being taken to a nearby field hospital and therefore unable to continue with the planned operation. Further along their path, between Paris and Caen the last two vehicles narrowly avoided the attentions of prowling RAF aircraft, hiding in thick roadside woods before the Allied fighter-bombers were able to attack.

The six remaining *Kampfschwimmer* and von Wurzian arrived in Caen without further incident and immediately set about organising their attack. They met with Oblt.MAdR Hans-Friedrich Prinzhorn, leader of MEK60 and *Einsatzleiter* for the forthcoming mission as part of Heye's Staff from *Marinegruppenkommando Süd*. The divers were split into two groups of three men each. The first, comprising *Feldwebel* Karl-Heinz Kayser, *Funkmaat* Heinz Bretschneider and *Obergefreiter* Richard Reimann, would transport one cylindrical charge to their target bridge over the Orne Canal. The second group, of Oblt.z.S. Sowa, *Oberfähnrich* Albert Lindner and *Fähnrich* Ullrich 'Uli' Schulz (an ex-human torpedo pilot), would carry an identical charge against the bridge over the Orne River, the canal and river bridges some 400m apart. Both groups were briefed to pass under the newly constructed bailey bridges and carry their attack forward against the bridges that had cost so much British and German blood on the morning of D-Day itself. While the attack was carried out both Prinzhorn and von Wurzian planned to remain on the bank of the Orne River, waiting near the spot where the divers were to return.

On the afternoon of 22 June the two 1,600kg heavy torpedo charges were prepared for action on the riverbank, but a brief flurry of British artillery fire scattered the group of men working around the torpedoes, save for the torpedo mechanic responsible for their smooth operation who doggedly remained working on the explosives as shells landed nearby. Within minutes of the barrage ending he activated the fuses, set to blow at 05.30hrs. Built and tested at Kieler Werft they were designed to have enough flotation to rest approximately half a metre below the water surface where divers could easily manoeuvre them into position. However, with the decreased density of fresh over salt water, the two charges promptly sank into the thick silt of the riverbed the moment they were launched. A makeshift solution was found after Prinzhorn sent his men racing to obtain empty petrol cans, which were then tied together with rope, the heavy torpedo slung between them and resting on the extra buoyancy.

The first group led by Kayser entered the canal water as night fell. Though less than a kilometre from the front line they faced an arduous swim of 12km to their target and the same to return. Kayser and Bretschneider took the lead, each pulling one side of the torpedo against the light current that they faced on the outward journey. Reimann took the rear position, guiding the torpedo and providing directional steerage to the unwieldy device. His transpired to be a nightmarish task as the rear petrol cans lost air allowing the stern of the torpedo to sink into the canal until it dragged once again in the silt. Reimann was constantly forced to submerge and lift the weapon, in the end resting the heavy torpedo on his straining shoulder as they inched up the canal with Reimann stumbling on foot through the thick silt.

> Then close ahead we sighted the first bridge, the one we were due to pass under. Visibility was poor; we heard what seemed a sentry's foot-steps on the wooden bridge. As a precaution we dived, passing under the bridge submerged. With the ropes we kept down the buoyant nose of the mine, while Reimann rested the tail on his shoulder.[42]

Eventually, amidst the dying echoes of a German artillery bombard-ment of that same bridge, their target materialised before them and the fatigued men quietly attached their charge to central pilings by embed-ding anchors into the river bottom that was thankfully more solid sand and gravel than silt. Once their weapon was positioned about a metre off the bottom, the timer already ticking steadily, the three men gently finned in the now currentless water towards the safety of the German lines as daybreak gradually crept into the eastern sky. They stayed together for the return, Reimann particularly exhausted by the difficult outward journey. Their mission was successful as the timer activated its charge slightly before its planned time, destroying what the Germans believed to be the main Orne Canal bridge.

The second mission was also successful and no less dramatic. The group made their way downstream towards their target in the Orne River aided by the current on their outward journey, Schulz and Sowa at the torpedo's head and Lindner pushing its tail. They had managed only a few hundred metres, still visible to their shore party when Sowa began to complain of sore feet, his fins apparently causing him great distress. Sowa immediately broke away and swam for the bank as the support personnel ran towards him. Encouraged to return to his comrades, Sowa's nerve broke completely and he began to weep while clinging to *terra firma*. Despite this unforeseen setback the two remaining men still with the torpedo and its ticking clock decided to press on.

The pair managed to negotiate a wooden barrier that lay across the river and soon afterward sighted what they believed was their primary target. Affixing the weapon to the riverbed they were dismayed to find the current too strong for their return, making little headway against it and threatened by the noise made as they finned harder and harder, frequently breaking the still surface of the water. Faced with little option they allowed themselves to drift slightly with the current, past their bridge and sought shelter on the riverbank – though the pit they chose was swiftly found to have once been an Allied latrine. With dawn breaking, they had no choice but to remain where they were and at 05.30hrs a huge explosion heralded success, the pair remaining within their stinking hiding place until night fell on 23 June. Faced with the same river current they made a difficult decision – to leave the river on its far bank, cross the 400m to the canal and swim back along its placid waters. Despite the obvious peril, their triumph was absolute and the two exhausted men were warmly received when they finally made landfall in German territory. However, Sowa was not amongst the men that greeted them. Ashamed of his breakdown he had waited anxiously for news of his comrades. When they failed to return that night or the following day he took it upon himself to enter the river and search for them. With British sentries alerted by the explosions to the possible danger of saboteurs he was seen and taken prisoner after being wounded in a brief burst of gunfire.

This baptismal raid had been successful – but not completely. As the first group had returned and were debriefed by Prinzhorn on the riverbank it became apparent that the planned target area and where the torpedo had actually been placed did not match. Due to what several historians have described as an 'incorrect sketch' of the target area, it appears that the wrong bridge was mined. There were apparently two bridges to negotiate before arriving at the one now called 'Pegasus Bridge'. Predictably, the same held true for the two surviving men of the second group, the nearby Pont d'Heronville still standing after the weapon's detonation.[43] Nevertheless, the *K-Verbände* had proved themselves equal to the task of commando raids. One man had been lost out of six and two bridges had been successfully destroyed.

There was little time to rest upon their newly-acquired laurels. From the beginning of the Allied landings in Normandy to the eventual collapse of the German front in France the *K-Verbände* frogmen would undertake twenty-four missions, the majority of them successful. Amongst the frogmen's achievements were the destruction of lock gates on the Orne by eight men led by the ex-SS man *Obermaat* Orlowski during July and the sabotage of captured German guns on 26 August by Prinzhorn and seven of his men. Earlier that month advancing British troops had captured the 15cm L/45 coastal guns of a battery at Vasouy that were originally designed to protect the mouth of the River Seine. Manned by men of MAA266, the guns and ammunition were abandoned without being disabled as British forces approached. Situated as they were between Honfleur and Trouville, the guns were perfectly placed within their concrete bunkers to bombard German-held Le Havre, only 7km away across the Seine river mouth. Prinzhorn and his men, led by an artilleryman familiar with the site, approached the formidable emplacement aboard two commandeered control Linsens and were able to land successfully less than 100m from the first bunkers. The artillery was situated above a bank that fringed the heavily-mined beach and Prinzhorn's assault party crept silently to their objectives, planting explosives in the gun barrels themselves and slipping through the narrow gap between gun and concrete to place other charges amongst the stored ammunition. Each bunker lacked an individual guard and the raiders were able to destroy the guns without challenge by the few British sentries that tramped slowly around the site and without loss to themselves.

However, all was not well within the ranks of Lehrkommando 700. In June 1944 Heye had placed the medical officer MstArzt Dr Arnim Wandel in overall charge of the *Kampfschwimmer* branch of the *K-Verbände*, replacing the colourful Friedrich Hummel. At first Wandel faced problems in winning the acceptance of the frogmen under his command, Hummel being held in high regard due to his obvious experience in underwater sabotage. Wandel on the other hand had served not as a saboteur but as a U-boat medical officer aboard *U-129* during 1941 before holding staff positions in the 26th and 11th U-Flotillas. Between April and June 1944 he had been attached to the *Einsatz und Ausbildungs Stab Süd* where he reported on the superb state of the training facilities and men at Valdagno and on the Venetian island of San Giorgio. Reporting back to Heye on his findings, the Admiral was impressed enough by the young officer to appoint him as commander of Lehrkommando 700 – despite the Geneva Convention forbidding medical officers to command combat units.

Wandel was later described as an 'extremely hard worker' but completely lacking in both the requisite technical knowledge and grasp of the overall tactical situations faced by his men. Furthermore, many felt that Wandel lacked the necessary drive and ruthlessness to forward the ambitions of the frogmen of Lehrkommando 700. On the other hand, these were skills that Hummel – and indeed the SS commando leader Otto Skorzeny himself – possessed in abundance. There remains some confusion as to the reasoning behind this unusual personnel change. Böhme later told Allied interrogators that he met Hummel in Paris on 10 August 1944 and the latter claimed to still be in charge of Lehrkommando 700, Wandel merely acting as a 'caretaker' senior officer in his absence. There is every likelihood that Hummel was actually removed from the post by Heye as he strove to eliminate the insidious and invasive presence of the *Abwehr* within his service. As we shall see he would soon also do the same with the SS men within the *K-Verbände*, attempting to regain complete control of the service rather than have the *K-Verbände* divided by such animosity and inter-service rivalry that elements within the Third Reich apparently thrived on.

With this uneasy tension affecting the Lehrkommando, Otto Skorzeny paid Valdagno a visit on 30 June, later also touring San Giorgio with Wandel. The potential of what he saw must have impressed the SS commando who also tested the diving equipment himself in the Venice Lagoon. He had already managed to convince Heye to accept SS men under disciplinary sentences into the *K-Verbände* and later the following month he despatched SS *Untersturmführer* Walter Schreiber to be his SS representative at Valdagno, a liaison officer between Himmler's organisation and the *K-Verbände*.

However, at the front there was little time for the frogmen of the *K-Verbände* to concern themselves with the internal wrangling of their service headquarters. The last mission of August 1944 for MEK 60 and MEK65 was undertaken in support of the Bibers of 261 K-Flotilla. After their disastrous committal to action on 30 August the Bibers were withdrawn and Prinzhorn's men were tasked with destroying any abandoned machines and their torpedoes as the rest of the Bibers retreated from Normandy. The MEKs were the last *Kriegsmarine* troops to leave the port of Fécamp, their own withdrawal to Ghent fraught with problems due once again to Allied air superiority and the *Wehrmacht*'s demolition of many water crossings and roads. The units were hurriedly moved on from Ghent on 3 September to Schouten near Antwerp and from there also pushed on to Utrecht due to enemy spearhead formations facing across Belgium.

The MEKs were scheduled for transfer to Denmark for rearming and reinforcement but the *Marinebefehlshaber Niederland* (Flag Officer Commanding the Netherlands), VA Gustav Kleikamp, demanded their retention for use around Antwerp. They correspondingly remained in Utrecht, reinforced by thirty officers and men from MEK 40 on 11 September and supplied with three Linsens, three Marders and demolition mines for future use. An original group of eleven frogmen from Sesto Calende that were due to also join them were delayed, replaced by ten frogmen from Lübeck instead, the men having recently transferred from Venice to the German port.

On 8 September, K.z.S. Böhme was appointed as commander of all K-Flotillas and MEKs in the Scheldt area. His brief was to employ his forces when opportunities presented themselves; his first task allocated by OKW being the destruction of the Kruisschans and Royer locks on the Scheldt in what would become 'Operation Bruno'. During the rapid fall of Antwerp to British armoured forces on 4 September the speed with which the advanced elements of the 11th Armoured Division had entered the city had completely surprised the German defenders. British troops, helped in no small part by Belgian resistance members, arrived to find the lock gates that controlled the rise and fall of the tide within the harbour basin largely undamaged, the *Kriegsmarine* Harbour Commander (*Hafenkommandant Antwerpen*), F.K. Joachim Syskowitz, being killed in a brief skirmish as he attempted to carry out the planned destruction of the lock and dockside equipment.[44]

The port of Antwerp was, and still is, one of Europe's great harbours, but it is not a natural one. Its expansive docks were dug to the northwest of the city centre, their first use recorded during medieval times. Though it rests some way inland on the River Scheldt it remains a tidal harbour and so the first canal lock was constructed in the port at the beginning of the twentieth century. The Royers Lock was 30m in length and 7m wide and allowed for the first time the round-clock usage of the port. As shipping grew in size new locks were required to allow access by the larger vessels and so in 1928 the Kruisschans Lock was added to the harbour entrance alongside its predecessor. Unable to deny the Allies the port of Antwerp, Böhme was instructed to investigate the viability of sabotaging the lock in order to render the harbour inoperative.

ABOVE: American troops inspect the remains of a Neger washed ashore near the Anzio beachhead. The element of surprise with its novel weaponry was soon lost by the K-Verbände.

ABOVE: The two Knight's Cross winners of the 361 K-Flotilla with their flotilla commander. *Oberfernschreibmeister* Herbert Berrer (left) was awarded the decoration on 5 August 1944 and is accompanied after the ceremony here by *Oberleutnant zur See* Leopold Koch (middle) the unit commander and *Schreiberobergefreiter* Walter Gerhold (right) who had won his KC on 6 July 1944.

RIGHT: German propaganda reported Gerhold's award after his sinking of an enemy 'cruiser'. Much was made in the German press of the effect that a single man could have on a large enemy warship.

Walther Gerhold, Schreiberobergefreiter (wegen Tapferkeit vorm Feind zum Schreiberobergefreiten befördert)

Er erhielt das Ritterkreuz des Eisernen Kreuzes

Keine Seegeltung ohne einheitlichen Staatswillen eines Volkes!

Adm. v. Trotha

ABOVE: The main improvement featured in the Marder was the ability to dive. On the left hand edge of the canopy was a small dive bubble to show the pilot the inclination of his machine.

LEFT: Young pilots such as these typified the K-Verbände's human torpedo service, often fresh from the fertile recruiting grounds of the Hitler Youth movement.

ABOVE: The Linsen explosive motorboat is unveiled to various military and Nazi Party officials. Among the audience is a Japanese naval officer, Luftwaffe General Adolf Galland and Albert Speer, the head of Germany's armaments industry.

ABOVE: A Biber submerges during a test run. This still was taken from German wartime newsreel.

ABOVE: *Leutnant* Alfred Vetter is congratulated by *Grossadmiral* Karl Dönitz after his award of the Knight's Cross on 12 August 1944 for service as commander of the 211 K-Flotilla in its actions off Normandy.

ABOVE: The cockpit of the Biber. This example was recently restored and remains the only working example of its kind in the world at Gosport's Royal Navy Submarine Museum.

ABOVE: The Biber prototype 'Adam' is readied for a test run.

ABOVE: View through the small hatch looking down at a Biber pilot. Their accommodation was cramped; their death rate alarmingly high.

RIGHT: A Biber pilot clears ice from his conning tower. Thick winter ice was a problem for the Bibers, many lost to damage caused by thick floes.

ABOVE: A Biber is wheeled into the water by hand for practice. The torpedo visible is a dummy weapon used for exercises and designated as such by its red and white striped inert warhead.

LEFT: A Biber is prepared for reloading of its torpedoes. This still was taken from German wartime newsreel as was the following photo.

RIGHT: The torpedoes are held in place aboard a trailer while the Biber is manoeuvred into position to receive them.

ABOVE: Bibers in harbour in The Netherlands being held in place by their 'ground-crew'.

ABOVE: A Biber found by Royal Marine Commandos of 30 Assault Unit on the Amiens-Bapaume road in September 1944. It had been damaged by air attack and abandoned by the retreating Germans.

ABOVE: The ill-fated Biber '90' photographed from HMS *Ready* as the British destroyer attempts to capture it.

ABOVE: A boat from HMS *Ready* prepares to take Biber 90 in tow, the pilot dead at his controls.

Maschinenobergefreiter Norbert Keller photographed aboard a 'snow-Linsen' in January 1945 at Gänserndorf near Vienna when he was serving with 217 K-Flotilla on the Eastern Front. The word 'Kuchen' was the name of Keller's section leader *Oberbootsmann* Kuchen. (Courtesy of Maurice Laarman)

ABOVE: Linsens being readied for an operational sortie from The Netherlands.

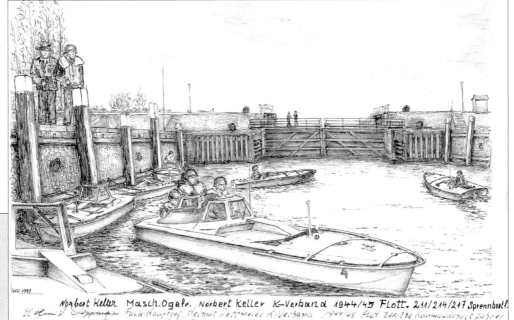

Norbert Keller Masch.Ogefr. Norbert Keller K-Verband 1944/45 Flott. 211/214/217 Sprennbootf.

ABOVE: A sketch signed by three veterans of the 211 K-Flotilla showing a similar scene. A three-man control boat is centre place. (Courtesy of Maurice Laarman)

ABOVE: Propaganda photo used in *Die Kriegsmarine* magazine showing an explosive Linsen moving at speed.

LEFT: German frogmen enter the water as they begin one of their river raids.

OPPOSITE TOP: A Panzerfähre IV tractor pulls a Molch armed with dummy torpedoes from the sea during trials in Germany. The Molch has received a new look – teeth painted on the submarine's bow.

OPPOSITE BOTTOM: A Hecht is lowered into the sea outboard of its depot ship in Germany. Ultimately unsuccessful they nevertheless provided valuable training machines for future Seehund crews.

RIGHT: Arthur Axmann, head of the Hitler Youth, decorates a young Neger pilot with Iron Cross First Class in Berlin as part of a recruiting drive in late 1944.

RIGHT: Otto Skorzeny (right) visits the frogmen of Lehrkommando 700 at the island of San Giorgio in the Venice Lagoon. The Lehrkommando's commander, Dr Arnim Wandel, is at centre of the photograph.

gkdos 19535-28 a Abzug 3

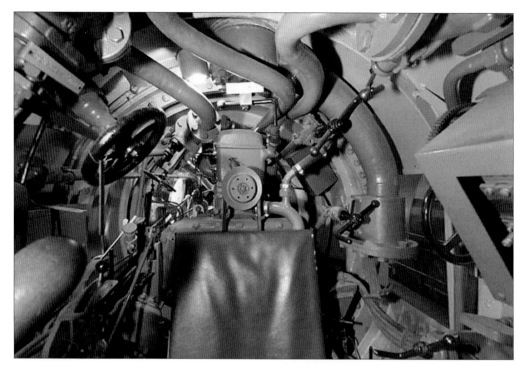

ABOVE: View from the pilot's chair looking sternward at the engineer's position. The diesel engine can be plainly seen immediately behind.

RIGHT: The Flotilla Engineer of Lehrkommando 300, K.K. (Ing.) Erhardt, helps Dönitz enter the cramped confines of a Seehund during an inspection visit.

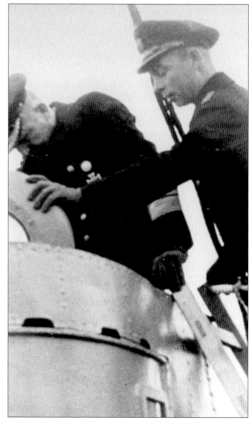

ABOVE: *Leutnant zur See* Ulrich Müller in the conning tower of his heavily camouflaged *U-5329*.

ABOVE: *U-5074* under way in Germany. The low silhouette of the surfaced Seehund is obvious. This particular boat was one of three that surrendered at the war's end in Dunkirk.

LEFT: *Fregattenkapitän* Albrecht Brandi (centre) sees off his Seehund men as they prepare to depart The Netherlands for action off England's coast.

LEFT: *Kommando Stab Süd* in Italy, August 1944. From left to right: Kaptlt. Schomburg, (Einsatzleiter) Kaptlt. Thiersch (Staff Officer), K.z.S. Hartmann (Commander), LzS Feiden (War Correspondent) and Oblt.z.S. Härting (Adjutant).

BELOW: An abandoned and partially stripped Biber found in a Dutch bunker at the war's end. Courtesy of Maurice Laarman.

ABOVE: Assembled Seehunds held by the Allies before testing and eventual destruction.

ABOVE: A surrendered Seehund at Toulon after being recommissioned into the French Navy. In the background is war prize *U-471*.

RIGHT: Two crewmen make a last journey as test pilots for the US Navy off the Florida Keys. If the weather had been like this in operational use, the effectiveness of the midgets would no doubt have been greater.

BELOW: Bibers carried aboard a Type VIIC in the abortive Operation Caesar attack on Kola Bay.

BOTTOM: The aftermath broken Bibers ashore near Narvik after the German surrender.

An initial reconnaissance carried out by a Linsen carrying men of MEK65 on 10 September showed that though the Royers Lock appeared to be jammed closed, the Kruisschans lock gates were largely undamaged and Böhme approached ObH. MAdR Prinzhorn with the potential mission. Prinzhorn studied the problem and soon accepted on behalf of his men. By destroying the main lock gate totally, Antwerp could be denied to the Allies for a considerable period of time. Aware that the mission would require precise targeting and that newly deployed protective nets would have to be negotiated, the only real option remained frogmen rather than an attempted attack using Marders. The attackers would be carried toward their target from Lillo, a small polder village close to the mouth of the Scheldt and near the Dutch–Belgian border, using Linsens with silenced engines. Two separate groups on duplicate missions would be used, thus doubling the chance of success.

On 8 September the problems within Lehrkommando 700 once again rose to the surface as Böhme encountered Friedrich Hummel in Utrecht. Hummel, calling himself by one of his many aliases, Hellmers, arrived at Böhme's headquarters in the uniform of an Army *Hauptmann*, stating that he was at that time working directly for the RSHA (*Reichssicherheithaupamt* – the Reich Security Department), ostensibly as part of Otto Skorzeny's *Jagdverbände*. He then proceeded to inform Böhme that he had been personally selected by Admiral Heye to carry out the mission against the Kruisschans lock and requested that the necessary men and material be placed at his disposal. Böhme was apparently extremely affronted by this declaration and refused point blank, stating that the mission had already been entrusted to Prinzhorn. After a brief and heated discussion Hummel departed, Böhme subsequently complaining to Heye about Hummel's behaviour only to be informed by his superior that Hummel had at no point been entrusted with the mission, though Heye had discussed the matter with Hummel and given him permission to go to Utrecht to act as an advisor to Böhme.

The arrival at Utrecht of the frogmen that would operate under Prinzhorn had taken longer than expected and the first planned mission date of 12 September was postponed for one more night. On schedule, one Linsen slipped from harbour at midnight followed by the second half an hour later. However, contrary currents forced a disappointing abandonment of the mission and the saboteurs returned to port. The following night they tried again, this time with greater success.

The attacking force comprised two Linsens from 216 K-Flotilla, each carrying an officer, group leader, helmsman and three frogmen with a single modified GS mine in tow. One Linsen was commanded by Prinzhorn himself, the other by *Leutnant* Dörpinghaus, the latter making better way than Prinzhorn's boat and soon the two had separated in the fog and darkness. Dörpinghaus followed the operational plan and hugged the east bank of the river, searching for the 'dolphins' – wooden pilings that marked the entrance to the lock itself. After hours of nerve-wracking probing, a disappointed Dörpinghaus ordered his Linsen to reverse course, fearing that they had somehow overshot the lock entrance. As the small boat eased back toward the centre of the wide river one of the elusive 'dolphins' loomed out of the hazy darkness. Discovered to be less than 1,000m from the lock gates Dörpinghaus secured his Linsen to the pylon, he and his men waiting for the time agreed with Prinzhorn in which to begin their final approach and thus co-ordinate their attacks. The moment finally arrived and the three frogmen, *Feldwebel* Karl Schmidt, *Mechaniker-maat* Hans Greten and *Maschinenmaat* Rudi Ohrdorf, eased into the water. Unhooking their mine from the Linsen the three saboteurs followed the line of 'dolphins' toward the lock.

> I [Schmidt] swam ahead, the other two steadying the tail of the mine in the eddies that played around the dolphins. We were passing very close to one of these, perhaps the seventh, when my suit got hooked on some obstruction jutting out from the structure. My suit was ripped and I felt the cold water filling it, driving out the warm air cushion. My comrades came to my aid and tried to persuade me to return to the waiting boat, but I was determined to go on and by letting some oxygen into the counter-lung of my breathing apparatus I managed to regain buoyancy.[45]

Schmidt, Greten and Ohrdorf carried on toward the lock gates, negotiating the first net barrage with ease but taking longer to circumvent the ensuing nets of finer mesh. The three men were forced to go around them, slipping through the narrow gap between net and shore with their mine in tow. Eventually the gate appeared in the darkness and the three men were able to rest alongside the stone pillars that flanked the huge metal gate. They could hear the steady footsteps of a sentry above them as they prepared to lay the mine against the sill of the lock. The mine was able to have its buoyancy adjusted by releasing air trapped in compartments at either end, a push button opening the required valve. Once on or near the seabed, a second button started the time fuse, the explosive force of detonation in theory concentrated by the water pressure against the target structure. Schmidt and Ohrdorf held an end each, gripping two small handles as they co-ordinated the release of the air. On Schmidt's signal they both pushed the button, the sudden weight dragging them swiftly underwater – so quickly that Schmidt's fins leapt out of the water with a resounding splash before he plummeted to the seabed. Behind him Greten froze, terrified that the sentry would have heard the disturbance. Seconds later he heard footsteps crossing the gate from one side of the lock to the other, but they were the slow measured tramp of a complacent guard; they had escaped detection.

> The sudden pressure on our heads due to the quick descent made Ohrdorf and I feel numb. It was now high water and we were still going down until at about 18 metres the mine bumped heavily on the sill of the lock. It lay well, so I pressed the fuse button and we immediately began to surface, too quickly for my liking. I drew air from the counter-lung and blew it out into the water to slow down the ascent, but both of us still bobbed up like corks, puffing and panting.[46]

Once more their luck held as the sentry had still not noticed them. After a brief rest the trio began to retrace their steps until Schmidt finally succumbed to the cold of his punctured suit after negotiating only one net. Despite his protestations, his two comrades held on and dragged him the remainder of the way back to Dörpinghaus and the waiting Linsen. Schmidt was manhandled aboard followed by the two other frogmen and the Linsen cast off, retreating into the darkness. The Germans sighted another motor boat heading directly for them as they headed for their base and so they abandoned caution and opened the throttle to maximum, managing to outpace the pursuing craft. As events transpired, the other boat was Prinzhorn's Linsen, still dragging its mine after they had failed to find the lock gates. The duplication of the mission plan had saved them from failure, Prinzhorn sighting the lock gate at the moment when Dörpinghaus' boat began to leave the scene and correctly guessing by their speed that they had laid their mine successfully.

A little after 05.00hrs a violent explosion shook the outer gate of the Kruisschans lock. *Luftwaffe* reconnaissance was later able to confirm that day that the gate was buckled and the harbour water level was falling with the ebb tide, signifying that the mission had succeeded and Antwerp was effectively, though temporarily, unusable, although by 13 October the subject of denying the use of Antwerp to the enemy was again high on the agenda of a situation meeting at Führer Headquarters, the *Wolfsschanze*. The same night that Prinzhorn and Dörpinghaus had attacked Antwerp's locks another group of ten frogmen had been scheduled to attack bridges in the Vught area south of Hertogenbosch, though German records do not record the outcome of their planned enterprise.

The German frogmen had once again proved their worth in combat and MEK60 was soon presented with a range of tasks to accomplish within the Scheldt. They were charged with the destruction of shipping at the Scheldt quay, which had failed to scuttle before the German evacuation; the scuttling of a German minesweeper lying off Fort Philip; the destruction of Scheldt navigation buoys by use of frogmen and Linsens; and an attack on a bridge south of Eindhoven. The men of 'Operation Bruno' were also ordered to demolish bridges and tunnels in the front-line area. The destruction of the minesweeper and Scheldt buoys between Hansweerth and Antwerp were successfully carried out on the night of 20 September, though one Linsen was hit by machine-gun fire from the south bank of the river.

Vizadmiral Kleikamp had in the meantime employed MEK65 as a reconnaissance unit as the military situation had deteriorated once more. On 17 September Field Marshal Montgomery made his bid for an armoured thrust over the natural barrier of the River Rhine and into the heart of Germany, threatening the industrial area of the Ruhr and aimed directly at Berlin. Code-named 'Operation Market Garden' the plan relied on the intact capture by airborne forces of three key bridges at Eindhoven, Nijmegen and Arnhem as well as several smaller crossings that the armour of British XXX Corps could pass over. History remembers the operation as going 'a bridge too far' but by 20 September Eindhoven had already fallen and Nijmegen Bridge was captured intact after a courageous river assault in broad daylight made by Americans of the 82nd Airborne Division. However, British troops at Arnhem were under extreme pressure by largely Waffen SS troops and the day after Nijmegen's fall were forced to surrender the bridge's northern end and became isolated within the city. In Nijmegen XXX Corps were forced onto the defensive and Montgomery's plan was failing.

MEK65 was engaged in reconnoitring the area around Arnhem–Hertogenbosch as Polish paratroops were dropped on the south side of the river to attempt to link up with the British troops trapped in Arnhem on the north side. The *K-Verbände* men also began the first of what would become many attempts to deny bridges to the Allies as they

84

prepared to demolish the Allied-held crossings at Nijmegen that consisted of a railroad bridge and the far more daunting road bridge. By this time the men of MEK65 were reinforced by Prinzhorn's MEK60 and the Germans established their headquarters in a barn near the Dutch–German border as they pondered their next move. The Rhine splits into two separate rivers around the Dutch–German border – the Waal, that flowed past Nijmegen, and the Lek, which was crossed at Arnhem. Due to the extreme current in the Waal and the size of the target Prinzhorn and MEK65's senior officer Kaptlt. Richard differed in their view on how best to destroy the bridge. Richard believed frogmen to be the only method by which to reach the bridge unobserved, though Prinzhorn maintained that Linsens were necessary in order to defeat the speed of the water flow. A sharp bend in the river about 150m upstream meant that frogmen would be badly placed to deliver the size of charge required to damage the thick bridge pylons.

Each one of the bridge pylons measured some 11m long and 4m thick, a formidable target to destroy using demolition charges floated downstream. There was little to be gained by exploding a charge alongside the foundations – the entire pylon would have to be lifted from its base to bring down the main span. Both Prinzhorn and Richard agreed that it could only be achieved by a pair of torpedo mines, each with 1.2 tons of explosive within the combined weapons and connected to each other by a length of thick rope. This rope would then be used to snag the weapon against the bridge pylon where they could be sunk to the required depth, one charge resting each side of it and co-ordinated to detonate simultaneously. They allocated one pair of mines for the rail bridge and two for the road bridge.

The two commanders continued to disagree on the method by which to deliver this hefty weapon to the bridges and therefore two frogmen, including one-time Brandenburger and member of *Jagdverbände Donau Hauptmann* Kurt Wimmer, volunteered to make a trial swim along the 35km length of river that would see them safely emerge once more in German-held territory. Their task was twofold; to reconnoitre the bridge area and test the current. The pair successfully completed their mission, entering the water near midnight and exiting the following morning at their correct preassigned position. However, the results were less than encouraging as the pair were swept swiftly past both of the bridges, unable to manoeuvre themselves against the current and between the central piers where the charges would need to be placed.

The problem returned to what kind of delivery method to use. At this point Friedrich Hummel once again made a not-entirely-welcome appearance. Brandishing a signed authorisation on the 'highest author-ity' Hummel assumed command of the operation in the name of the RSHA. According to the German author Cajus Bekker Hummel ignored in his swiftly hatched plan the need for silence and secrecy to carry out the operation and instead declared that a combined force of assault boats and frogmen would attack the bridges. While the assault boats drew the enemy's fire, the frogmen would lay their charges. If true, this notion was ludicrous and at the very least Prinzhorn was unhappy to see his *Kommando* commandeered by the SS and telegraphed his con-cerns to Admiral Heye. However Hummel's authorisation by Hitler to control the task was genuine and Prinzhorn departed shortly afterward to oversee the aforementioned attack on the Kruisschans Lock leaving Hummel in charge.

Hummel began planning for the attack almost immediately. He would use the twin-torpedo charge that Prinzhorn and Richard had put forward, the weapon requiring four men to control in the water; one at each end of a mine holding onto lines strung from the torpedo bodies. Again, according to Bekker's account, Hummel decided to make his own study of the target bridge and took two assault boats to study the Nijmegen crossing, attracting heavy fire and alerting the British guards to the danger posed by frogmen. If true this would display a bizarre lapse of judgement on behalf of such an experienced saboteur. Nevertheless if true it also proved the impossibility of hoping to approach the bridge in boats. Frogmen were the only method by which the attack could be mounted. At some point immediately after Hummel's alleged botched reconnaissance the British flooded the area upstream of the road bridge with arc- and searchlights to deter any possible attacks. British and Canadian units were posted along the Waal riverbank and authorised to fire at anything vaguely suspicious. The Allies would not relinquish the bridge that so many men had died to take despite the fact that by 25 September the surviving British troops of the 1st Airborne Division had withdrawn over the Lower Rhine from Arnhem, leaving the majority of their strength behind, dead or captured. 'Market Garden' had failed and the Rhine remained inviolate at the crucial final bridge.

Regardless of whether there is in fact substance to Hummel's alleged behaviour, the attack was finally launched on the night of 28 September. The first group comprising *Funkmaat* Heinz Bretschneider (veteran of the Orne bridge attack), *Obergefreitern* Walter Jäger, Gerhard Olle and Adolf Wolchendorf took to the water about 10km upstream of their target lugging the mines destined for the railroad span, the two cylinders joined together for ease of transport. The four men passed submerged under the illuminated road bridge and made ready to snag their mine against the pylons of the rail bridge when the unexpected obstruction of a pontoon crossing loomed from the darkness. Frantically diving to avoid the obstruction the men were nearly separated from the mines as they snagged on one of the pontoons. Their situation was precarious in the extreme as the four Germans clung to the guy ropes and were compelled to surface as quietly as possible and try to free the trapped weapon. Bretschneider remembered reaching the water surface and being able to see the shadows of British engineers working on the roadway above him, the glow of their cigarette-ends plainly visible.

Almost miraculously the four Germans were able to free the weapon without attracting the attention of the enemy above them and drifted onwards to the rail bridge. They had little time in which to pull apart the two mines, two men on each as they separated them enough to allow the rope trailing between them to act as anchor for the weapon. They were able to snag their weapon against the stonework of the pylon and sink it into place activating the timer and then drifting away with the current. Freed from their cumbersome charge the four men gradually became separated as they allowed the Rhine to deliver them to German lines once more. Bretschneider again remembered the sporadic firing of white signal flares agreed upon beforehand to show the frogmen where friendly territory began. With daylight creeping into the east he searched for a place in which to conceal himself, alighting upon a derelict fishing boat where he slept the daytime hours away, resuming the swim to safety once night had fallen again. Finally, using the signal flares as a guide he clambered from the cold water to be greeted by his comrades, Walter Jäger amongst them. He too had been forced into hiding during the previous day, narrowly escaping capture by two soldiers whom he was forced to fight unarmed before taking flight and later hiding himself within a hollow tree stump. They were, however, the sole members of the team to return, Olle and Wolchendorf both having been detected and captured by the British.

The second and third groups that were destined for the road bridge had less fortune. The first of these was forced against the shore by the sudden bend of the Rhine, unable to control the ponderous mines as the current caught them. Stranded in barely waist-deep water they desperately tried to inch the weapons back into the deeper river water, wary of the British guns only metres away on the riverbank. A fusillade of shots suddenly rang out across the Rhine as the last group also washed against the river bank slightly upstream, spotted and fired on by British troops of 5th Battalion (Gloucester) who killed one man and wounded two others. The three survivors were dragged from the water, their mines abandoned and sunk behind them.

The four men of the second group, *Bootsmaat* Henze and *Unteroffizieren* Krämer and Kammhuber led by the formidable commander of SS *Jagdverbände Donau Untersturmführer* Walter Schreiber, laboriously moved towards open water, braced for the inevitable fusillade of shots. Schreiber activated the timer on the mine lest they be discovered although their silent struggles were finally rewarded as the mine floated free with the current once more. However, they had also finally been seen. Bullets splashed into the water around them as they despairingly realised that the current would not allow them to position their mines against the bridge pylon. With little option left open to them they flooded the chambers and allowed the mines to sink into the Rhine, too far away to do any real damage to the Nijmegen Bridge. Schreiber, Krämer and Kammhuber would subsequently reach friendly lines, but Henze was captured later that day by a British riverside patrol.

In due course Bretschneider's mines exploded and the rail bridge was demolished, though *Luftwaffe* reconnaissance aircraft later showed only minor damage to the road bridge by Schreiber's misplaced mines. Bretschneider and Jäger were awarded the German Cross in Gold for their successful attack. German propaganda in turn trumpeted the achievement, illustrations drawn to show frogmen placing the huge charges giving credit where credit was indeed due to the courageous commandos. Even the British Press were impressed, the London *Times* reporting on 6 October that the Nijmegen attack was one of the 'most daring operations of the war'.

Elsewhere the campaign waged by the *Marine Einsatz Kommandos* continued apace. The Antwerp operations had been successfully executed and smaller missions in support of Scheldt operations carried out. As the Allies had advanced with 'Market Garden' the Linsens and Marders that had been based at Lillo were withdrawn to the more secure area of Groningen. A further attempt was also made on the Nijmegen road bridge by MEK60 using two borrowed Linsens and two likewise purloined Marders. The small force departed from a point three kilometres west of Tolamer at 19.30hrs on 15 October, the Linsens towing one mine each. After travelling for 9km the mine tows were transferred to the Marders, which in turn were supposed to continue to the bridge, affix the mines (by a method unspecified in reports) and then return to Zaltbommel. The Linsens discharged their mine tows to the Marders as planned and returned, though the human torpedoes subsequently aborted the attack for reasons that were not mentioned in German records. A second attempt was planned though this time the mines were lost in transit from Utrecht due to Allied air attack and another attempt was not able to be launched until 23 October, though this too was defeated as the Linsens failed to drag the mines freely into the current, the heavy mines becoming embedded in thick mud and later destroyed.

A fresh attempt on the Nijmegen Bridge by the newly raised MEK40 that had arrived in the Netherlands to relieve MEK60 and 65 was aborted on 14 November though the following night Prinzhorn's MEK60 demolished a bridge at Moerdijk over the Holländsche Diep. MEK40 became embroiled in fighting within the Scheldt, a small raiding party sent to North Beveland failing to return in late November.

The flooding of the Rhine in December and the subsequent loss of suitable landmarks precluded further attempts against the Nijmegen Bridge. Nevertheless a detachment from MEK40 and twenty-four Bibers were being held in readiness for another attempt once the flood-waters had subsided. The remainder of MEK40 were spread between Rotterdam, Zeist and Biebosch islands, the latter involved in the elimination of an enemy machine gun post and capture of a boat carrying eight Allied agents during December.

Towards the end of 1944 and perhaps in no small part due to the antipathy with which many officers within the *K-Verbände* viewed Hummel, Admiral Heye moved to completely eliminate any presence of the *Abwehr* and SS within his service, during November ordering the removal of all such personnel from the *K-Verbände*. Böhme was convinced that this decision was due to Hummel's actions at Utrecht, which Heye may have interpreted as an attempt by the SS to steal the 'glory' due to the *K-Verbände*. It could also not have been helped by resentment that had grown in Lehrkommando 700 regarding the incorporation of SS probationary troops being posted to Wandel's unit. The annoyance of the *K-Verbände* officers and men rested predominantly on the fact that the SS men thus transferred by Skorzeny were usually being punished for some misdemeanour at the front, their degradation in rank and dangerous new employment viewed as a way to regain their honour. Many of the *Kriegsmarine* personnel were at first unaware of this and when they learned the details, including what have been described as several 'unpleasant incidents' they viewed it as a perceived slight on the elite and honourable status of the *K-Verbände*. By the month's end the weeding out of the SS and *Abwehr* men had been completed, at least fifty SS men removed from six *K-Verbände* units and returned to their original service. Many would subsequently use their experience for Skorzeny within his *Jagdverbände*.

In January 1945, to placate those officers and men that still considered the young medical officer as unsuited to the task, Wandel was finally removed from command of the Lehrkommando 700 and his place taken by K.K. Hermann Lüdke. The base for the Lehrkommando had already moved due to the inexorable advance of Allied troops, the Venetian units having relocated to Sylt on 21 October 1944, Lehrkommando 704 following shortly afterward.

It was not just within the West that German frogmen had found employment during 1944.

> December 10, 1944; 15.00hrs: The Chief of the General Staff, Army, emphasises the importance of destroying the Russian Danube bridges south of Budapest. The C-in-C Navy comments that Naval Shock Troops are available for such tasks in the area of the Southern Army Group, and that it is the responsibility of the local authorities to plan and execute the details.[47]

A similar request had also been issued by Army Group A for *K-Verbände* units to be used against bridges across the Vistula where the German Army held a rapidly crumbling front. Russian bridgeheads across the Vistula and Danube Rivers posed great threats to the beleaguered *Wehrmacht* and Waffen SS men that fought to contain them, though they remained largely static until January 1945 as the Red Army sought to consolidate its positions before exploding into the final drive for victory.

The most extensive Russian bridgehead was that which straddled the Vistula, nearly thirty bridges having been taken and held by the Russians. Frogmen were deemed unsuited to the task so eighty-four Linsens were despatched from Plön to Krakow, their deployment overseen by Lüdke himself. The boats were transported under great secrecy to the Vistula and assembled awaiting the order from Army Group A to begin. The plan was absurdly simple. All eighty-four boats would race along the Vistula, each bridge being rammed by two of them which would sink alongside and be detonated by time fuses until the entire force was spent. It was, at best, wildly optimistic.

Regardless, the force was ready for action as Lüdke impatiently awaited the order to start, aware that the temperature was steadily dropping and ice on the river would render the light hulled boats useless. *Generaloberst* Josef Harpe finally approved the operation on 19 December, but as the Linsens were being put into the water, the plan was scrubbed. *Luftwaffe* photographs had shown thick ice forming around the first pair of bridges.

Men of MEK71 had also been allocated to the Russian front, passed to Army Group South for the Danube operation. Though MEK71 was based within the Adriatic, fourteen men (including four divers) had been withdrawn to Weissenburg in Bavaria where they were first scheduled to operate against bridges on the Danube (Donau). The group led by *Oberfähnrich* Schulz was soon augmented by sixteen more men, commanded by *Leutnant* Tegethoff, the whole unit officially departing the strength of MEK71 and becoming 'Kommando Wineto'. Their first use by Army Group South came on 4 December when they attacked the bridge at Paks south of Budapest with floating mines though the result of this attack is unrecorded.

The year 1944 had seen the final shattering of Germany's military on all fronts. The final path spiralled downward into oblivion, though the *K-Verbände*, like most of the *Wehrmacht*, remained determined to make their enemies pay dearly for their advances.

91

CHAPTER SIX

The Southern Front
The K-Verbände *in the Mediterranean*

The baptism of fire of Bartels' Biber unit in France had resulted in little of worth to the *Kriegsmarine*. Decimated during the chaotic retreat across the Seine to Germany, the Bibers required significant reinforcement before being recommitted to action.

Meanwhile, a second German one-man submarine design had also been released into active service. The TVA at Eckernförde, responsible for the Neger and Marder designs, had been busy putting together their own model of proper midget submarine. Aware that the Neger had suffered considerable losses through their inability to submerge and easy sighting of the Plexiglas dome, they had designed a vehicle that was fully submersible and carried two torpedoes into action.

Initially designated Thomas II, the completed vehicle was eventually named the Molch (Salamander) and was an electrically-propelled torpedo carrier. Using a similar powerplant to the unsuccessful Hecht design, the Molch was constructed using as many available torpedo parts as the TVA could use, simplifying its future construction capacity. The 11m long Molch even resembled an enlarged torpedo with the pilot compartment situated towards the stern of a long streamlined body. Being solely battery-powered it carried twelve troughs of the sort used in the Biber, Type 13 T210. These rested in the forward area of the craft. The stern section contained what was in essence the after part of an electric torpedo, though with larger stabilising fins and hydroplanes, their use facilitated by the submarine's lower speed.

Due to the high weight of the batteries the Molch displaced considerably more water than the Biber, weighing 8.4 tons without torpedoes. While the total radius of action for the Molch was considerably less than that of the Biber its underwater capabilities were outstanding, a range of 50 nautical miles at 3.3 knots (dead slow) plus 50 nautical miles at 5 knots (three-quarters speed) achieved by the 13.9hp electric

92

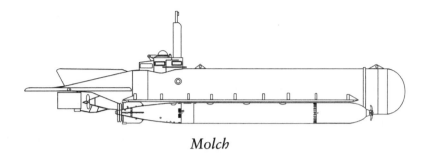

Molch

motor that turned a single three-bladed propeller. However, though highly manoeuvrable underwater, the oversize hydroplanes were battered by anything but the calmest seas if surfaced, leading to great handling problems for the pilot. In addition, there was a stunning constructional problem as due to their overlap the rudder could only be used when the hydroplanes were horizontal. This meant that the boat could not turn unless surfaced or at a constant depth. The Molch's superstructure consisted of a cupola only 30cm high, with small Plexiglas windows all around. Because of problems of carbon dioxide build-up inside the Molch, the pilot once again wore an oxygen mask and utilised six oxygen tanks, without which the operator could only safely function for 30 minutes.

The maximum recommended dive depth was 40m, though the deepest recorded dive depth was eventually taken as 60m, off the scale of the depth gauge inside the conning tower that was marked to 50m, a large scale gauge alongside marked up to 15m. Scuttling charges were also provided, triggered by pulling a cord when abandoning ship. Two pedals in the cockpit released blocks on the torpedo holding rails and at the same time started the weapons' motors, firing the two underslung torpedoes. Only a slight list was reported when one torpedo was fired, although apparently unless the boat was deep it was essential to quickly flood tanks and use a lot of hydroplane to prevent the Molch from breaking the surface.

Like the Biber, the Molch pilot suffered from only having a forward-facing periscope, capable of only 30° view either side of the centreline. They were also equipped with the same basic magnetic compass situated on a mast that protruded alongside the periscope. The Molch lacked any kind of underwater detection equipment, only a small number of test vessels being fitted with automatic course-keeping mechanisms and a listening device. However, an improvement on the Biber was the equipping of the Molch with a combination of diving, compensating and trimming tanks that required exact adjustment before sailing but theoretically allowed easier use in areas of differing salinity.

Initially trials proved unsuccessful, a first attempt on 19 March 1944 leaving the Molch stranded on the surface, its large forepart incapable of submerging. However, by 12 June this fault had been remedied and the Molch successfully used at Eckernförde. Placed immediately into construction at Bremen's Deschimag AG Weser yards, the first three boats rolled off the production line in June 1944, sent immediately to Suhrendorf for compass adjustment.[48] The first Molch unit – the forty-six boats of 411 K-Flotilla – formed in July 1944 at Suhrendorf, commanded by Oblt. Heinrich Hille. The flotilla's support staff (*Bodenstaffel*) was trained initially at List on the island of Sylt (*Weisskoppel*), the pilots at Lübeck (*Steinkoppel*) before the unit was decreed ready for action on 20 August at Gettdorf.

The following summary written by US Naval Intelligence was gleaned from the interrogation of captured Molch pilots, providing a basic overview of the establishment of the 411 K-Flotilla:

The 1st Flotilla (411 K-Flotilla) was divided into eight groups of which two, under the supervision of one officer, were always taken together for practical training. Theoretical training consisted of a number of lectures, one of which is believed to have been given by the designer of the Molch.

Practical training originally took place at Eckernförde and the Molch lay in the TVA (Torpedo Experimental Establishment) on the right hand side of the harbour on entering. In late July there was only one Molch available for training, but by early September there were three. It was eventually found that Eckernförde was too far from Suhrendorf: the boats were transferred to Suhrendorf where all training was thereafter carried out.

One prisoner made some ten to twelve runs in a Molch during training, the longest of which lasted 2½ hours, and made two practice attacks on the old minelayer *M.T.1*. Other targets were the *Glücksborg* and normal battle practice targets. Another prisoner, who did not arrive at Suhrendorf until 26 August, only went out in a Molch five times, the longest trip lasting half an hour. He said that parties of five men at a time would be taken out in a motorboat to a point two miles off shore where they rendezvoused with the Molch.

Numbers trained

At the end of July, 1944 the 1st Molch (411) Flotilla consisted of about 33 men. At a later date five or six more joined while others left or transferred to the 2nd (412) Flotilla. By the beginning of September when training was complete the 1st (411) Flotilla had 32 men trained in handling the boats.[49]

As the *Wehrmacht*'s debacle in Normandy became a virtual rout of German forces, the 411 K-Flotilla Molchs were readied for transfer to the front, via Tournai. However, after the rapid collapse of the German lines and the withdrawal of *K-Verbände* units to Belgium and Germany, these orders were cancelled and the flotilla held in readiness for transfer instead to the Mediterranean to join the human torpedoes already destined for that front. On 1 September – as twelve Marder Is of 364 K-Flotilla arrived in Genoa ready for transfer to San Remo and commitment to the Mediterranean – the fifty Molchs of the 411 Flotilla began to entrain at Gettdorf near Kiel. The flotilla was to be split:

> Twenty craft of the *K-Verbände* Flotilla 411 will be transferred to San Remo for action along the southern French coast. Thirty craft of the *K-Verbände* Flotilla 364 (Marder) will transfer to the Padua area [alongside the remainder of 411 K-Flotilla] for action in the northern Adriatic Sea.[50]

The completely motorised flotilla, nearly 400-strong, departed Germany, *en route* to Italy encountering a three-day delay due to Allied bombing of the beleaguered transport system. Despite this initial setback they reached Capo di David, outside of Verona, ahead of schedule on 13 September, remaining there for a week awaiting petrol for their motor transport. Here the flotilla was split into the two groups specified in the SKL's diary. The larger group of thirty Molchs and support crews left first for Padua (near Venice), the remainder moving out the following day, transported by bus and truck to San Remo, travelling mostly by night because of the danger of attack and arriving in the afternoon of 24 September. The men were quartered in a hotel set on a hillside away from the coast while their Molchs were prepared for action.

In the time that it had taken Hille's unit to reach its forward staging area, the Marders had been committed to action and then withdrawn in the face of abject and costly failure. The twelve spearhead Marders of 364 K-Flotilla's 'Group 1' had reached San Remo on 3 September after a two-day transit from Genoa. Their journey had been fraught with problems. After the crewmen left Suhrendorf they had rendezvoused with their Marders at Saalburg near Rudolstadt. From there they had loaded first onto lorries and then train for transfer ultimately to Genoa. A destroyed bridge in the mountains of the Trentino

Altoadige near Bolzano forced a halt in the march. Using the River Isarco instead, the Marders were transported by pontoon to Mezzolambardo where they were loaded onto train to Trient, onwards to Verona and ultimately Genoa. Once assembled there they had transferred to the small village of Menton, 1km east of Monte Carlo near San Remo. This was to be their supply base for the ensuing operation, pilots billeted in a hotel in Ospedalette while mechanics and other shore personnel were assigned another hotel nearby. The Marders themselves and all ancillary equipment were placed into a disused railway tunnel that ran from Caponero. Oblt.z.S. Berger's flotilla was readied for action, torpedo officer L.(Ing.) Worm and his small engineering crew checking the weaponry for mechanical problems before action.

The planned target for their first operation was the massed Allied landing support force off the French Riviera, particularly the bombarding cruisers and destroyers that were harassing *Wehrmacht* troop concentrations on the Franco–Italian border. Immediately prepared for action, the entire complement of twelve craft were committed to the attack, though familiar problems with launching the craft meant that only five actually got to sea. Of these only one returned, the pilot having made a badly-aimed attack on a *Fantasque* class destroyer. The American destroyer USS *Tudlow* and French destroyer *Le Malin* had sighted the attacking Marders and destroyed four of them off Cape Ferrat with depth charges and concentrated machine gun and cannon fire, three German prisoners being recovered from the sea.

While Group 1's Marders were put into action, Oblt.z.S. Hans-Georg Barop's 365 K-Flotilla and Oblt.z.S. Paul Heinsius' 366 K-Flotilla were also despatched from Germany to the Italian front. Meanwhile, by 7 September fifteen more Marders of Group 2 had arrived at San Remo after being held up by a demolished railway tunnel near Savona, raising the flotilla's serviceable number to twenty-five. They went into immediate readiness at Ventimiglia, though the decision to commit them was delayed for a day or two while German and Italian assault boats tried their hand on the night of the new Marders' arrival – also to no avail.

A combined assault boat and Marder strike was planned for 8 September against Allied destroyers off Menton. However, bad weather forced a postponement and it was not until the following night that the attack was launched. Fourteen Marders, three German and two Italian two-man assault boats and one Italian one-man assault boat were used in the attack. Only four of the Marders returned. The assault boats reported clashing with Allied MGBs, one of their number being damaged by gunfire. However, there had been

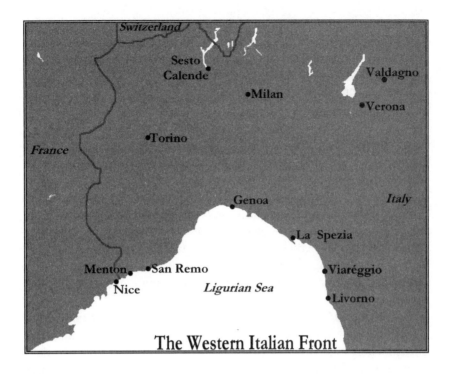

The Western Italian Front

no successes for the Marders and though some explosions were reported, none of the survivors claimed hits. The destroyers USS *Madison* and *Hilary P. Jones* of Destroyer Squadron 7 (DesRon 7) and a supporting PT boat sank ten of the attackers between them, the glinting canopies of the Marders providing easy targets for the defenders' gunners.[51] One of the survivors had been slightly wounded by small-arms fire from *Madison*, nursing his damaged torpedo with shattered Plexiglas dome to his base where the flotilla surgeon *Marineoberassistenarzt* Dr Jung treated his wounds.

The American defenders were recognised for their stalwart defence. The USS *Hilary P. Jones* became one of only two destroyers to be awarded the Navy Unit Commendation, in part for:

> Operating in bold defiance of enemy coastal batteries and further menaced by submarines, E-boats, explosive boats, human torpedoes and midget submarines . . .

Likewise the commander of USS *Madison*, Commander Daniel A Stuart, received commendation. Awarded the Silver Star on 23 December, Stuart's citation included the neutralisation of the Marder attack.

On 10 September 1944 when a large number of human submarines were sent out to attack the USS *Madison* and its accompanying destroyer, ten of these craft were positively and one possibly sunk in the ensuing action. By his skilful manoeuvring and intrepid prosecution of this action, Commander Stuart avoided all attacks on his ship and was responsible for at least four of the sinkings.

The remaining eleven serviceable Marders were withdrawn to San Remo. There Groups 3 and 4 joined them, the former having suffered five minor casualties in an air raid as well as the destruction of their train's locomotive and one heavy truck used to haul the vessels. Group 4 had also had to contend with a destroyed bridge over the Po River, bypassed using boats once again, another air attack on 5 September wounding twenty of their number. The Marders were judged to have been ineffectual against moving targets and so were instead held in reserve for use against stationary targets or in the event of fresh Allied landings.

Assault boats had meanwhile launched another ineffectual mission on the night of 14/15 September, returning without any sight of the enemy. Their next brush with the prowling destroyers was two days later, though they were powerless to resist as the American warships bombarded their base at San Remo destroying three boats and damaging three more before any could be launched. Another bombardment the following day destroyed a further thirteen craft, rendering the total available strength a meagre seven boats in total. San Remo remained vulnerable to Allied shelling, though several Molchs arrived at the port on 19 September to capitalise on the tempting target that the port presented to the Allies. Despite their planned numbers reduced by transport fuel shortage plans were already in hand to use them against the destroyers. There would be no need to seek the enemy – they would come to the Germans.

Verona soon became a concentration point for the *K-Verbände*. To augment the Marders already present, the second group of ten Molchs arrived there on 20 September *en route* to join the advance group in San Remo and the same day that the Linsens of 213 K-Flotilla entered Verona, withdrawn from Western France two days previously and *en route* ultimately to Padua. The Linsens were soon moved onward to the Ravenna area where launching sites were being prepared for them south of Porto Corsini and north of Cesenatico. The Marders in turn were ordered to Treviso while they awaited completion of launching sites at Garibaldi.

While the Marder was experiencing its nadir in action, the fresh Molchs of 411 K-Flotilla were being readied for their baptism of fire in San Remo. Once again it became rapidly apparent that the difference in salinity between the Baltic and the Mediterranean required compensation, the first Molch launched sinking uncontrollably to 60m after flooding the forward diving cell. The midgets were serviced in the railway sidings, a full two-thirds of the flooding cell being packed with material to reduce their volume and thus allow less water to enter the craft when flooded.

Kommando Stab Süd commander, the U-boat Ace K.z.S. Werner Hartmann, arrived in person to hand the mission orders for 411 K-Flotilla to Oblt.z.S. Heinrich Hille. During the night of 25/26 September nine Molchs were to sail against patrolling Allied warships off Nice and Menton. Each man of the attacking force was given full individual instructions on courses to steer, targets to attack and the designated time to return. Deviation tables for each Molch (from which the men for the first time discovered the numbers of their boats) and small pencil sketches of the section of coast off which they were to operate, were issued. Hille even took his men by road as far as Ventimiglia near the Franco–Italian border to give them an idea of the coastline's appearance.

However, despite the exact briefings, the first and last operation by Hille's unit ended in disaster. Nine Molchs departed San Remo, *M58* returning half an hour into its voyage at 21.30hrs after the pilot noticed water entering through a flange round the base of the periscope. Quickly repaired he departed once more at 23.30hrs as the sixth boat to leave. Only two of the attackers would return. Patrol and sinking reports from three survivors of the attack illustrate the disaster that befell them.

M58 left at 23.30hrs and proceeded dead slow for 1½ hours with periscope visible. The coxswain then took her to 5 metres and maintained the same speed until 03.00hrs, when he increased to ¾ speed (7 knots). At 04.00hrs he arrived in his operational area off Nice, some 4–5 miles southwest of Cap Ferrat, having steered 230° throughout. He took his boat down to 12 metres and slowly circled around. Shortly before 06.15hrs, it became evident that the boat was bow heavy, and the coxswain was unable to trim her . . . he came to periscope depth, and was almost immediately sighted by an aircraft which dropped a number of smoke floats near him. Destroyers soon approached and made contact; the coxswain, believing that depth charges would be set much deeper, decided that it would be safest to remain at 5 metres. Eighteen to twenty depth charges were dropped shortly afterwards, but all exploded beneath him. Two more series followed, and the last depth charge to explode caused a water entry on the port side below the Control Room. The boat became stern heavy, and after setting the scuttling charges, the coxswain opened the cupola and abandoned ship at 08.45hrs.

M54 sailed between 23.00hrs and midnight and set course 274° at the same depth and speed as *M58*. At 03.00hrs the coxswain went to 15 metres. At 06.15hrs he came to periscope depth and at 07.00hrs sighted a destroyer approaching from seaward 2–3 miles away. He closed, and at 07.16hrs, when the destroyer [probably USS *Madison*] was at 600 metres, fired his starboard torpedo. The destroyer turned hard to port and the torpedo missed. The Molch was immediately picked up by asdic and depth-charged: the coxswain, realizing that he had been detected, decided to dive to 30 metres. No damage was caused until, at a depth of 25 metres the cupola burst. The coxswain then pulled the cord of the scuttling charge, abandoned ship and came to the surface.

M50 sailed at about 23.00hrs, proceeded for three hours at ¾ speed and then dead slow until 06.00hrs maintaining a depth of 5 metres throughout. By dawn, she was just within sight of the coast. The coxswain cruised around for some time, at intervals coming to periscope depth in search of shipping. Without having sighted any ships, he suddenly heard about ten depth charges exploding comparatively near, and dived to 20 metres where he circled for a while, before rising once more to 10 metres. About an hour later he heard another series of 6–8 charges, came to periscope depth and sighted a shadow at which he fired his port torpedo. The torpedo missed and soon afterwards when another and much closer depth charge attack followed the coxswain went to 30–35 metres. The steering gear was damaged and the bow got out of control: the starboard torpedo broke away aft and hanging from the bows made the boat bow heavy. At 30 metres water entered through the cupola and the coxswain blew all tanks. For some time *M50* failed to surface and water rose in the Control Room as far as the coxswain's chest: she rose gradually, however, and at 5 metres the pilot fitted his escape apparatus, pulled the cord of the scuttling charge and abandoned ship.

The French destroyer *Forbin* obtained contact after sighting a conning tower, and dropped depth charges at 07.55hrs on 26 September, probably sinking two Molchs. Eventually only one survivor was picked up by *Forbin* and two by *Madison*. It had been a disaster for 411 K-Flotilla.

The calamity was attributed chiefly to a failure among the personnel crewing the Molchs, exacerbated by the strain of the journey from the launch site to the area of operations. The Molchs' short tenure in action was over and they were withdrawn from action to Trieste and then a concentration area at Sistiana, where they alternated between overhauling the equipment and practising attack runs, their place in the front line taken by assault boats. In a radio message from OKM to Heye on 30 September, the former ascribed general failure of *K-Verbände* operations to the use of insufficient numbers of craft and inadequate crew training. However, they were at least deemed to be of value for the tying down of Allied warships assigned the task of combating the German menace.

The much-criticised training for the *K-Verbände* was carried out in varied locations and to varied degrees of thoroughness throughout the war. As conditions deteriorated for the *Wehrmacht* instruction was either deliberately curtailed or rushed to completion in order to get the operators of the new weapons into action as soon as possible. For example, Biber training officially was six weeks from beginning to end, though several prisoners captured by the Allies during the war stated that they had been sent into action with as little as two weeks of intensive schooling.

The forced expansion of the *K-Verbände* to incorporate a variety of weapons and so theoretically maintain the element of surprise against the enemy, meant that nearly every device to be used required its own specialist instruction, thus there was very little overlap between crews and pilots of the different weapons.[52] Therefore separate Lehrkommandos, each specialising in its particular weapon, eventually carried out each training programme:

Lehrkommando 200 – Linsen.
Lehrkommando 250 – Biber.
Lehrkommando 300 – Seehund.
Lehrkommando 350 – Human torpedoes (Neger and Marder).
Lehrkommando 400 – Hecht and Molch.
Lehrkommando 600 – MTM and SMA assault boats.
Lehrkommando 700 – *Kampfschwimmer.*
MEK zbV – Commando troops.

Prior to September 1944 the sole purpose of the various Lehrkommandos was to establish the cadres of instructors to use in the training of the flotillas' troops, develop the technical design of the various weapons through experiment and experience and the administrative task of forming combat flotillas. However, after September when the *K-Verbände* had expanded to nearly 8,000 men, *K-Verbände* command (KdK or *Kommando der Kleinkampfverbände*) decentralised some of the administrative and supply issues from its own control and transferred them to the various Lehrkommandos. Previously, Heye's staff had directly controlled the fighting units, but henceforth the Lehrkommandos would increasingly carry this burden. By November 1944 they had also taken charge of the issue of supply of boats and related German manufactured equipment for the flotillas.

Logistically the *K-Verbände* relied on a combination of Army and Navy stores. For petrol, naval craft drew exclusively from naval supply dumps through MOK Süd, which suffered no shortages until the end of January 1945 due to ample accumulated regional stocks. On the other hand all motor transport requirements were drawn from Army supplies and were sporadic at best throughout their deployment. By the war's end the situation regarding motor vehicle petrol was considered 'hopeless'.

The presence of the *K-Verbände* in the Mediterranean burgeoned during 1944 and into 1945. As the headquarters of *Einsatz und Ausbildungs Stab Süd* was relocating from Castelletto to Meina in September 1944, Schomburg was relieved of command and replaced by the highly decorated U-boat Ace, Kapt.z.S. Werner Hartmann, who was subsequently made responsible for all *K-Verbände* units in the Italian theatre of operations, including the aforementioned Molch fiasco. Thus the *Einsatz und Ausbildungs Stab Süd* was renamed once more, this time to *Einsatzstab Hartmann* and would control the following units: *Ausbildung Stab Süd* (training staff south), Lehrkommando 600, Lehrkommando 700, *Maiale Gruppe* Lehmann, 213 K-Flotilla, 363 K-Flotilla, 411 K-Flotilla, 611 K-Flotilla and MEK 80. Later the following additional units would also be transferred to his command: 612 K-Flotilla (in October 1944), MEK 71 (in October 1944), 364 K-Flotilla (in December 1944), 613 K-Flotilla (in January 1945) and *Gruppe* Dexling (in February 1945).

Schomburg was moved in order to take charge of the purely training office of *Ausbildung Stab Süd* at Meina, catering for the formation and training programmes for Lehrkommandos 600 and 700 and the *Maiale Gruppe* Lehmann. Schomburg also oversaw the regional supply section. It was not until November 1944 that *Ausbildung Stab Süd* was disbanded after Lehrkommandos 600 and 700 were transferred to Germany.

Hartmann too departed Italy late in 1944, relinquishing his post in October and being replaced by the erstwhile *Kommando Stab West* senior officer Kapt.z.S. Böhme. Hartmann returned to Germany to take charge of the *Volkssturm* in Danzig and West Prussia, later commanding Marine-Grenadier Regiment 6 with whom he fought till the war's end.

With Böhme's arrival the Italian *K-Verbände* headquarters were renamed once again, this time to *Kommando Stab Italien* and in December 1944 to *Kommando Stab Süd*. Its final relocation was on 25 April 1945 when it moved to Vigo Di Fassa. Like all regional commands, the operations of *Kommando Stab Süd* required sanction by Heye or his Chief Of Staff Frauenheim. The operational details were required to be submitted by courier, teleprinter or wireless. This in itself actually posed no real problem for Böhme as attacks were generally planned at least a fortnight ahead of time. In turn KdK would transmit a single prearranged codeword to signify approval of the plan. It was only in the case of special emergency, *ie* enemy landings, that Böhme was free to commit his flotillas without first consulting KdK. In actuality this would only happen once, on 23 April 1945 when 611, 612 and 363 K-Flotillas were sent into their last actions without previous authorisation. In turn no commander of a subordinate *K-Verbände* unit was allowed to carry out an independent mission except in a case of 'grave danger', a term subject to a certain degree of elasticity in its interpretation. Generally, offensive missions were approved even if retrospectively. Such endorsement would generally state Heye's conviction that the actions taken were 'in keeping with the spirit of the *K-Verbände*', which fostered initiative and independent thinking.

The regional *Kriegsmarine* command, *Marineoberkommando Süd*, was also required to give its approval to any proposed mission. These negotiations were conducted between Böhme and the F1 at MOK Süd, Kapt.z.S. Günther Wachsmuth or his successor Kapt.z.S. Alberts after April 1945. In turn MOK Süd were able to suggest operations to Böhme as they had a greater vision of overall naval strategy and dispositions within the region. However they exercised no authority other than advisory (*weisungsberechtigt*) over Böhme and both he and Heye could veto any such suggestions. Among MOK Süd's requests were facilities to be provided for the landing of agents behind enemy lines. Each case was handled on an individual basis and if Böhme, and ultimately Heye, agreed in principle to the proposed operation the mission was handed over to the K-Flotilla or MEK concerned who would then co-ordinate planning with the agents' parent unit.

One of the more unusual units of the Italian-based *K-Verbände* was *Maiale Gruppe* Lehmann, which Oblt.z.S. Lehmann had been despatched from Germany in March 1944 to form. Lehmann, accompanied by *Oberfähnrich* Wirth was charged with establishing facilities for the training of German operators for the Italian *Maiale*, which had hitherto only been used by the Italian Navy. Lehmann and Wirth took eight men of the *K-Verbände* with them, these eight planned to form an instructional cadre with which to teach further operators. The small group established themselves at the old seaplane base on the island of San Andrea at Venice where they underwent instruction from Lieutenant Tadini of the *Decima Mas*. Lehmann himself was also taught, later handling the training of the other nine men, though Prince Borghese commented to Böhme in March 1945 that he considered Lehmann to be unqualified to teach, never having been fully trained himself. Relations between Lehmann and Tadini were at first cordial though they swiftly became strained after Lehmann assumed greater control of the unit's schooling. He was of course still dependent on Tadini for supplies of equipment and tools but their relationship never improved. Manfred Lau was one of Lehmann's second batch of recruits brought in to operate the *Maiale*.

> In the transit camp at Kappeln I was waiting with my comrades as a section leader until I could begin training to use the small Seehund U-boats. Since this was taking so long – it was late autumn by then – we volunteered ourselves for underwater salvage work in the Mediterranean. With 26 comrades of different ranks we found ourselves part of the German test group headed for Italy. Our destination was the diver school at Valdagno . . . Our new Chief, Oblt.z.S. Lehmann, told us at our entrance examination that our *Kommando* had the highest security and secrecy rating. Also, in view of the high physical requirements we would be subject to stronger medical control and classified under the highest food supply stage, complete with an additional butter ration.[53]

By November 1944 the group was fully prepared, though they lacked practical experience. Exercises were suspended between October 1944 and January 1945 as the water temperature was considered dangerously low, the men instead overhauling their four old-type SSC Chariots and two newer SSB models. An order had been placed with the Caproni firm in Milan for sixteen SSBs, due for delivery in March 1945.

Such local equipment was supplied to *Kommando Stab Süd* after requests for Italian hulls and boats were passed to Heye's KdK and from there onwards to the *Hauptausschuss Schiffbau* at OKM in Berlin, which in turn issued the necessary orders to the *Abteilung Schiffbau* of the RuK (*Rüstung und Kriegsproduktion*, or Armaments and War Production) Milan. This last organisation held responsibility for the placing of orders with Italian companies and supervising such construction. RuK Milan, headed by merchant navy officer *Kapitän* Sembt, assisted by *Oberbaurat* Kertscher, from an office at Milan's 2 Via Mascheroni, also took delivery of the completed units, which were either despatched to Germany or delivered to *Kommando Stab Süd* for distribution among the requisite flotillas.

In August 1944 as a result of the deteriorating war situation, K.K. (Ing) Burckhardt had been appointed liaison officer between *Hauptausschuss Schiffbau* (Shipbuilding Head Office) in Berlin and *Abteilung Schiffbau* of RuK Milan with the brief to ensure that all available resources of Italian industry were correctly harnessed for the benefit of *Kommando Stab Süd*, in particular the construction of SMA and MTM assault boats. Burckhardt was further ordered to keep close watch on Italian technological developments while developing new ideas of his own.

All other equipment apart from boats and hulls were claimed by *Kommando Stab Süd* through the *Sonderstab Marine* at Como, the latter an affiliate of RuK Milan and directed by F.K. Carl Siegfried Ritter von Georg, a veteran of the First World War and holder of the Pour Le Merité, awarded on 24 April 1918 for service as commander of U-boats *U-57* and *U-101*. The following firms supplied equipment for *Kommando Stab Süd*, occasionally subcontracting for their own production efficiency:

Siai-Marchetti, (Sesto Calende) – MTM and SMA boats.
Cabi, (Milan) – MTM and SMA boats.
Alfa Romeo, (Milan) – Engines for MTM and SMA boats.
Isotta Fraschini, (Milan) – Engines for new S-Boats (Isotta Fraschini 183 and 184D).
Caproni, (Milan) – Boat hulls and *Maiale*.
Pirelli, (Milan) – Equipment for *Kampfschwimmer*.

During October 1944 Heye had issued fresh instruction for the use of *K-Verbände* forces based in the Mediterranean.

Effective results are to be expected by mass actions only. Therefore, the stocks must not be expended prematurely but must first of all be filled up for mass actions. The prospects for success are deemed by the Admiral . . . more favourable in the Ligurian Sea than in the Adriatic Sea.[54]

A new assault boat flotilla was formed in October for use in the Mediterranean, 612 K-Flotilla, with men from Lehrkommando 600. Comprising thirty MTMs and fifteen SMAs from Sesto Calende the unit was placed under the control of VI K-Division during November 1944 and co-operated with MEK71 and the 1st S-Boat Division in landing agents behind Allied lines on the Dalmatian and Italian coasts. The flotilla was not involved in anti-shipping operations.

As Linsens and assault boats continued their battles against the enemy during the rest of September and into October 1944 they fared no better than their counterparts in Normandy. Often boats were lost due to grounding and fuel shortage without even sighting the enemy. Their bases at San Remo and Corsini continued to be attacked by naval and air forces and the gradual rate of attrition through this unrelenting bombardment gnawed at their effectiveness. A planned mass assault by Linsens and assault boats scheduled for the night of 20 October was to be the masterstroke of that month in the Mediterranean. However, the use of the assault boats was soon cancelled as their strength lay below the desired number. Nevertheless, forty-eight Linsens were moved to San Remo from Corsini on 18 October, the boats hidden with their motor transport in a covered market while they were prepared for use. Two days later, on the day of their scheduled launch an Allied destroyer bombardment hit the port, a shell landing in the market and destroying the entire stock of Linsens and their transports. To add insult to injury four assault boats in the port were also destroyed.

A last gasp for that month saw the largest number of assault boats deployed thus far put into a raid on the Gulf of Juan on the night of 23 October. Two groups, one of twenty German boats and the other of six Italian, were launched. From this considerable force, eleven German boats failed to return, five heavy detonations being heard but no claims made after they skirmished with enemy ships. The Italians failed to sight anything and returned intact. This futile raid, coming at the end of a disastrous month, broke the backbone of the assault boat and Linsen units, their strength requiring significant rebuilding and never truly recovering.

On 18 October the withdrawn Marders stationed at Treviso were ordered forward to Savona, though diverted to Venice while *en route* for an overhaul of batteries and equipment. There they remained until the first week of November, during which period their initial orders were cancelled and they were relocated to Trieste in anticipation of Allied landings on the north Adriatic coast.

October saw the evacuation of a number of training areas held by the *K-Verbände*. The Lehrkommando 700 (Valdagno) and Lehrkommando 701 (San Giorgio, Venice) frogmen training centres were transferred to List on the North Sea island of Sylt on 21 October. The Venetian school was planned to reopen in the spring of 1945 if the military situation permitted, so Kummer's flak unit remained behind under the cover name 'Rothenburgsort'. The island was renamed '*Ausbildungslager* Venice' though no more training was ever done there. The reason for abandoning Valdagno was more prosaic – the water temperature in the pool was too cold, reliant on heating from local factories that had ceased to function due to a lack of coal.

Lehrkommando 600 was also moved to List during that month where their training policies were dramatically altered after Kapt.z.S. Böhme criticised the fact that previous instruction had taken place on placid lake waters. The emphasis was now switched to sea and night training. Schomburg accompanied the unit as Lehrkommandos 601 and 602 were dissolved in the face of the advancing enemy. A small supply cadre remained at Sesto Calende to take possession of SMA and MTM boats due from the Siai-Marchetti and Cabi firms. As Lehrkommando 600 units were now totally equipped with Italian assault boats there were constant requests for these craft from their Italian manufacturers, though eventually, by March 1945, any that were despatched from Sesto Calende for Germany were doomed to never reach their destination due to the extreme transport difficulties.

Seven weeks passed between the last abortive attack by the Italo-German assault boats in October and renewed activity by the *K-Verbände* in the Mediterranean. This idleness was officially attributed to a 'lack of suitable targets' though the depleted ranks of the units contributed. Activity was resumed on the night of 9 December when three German-manned Italian S-boats and twenty-one assault boats departed San Remo to attack a convoy reported by intelligence to be travelling from Marseille to Villefranche. Another debacle ensued as the assault boats were forced back to base in bad weather, one of them being swamped and sunk, and the S-boats clashed violently with Allied forces where one was boarded and captured.

The Adriatic Battleground

Meanwhile reinforcements had arrived for the human torpedo units. Sixteen Marders of 363 K-Flotilla, a fragmented group commanded by L.z.S. Münch, had entrained at Suhrendorf on 5 December bound for San Remo. The remaining forty-four Marders would depart five days later to reunite with their spearhead unit. While in Italy, 363 K-Flotilla had a transport column from the *K-Verbände Kraftfahr* Regiment placed at its disposal, comprising thirty 3-ton trucks, three private cars, one wireless truck and three motorcycles.

While the remainder of the flotilla was on its way, K.z.S. Böhme visited Münch and his second in command L.z.S. Köhn on the night of 17 December to issue fresh instructions. The following night, 18 December, fifteen of the Marders attacked the Allied cruiser and destroyers off San Remo that continued to harass German troop concentrations with precisely targeted bombardments. The Marder pilots were given precise courses to follow, instructed to head between 210° and 230° from port for a period of five hours at 3 knots, after which they should be on station and were to await contact with the Allied ships. Fourteen of the Marders were successfully launched a little after midnight, guided from harbour by a pair of searchlights, one mounted on a blockship inside the harbour area and the other atop a wreck outside. The fifteenth pilot was unable to put to sea on account of an injury to his hand suffered while preparing for the mission. From the fourteen deployed, only six pilots returned from the unsuccessful sortie. Five of the survivors reported missing their targets either through their own inaccuracy or torpedo failure. One of the missing Marders was captured intact by American troops. Its pilot, 19-year-old Wolfgang Hoffmann had been a naval artilleryman before volunteering for the *K-Verbände* on 20 June 1944. His Marder had travelled from San Remo for nearly six hours before Hoffmann realised that he had been following an incorrect course, hugging the coastline the entire time. Blaming a faulty compass the hapless German attempted to retrace his steps as dawn approached, sighting a distant beacon in the early morning. Closing the light at approximately 08.30hrs he identified the area of Cap Martin indicating that he was hopelessly off course. Hoffmann followed standard operating instructions in the event of no targets found and fired his torpedo to seaward. Following a path for an anchorage he believed to be held by the *Wehrmacht*, Hoffmann entered Menton Harbour at around midday, grounding in shallow water near Antibes. Apparently confused, Hoffmann then attempted to swing his Marder around and retreat to sea but sighting enemy troops approaching he then struggled to wriggle free of his cockpit and scuttle the Marder trapped in glutinous wet sand. Swiftly surrounded by the patrolling American troops, Hoffmann was taken prisoner after his vain effort to pull the toggle that would fire the torpedo's scuttling charge failed.

Hoffmann's detailed three-day interrogation that began on 2 January 1945 yielded much valuable detail for Allied intelligence though Hoffmann was at first evasive in his answers. Among the observations they recorded was that Hoffmann:

> . . . estimated the average age of the torpedo operators in the flotilla at 21. They were all enthusiastic and strong Nazis and certainly also attracted by the comparatively easy life while on shore and the privileges which were granted them. Torpedo operators had no responsibility for the care and maintenance of their equipment, which was entirely

seen to by the attached mechanics. They were also exempted from guard and admin duties. Rations were also superior to those found in other naval units.

Hoffmann also indicated that the lure of instant glory might have also attracted young idealists to the K-Verbände.

The usual award for the destruction of a merchant vessel or a destroyer is the German Cross in Gold, while the destruction of a cruiser is usually the occasion for the award of the Knight's Cross. The Iron Cross (1st Class) is given as a rule for successes against smaller units, such as MTBs, landing craft etc. The Iron Cross (2nd Class) is awarded to all crews who have participated in an operation, irrespective of success. They are also given a fortnight's leave after every operation.[55]

Hoffmann's loss was not the only catastrophe for the spearhead of 363 K-Flotilla – a majority of their pilots were now missing in action, including the senior officer L.z.S. Münch and his deputy L.z.S. Köhn. The survivors were shortly afterward returned to Suhrendorf.[56]

A final abortive Marder attack was launched by 364 K-Flotilla on New Year's Eve against Allied shipping off Villefranche, only a single Marder being lost in this attack despite heavy defensive fire. One pilot reported an attempted attack on an enemy patrol boat, another against convoy traffic sighted, though neither claimed success. Finally the surviving Marders of the front-line flotillas were withdrawn to Saonara near Padua. Others held in reserve in Treviso, a small village 30km north of Venice, were ordered to Savona, later onward to Grenze on the northern Adriatic coast. Their war was nearly over; save for one last gasp in the twilight days of April 1945.

MEK80 was also active within the Mediterranean during the final months of 1944. During October the commando unit was located at Stresa on the Lake Maggiore, northwest of Sesto Calende. At that time its complement numbered about 160 men and a staff of six officers, including Senior Officer Kaptlt. Krumhaar. It was there that, against the express wishes of Heye and Böhme, the unit was ordered into action against Italian partisans, becoming embroiled in the bitter and savage nature of such action. To show his displeasure, Heye withdrew half of Krumhaar's men and posted them to MEK zbV for use in German waterways.

In mid-December thirty men of MEK80 moved to San Remo, a fifty-strong rearguard posted shortly afterward to Meina to guard troops of the K-Verbände supply section. These men would also soon come under partisan attack. Meanwhile, Krumhaar carried out one commando raid behind enemy lines at Menton during mid-December. Requested by General Lieb, the object was to bring in an Allied POW for questioning, though, as with so many of the *K-Verbände*'s Mediterranean ventures, it was unsuccessful.

CHAPTER SEVEN

New Weaponry
Hecht and Seehund

Within the labyrinthine organisation of design offices that worked for the benefit of the *Kriegsmarine* there existed as early as 1942 a 'K' Office, tasked with designing small submarines for possible production. Despite the earlier rejection of Dräger's idea for midget submarines to be built on a revolutionary new production line, the 'K' Office continued its planning, finishing a blueprint for a small U-boat at the beginning of 1942. Displacing 97.95 tons, the craft vaguely resembled the Japanese *Ko-Hyoteki* midgets that had been employed against American forces at Pearl Harbor, reports of their success being somewhat exaggerated by an enthusiastic Japanese military. The project was shelved, however, and it was not until the recovery of wrecked X-Craft responsible for the successful attack against the *Tirpitz* in Norway in September 1943 that the 'K' Office was once again spurred into action.

This time their brief was to develop a two-man submersible, capable of delivering a limpet-mine warhead against its target. In due course they designed a submarine considerably smaller than the X-Craft and able to approach its target submerged only. The boat, designated Type XXVII, would thus have to be transported to a suitable 'jumping-off' point by carrier vehicle. The projected combat radius was 145km, but as no suitable small compass was immediately available and designers deemed it essential that a large gyroscopic compass with its transformer be provided, the submarine's size was increased, with a corresponding reduction in range to 61km at 4 knots as more energy was required to propel it. This vessel was known as the Hecht (Pike).

As before in the German midget programme, elements of the Hecht were extremely primitive. As designers envisaged the boat having to penetrate torpedo nets to attack enemy shipping, there were at first no hydroplanes fitted. Instead, trimming was done using adjustable weights on spindles within the interior – a system used in the pioneering *Brandtaucher* submarine of 1850! This arrangement was swiftly found to be impractical. Instead the Hecht was fitted with forward hydroplanes and stabilising fins at the stern, though this last-minute solution did not provide any kind of steady depth-keeping ability. No diving tanks were fitted as the boat was meant to operate continuously submerged, the crew able to board the vessel by its natural positive buoyancy, counteracted underwater by the flooding of 200-litre compensating tanks flanking the forward operator's position amidships. The nose of the submarine comprised a detachable limpet mine weighing 800kg. The battery consisted of five torpedo troughs, with three lying horizontally at the forward end of the hull, another above and one more below along the centreline, all five reinforced with stronger plates to allow a greater charge capacity and longer life. These powered the 12hp AEG electric torpedo motor that was the only means of propulsion.

After the Hecht design had been completed, SKL made an additional demand of it. They wanted the craft to be able to carry torpedoes as well as mines. The need for a 'special forces' mine delivery vehicle had diminished and they required more conventional weaponry for the *K-Verbände*. As the boat's displacement was only 9.47 tons, only torpedoes without negative buoyancy could be used lest the Hecht be dragged to the bottom by the additional weight, the same problem suffered by all German midgets and human torpedoes. Consequently the Hecht was either to carry a single under-slung torpedo or a mine, but not both together. If armed with a torpedo the detachable nose of the Hecht where the limpet mine attached was replaced with a compartment containing three additional batteries, allowing extended range. Regardless of this makeshift solution it would never suffice for effective torpedo patrols. Designers soon understood that the time they would require to redesign the Hecht to a degree where it could fulfil its new multi-function purpose would in fact be better spent on a fresh idea. There then arose difficulties equipping the submarine with a suitable mine and ultimately before the Hecht could be used operationally, the whole project was dropped, those midgets completed being relegated to training duties. The use of the Hecht was remembered by Harald Sander, later an engineer aboard a Seehund:

> . . . I went to Gotenhafen . . . for my first training course as head engineer on board a VIIC boat. This was one of the standard submarines

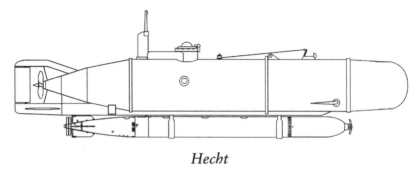

Hecht

that were in service. So we completed our training on these boats in the
Baltic Sea, first in Gotenhafen and then there was a second course in
Pillau . . . Of course, coming to Neustadt was quite special. So what
were we in for? *Ach* so, we hadn't even finished the beginning [train-
ing] yet.

At first we didn't even have the finished *Seehund* – the small submarines. Instead we initially had the two-man submarines, which only
operated with an electric motor. This boat wasn't as large as the other
later ones operating with both diesel and electric motors and we started
practising on it there, at sea. Then there was this fuss with the shooting of torpedoes. Of course we had a torpedo attached underneath the
boat and we sailed around Neustadt Bay, which is not very deep. When
we wanted to stop for a while we settled on the seafloor. There were
these windows up in the tower so that we could look out at the fish
swimming around. That was the initial period.[57]

Coupled with the battery modification to the detachable nosecone that
had been developed already, further experiments were undertaken to
modify a detachable nose compartment that could accommodate two
frogmen for covert operations though development never passed
beyond the blueprint stage.

Nevertheless, as the disappointing Hecht design took shape, Dönitz
discussed the feasibility of producing it in large numbers and obtained
Hitler's permission to build fifty for both torpedo attack and minelaying. Kiel's Germaniawerft were contracted to build a prototype and on
28 March 1944 given a further order for fifty-three machines. The first
two were completed in May 1944 and almost immediately the poor
manoeuvrability and handling qualities combined with the confused
purpose of this minelayer–torpedo carrier combined to doom the
project. Fifty-three were indeed eventually constructed as ordered,
providing the perfect introductory craft for men destined to crew a far
superior midget submarine – the Seehund.[58]

slightly over a metre in length that was projected on to a plate immediately in front of the engineer. A standard magnetic compass was also provided, situated immediately in front of and above the engineer. This compass was mounted within an elevated watertight tower so as to remove it from the magnetic influence of the boat itself.

A sound-powered telephone was provided to allow the engineer to communicate with the coxswain if he was above decks on the superstructure, the outside of the boat reached through a small hatch in the middle of which was a 30cm Plexiglas dome. When the hatch was closed this dome allowed enough room for the coxswain's head that all-round visibility was possible. Two framework sights were rigidly mounted on either side forward of the dome, giving a 30° angle either side of the centreline, with four uprights calculated to show 15°, 25°, 35° and 45° angles on the bow. These were for the use of the commander if making a surface attack. The hatch itself was dogged shut by three clips mounted on a toothed ring turned by a cog on the single hatch handle. This could also be opened from the outside by a 't-shaped' handle.

For submerged attacks a monocular fully rotatable but non-retractable or extendable 1.5-metre periscope was provided. It also included an elevation of 50° for air-search. The periscope had a magnification factor of 1½ to 2, the aiming point being a single vertical line in the eyepiece. Deflection was calculated with simple tables and set on the periscope, the entire boat turned to the relevant bearing in order to fire. The weapons used for the Seehund were TIIIc, a modified G7e torpedo with the same reduced battery capacity that was used from the Neger onwards to reduce the negative buoyancy of the torpedo. The engineer fired them after he received targeting instructions from the coxswain. Though the boats were eventually equipped with a basic underwater listening apparatus, there was no radio equipment for communicating either with fellow Seehunds or headquarters. At the tapered bow, the Seehund had a free-flooding casing that extended past the pressure hull, much like a standard U-boat. In the bow of the pressure hull were diving tanks and trim cells, with six of the battery troughs behind them.

It soon became apparent that the Seehund possessed some excellent assets for its role as an attack submarine, not least of all the fact that the boat's surface silhouette was so small that it was barely detectable by optical or electronic instruments. It possessed outstanding seakeeping qualities in weather below sea state 4, though the steering was sometimes difficult as already mentioned. This, however, was allevi-

The development of the Seehund marked the high tide of German midget plans. As the shortcomings of the Hecht became apparent, the K Office produced numerous fresh design ideas with increased range and heavier two-torpedo armament. Originally designated Type XXVIIB, Seehund, was an antidote to the previous midget designs, none of which truly met the minimum requirements of a submarine but were rather emergency measures to meet the threat of invasion. An initial design proposed by the Hamburg Shipbuilding Test Institute resembled the Hecht but with the addition of a foredeck for surface travel and saddle tanks amidships. The keel had also been enlarged to accommodate battery troughs. Almost simultaneously, Chief Naval Construction Adviser Kurzak, OKM's representative for closed-cycle development at Kiel's Germaniawerft, himself designed a midget submarine that could utilise the embryonic closed-cycle drive that had first been successfully tested at Stuttgart's FKPS (Research Institute for Motor Transport and Motor Vehicle Engine Construction) by Dräger who had planned its use as part of his small U-boat research programme in 1941. His initial model was known as 'Kleine U-Boot K', which bore little resemblance to any previous midget design that the Germans had created. Its hull was suitable for surface travel and diving cells were arranged on each flank of the craft, partially enclosing the torpedoes, two of which were carried. By doing so, a considerable reduction of the drag created by side-slung torpedoes was achieved. However, as Dräger himself had found years before, for the closed-cycle power plant to be used in such a small vessel its efficiency would have to be improved beyond current standards. Accordingly, though the project was discussed at an OKM meeting chaired by Heye on 21 May 1944 and Kurzak later tasked with creating a more appropriate and refined closed-cycle unit for the projected boat, the 'Small U-boat K' was never produced.

However, it did have a powerful influence on the design of the more conventional single-hull Seehund that was evolving under the auspices of Marinebaurat Grim. Designated the Type XXVIIB5, later changed to the Type 127, the Seehund strongly resembled Kurzak's boat. Sporting a relatively powerful diesel-electric power plant the Seehund was truly a miniature U-boat throughout, sporting all of the main installations of its larger cousins and carrying two out-slung torpedoes. The diesel engine was a standard six-cylinder Bussing 60hp truck engine, adapted to marine use, providing 1,300rpm and capable of propelling the boat at 7.7 knots when surfaced. The Seehund's electric motor was a 25hp AEG delivering a submerged speed of 6 knots.

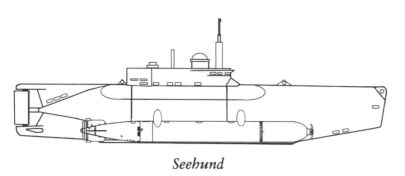

Seehund

With the standard 500-litre fuel tanks aboard the Seehund it was capable of 270 nautical miles at full speed on the surface, although the later addition of saddle tanks increased the fuel bunkerage enough to allow a further 230 miles. The eight battery troughs (six in the nose and two in the keel, each trough carrying thirteen cells) of 7 MAL 210 batteries allowed a submerged range of 63 nautical miles at a sedate 3 knots or 19 nautical miles at top speed. As with its larger cousins the Seehund was more a submersible than a submarine – designed for surfaced travel except when actually in attack and defence. The diesel was immediately behind the engineer so when in use it became almost unbearably hot for the luckless crewman. Correspondingly, upon diving the temperature rapidly dropped within the small submarine and both crewmen were compelled to wrap up warmly lest they suffer hypothermia.

Once the rough design had been worked out it was handed over by Grim to the *Ingenieurbüro* Glücklauf (IBG) where *Marinebaudirektor* (Director of Naval Construction) Dr Fischer and his staff finalised the details of the design and farmed it out to shipyards for prototype construction. Three were to be built by Howaldt-Kiel, the contract agreed on 30 July 1944. Indeed most of the numbers and construction orders were handed out by April 1944 before the design had been completed. Construction was scheduled to take place at Germaniawerft, Schichau Elbing, Klöckner-Humboldt-Deutz in Ulm and CRD in Montefalcone.

Armaments Minister Albert Speer added the Seehund to his list of manufacturing priorities and issued instructions on 1 June 1944 that a total of 1,000 Type XXVIIB midgets were to be produced, Elbing supplying forty-five and Germaniawerft twenty-five per month. His initial plans were to only utilise these construction firms as he balanced the necessity for Type XXI and XXIII construction at other shipyards. Once Germaniawerft began planned production of the

Type XXIII it was to hand over its Seehund manufacturing to southern German firms, to be completed by May 1945. However, by January 1945 this target had been revised and the construction at Ulm and Hall were to be accelerated, also continuing to use Germaniawerft as a key builder. Speer was soon forced by the exigencies of total war to instigate an emergency building programme that allowed only repair work and the construction of U-boats whose production time was as short as possible, notably the sectional Type XXI and XXIII. Completion targets for the Seehund were reduced to a total of 600 and as Germaniawerft's Konrad shelter was no longer required for the new U-boat types it was given over completely to Seehund construction. Work at Ulm never really got going, as transport links were poor, work in Hall also never commencing. Ultimately 285 Seehunds would completed by the war's end, principally from Germaniawerft and Elbing's Schichau, the three prototypes the only ones constructed elsewhere at Howaldt-Kiel.[59] A shortage of battery accumulators was among the many problems that hampered production of all U-boats including the Seehund.

The finished Seehund measured 11.86m in length, 1.68m beam displaced 14.9 tons. With a 5mm pressure hull it had a rated diving depth of 30m, though in actual service depths of up to 70m were achieved without problems. A simple joystick controlled direction, initially a profile rudder used for the Seehund. The turning circle then found to be inadequate and a Kort nozzle rudder was planned replace the older style. This too proved imperfect; an example captured by the Allies reported as being 'heavy to work' and eventually two-surface rudder (box-rudder) was used.[60] This too was liable flutter when in use making the coxswain's job of keeping it control more difficult than necessary. Coupled to the forward of the steering shaft was an automatic steering device that consisted semi-gyro connected by leads through a relay box and operated electric motor. A remote control steering switch was linked to the by a length of cable and could be carried by the coxswain either outside on the casing or in his normal control position. The control consisted of an on-off switch and a port-starboard switch diesel engine was not reversible so all such manoeuvring was using the main motor.

The semi-gyro compass used for the automatic pilot was set coxswain's panel and was electrically driven. Another compass magnetic projector compass in a brass tube similar to that used Biber, comprised an illuminated card at the top of a 8.8cm brass

ated somewhat by the superb automatic pilot system that allowed the gyrocompass to steer the boat, relieving the crew from this arduous task during travel. It also possessed an extremely good diving time of only two to three seconds.

However it was not without imperfections. As well as its limited radius of action, the interior was largely given over to functionality rather than habitability. There were no WC facilities on board and the crew were limited to the same special diet that had been employed by Biber pilots, using empty tin cans from their rations for storing whatever human waste they accumulated during missions that could last up to a week.

> We drank, but did not excrete much. Beforehand we were supplied with food so that digestion was slowed down, because this was a kind of problem. Our food came in large tin cans and these had to be used for excretion and then thrown overboard, but when the seas were so rough it wasn't possible. But in the first two or three days it could happen that there was no need to go, just like in normal life, and that was okay then. As far as the little things went, as a man one was better off, if I may say so – put it to one side and then it was done. We did it in a similar fashion to the way the cyclists do it today in the Tour de France. They do it quickly.[61]

Of course there was also the same problem that all midget submarines faced as well – the viewing horizon was so low that finding targets relied on their being in close proximity. Airborne reconnaissance would aid this problem – but that was scarce in the extreme by the time that the Seehund sailed into action in early 1945.

Initial training for the Seehund crews was undertaken aboard the Hecht midget submarines as part of Lehrkommando 300 in Neustadt (*Neukoppel*) in barracks at the edge of Wiksbergkaserne, home of the 3. *U-Bootslehrdivision*. Crews immediately under training were also accommodated aboard the motor ship *Frida Horn*, a 3,184-ton Hamburg-registered freighter that had been surprised by the outbreak of war in 1939 while returning from Trinidad to its home port, lucky to reach Germany through an increasingly tight British blockade.

Gradually the Seehunds would replace the Hechts as training vessels as more and more became available, and by December as many as twenty-five Seehunds were on hand at Neustadt. Training comprised a theoretical four weeks devoted to handling the boat at sea, followed by two weeks of torpedo practice. The men were divided into groups of ten for the purpose of their instruction and all available

Seehunds were meant to make a three-day sea trial within the Baltic in December 1944 before leaving for operational deployment. It is believed that as many as five of these boats failed to return from this training voyage.

Established in June 1944, the group's first commander was L.z.S. Kiep, himself undertaking watch-officer training for the U-boat service. However, by July he had been replaced with the far more prestigious figure of Knight's Cross winner and U-boat veteran Kaptlt. Hermann Rasch as Kiep joined the ranks of the coxswains as Flotilla Senior Officer. His engineer, Oberleutnant (Ing.) Palaschewski, was correspondingly the Flotilla Engineering Officer.

By no means were all the Seehund pilots and engineers volunteers. Eugen Herold, an *Obermaschinist* in early 1944, remembers his induction into the *K-Verbände* clearly.

> I was training to be U-boat crew. The sea had fascinated me since before the coming of the war when I had spent summer in a boys' camp on the Elbe near Hamburg. For a native Bavarian it was a wonderful experience. However, after weeks of training aboard a Type VIIC I received my posting – the *K-Verbände*.[62]

Under Rasch's auspices the first batch of recruits was soon formed into the first operational Seehund unit – 312 K-Flotilla. On 24 December the first twenty-five crews departed Neustadt for Wilhelmshaven (*Graukoppel*) by train. There had already been twenty-four Seehunds shipped to Wilhelmshaven where the Deutsche Werke carried out final adjustments.

> The journey from Neustadt to Wilhelmshaven was very elaborate. Through Lübeck, Hamburg, Bremen and Oldenburg by Autobahn. In these long war years we were often halted for periods due to air attacks. In Hamburg alone we were stopped for five days and every night we were on the streets and roofs on air-raid defence duty. Phosphorus rained from the sky, fires raging day and night, we had to gather together terribly mutilated people. Anyone who was in Hamburg at this time knows what I am talking about.
>
> When we arrived at Wilhelmshaven it was only shortly after an enemy aerial bombardment. We stumbled through burst walls, bent steel girders and scattered metal sheets and climbed over iron bars and tangled wire. In some places it burned still and smoke covered the dockyard.
>
> Then we saw the new midget U-boats. They were hidden under camouflage nets where some were being welded. So, these were our Seehunds. We had left the idyll of Neustadt behind. Here was the front-

line. We had spent the last bombing raid in a shelter. From now on bunkers and shelters became daily places of residence for us.

We numbered about 30 officers, NCOs and enlisted men. For the time being, we were all 'machine people'. The sailors were ordered to have still more special training, however we were pushed through it in only a few days. We had to bring the new boats in here and also set up new crews for them so without delay we began to familiarise ourselves with the boats.[63]

Somewhat strangely, the bonds between crews that had been forged during their Hecht training were now broken as commanders and engineers were reshuffled upon arrival in Wilhelmshaven. The boats lay in the northeast corner of the Tirpitzhafen, near the Jachmann Brücke, some in the water and the remainder under the netting with work being completed on them. While maintenance men for the Seehunds were quartered in the *Seefliegerhorst* barracks, the actual crews were quartered in the Roon barracks, spending two days in the yards getting acquainted with their boats and having each craft compensated for their individual weights. The Seehunds clearly impressed their new operators who waited impatiently for them to be released for service. It was also in this period that the young recruits met the man who was soon to take command of the Seehund operations in Holland, one of the two most highly decorated men of the *Kriegsmarine*, U-boat veteran F.K. Albrecht Brandi. The arrival of this illustrious figure helped to foster the sense of belonging to an elite service that Heye had strived to imbue his men with. However, despite their esteemed commander, it was still the 'nuts and bolts' of using the Seehunds that truly inspired the men of the flotilla.

As well as manoeuvring practice they undertook torpedo-firing drill, both surfaced and underwater. Tragedy of a kind familiar to trainee human torpedo pilots nearly overtook at least one crew as *Oberfähnrich* Pettenkofer and *Oberbootsmaat* Werner Schulz attempted their first submerged torpedo shoot.

> I looked one more time at the compass, yes, it is all clear and I gently pulled the lever backwards. It refused to move. I pulled harder. Nothing happened, the handle was stuck, I couldn't move it forwards or backwards. However, the torpedo propeller was turning, I could hear it clearly . . . but it wasn't running off! I pulled more. No, it refused to move from its place.
>
> 'Herr *Oberfähnrich*, the torpedo has not released!'
> 'What?' shouted the *Oberfähnrich*.
> 'The torpedo hasn't released!'

'Are you mad?'

And then – the boat took off. Well, clearly the torpedo did, but with us attached! I can't stop the boat, we are going on a ballistic trajectory!

'Ten metres depth' I said, surprised we had gone so deep.

'Surface!' ordered my commander.

I put the hydroplanes to rise and the boat obeys immediately, but what is that? A tremendous crash, it cracks like a grenade, we had hit an obstacle. The boat tumbles, I switch the electric motor off. The boat spins like a roundabout, we had hit steel.

'Water leaking' said the *Oberfähnrich*. Now what?! Water came from the periscope shaft, not much, but enough. A connecting joint must be leaking.

'See if you can screw it more tightly' I say. It works. The boat is not moving anymore. But we can't rise either. Something is holding us down.

Then to add to the misfortune the lights went out, only the dull glimmer of emergency lighting flickered.

'What's the matter now?!' screamed the *Oberfähnrich*.

'Yeah . . . what now?' I called back.

I changed the fuse and the lights came back on. Well, at least we have that. I am really frightened. The sweat stands out on my forehead. Pettenkofer's face is distorted. But then that's probably how I look too.

'Where are we then? Where can we have ended up?'

'Shit!' shouts Pettenkofer, 'complete giant shit! We are stuck under the harbour lock gates!'[64]

The Seehund had swung to port with the sudden burst from the torpedo motor, before crashing beneath the harbour lock. The two terrified men were finally able to nudge their boat free using their electric motor and the Seehund surfaced once more, the shaken crew rejoined their flotilla and later earning praise from Brandi for their handling of the situation.

The gruelling training continued for the prospective Seehund crews until orders arrived for them to prepare for posting to Holland from where they would attack the Allied convoy traffic within the Scheldt estuary. Their area of operations would span the width of the eastern end of the English Channel, ranging from Holland to northern France and the opposite British coastline. Harald Sander later recalled his own period of time spent familiarising himself with the new submarine and their subsequent relocation to northern Holland:

The boats we were to use . . . were in Wilhelmshaven. I was assigned a commander and we were a crew and we had to agree that we wanted to sail together. We were given a boat and learnt to operate it there in

North Sea

Great Yarmouth

Lowestoft

Ijmuiden

England

Amsterdam

Felixstowe

Rotterdam

London

Thames Estuary

Margate

Zeebrugge

Dover

Antwerp

Dunkirk

Seehund Operational Area

Wilhelmshaven. We carried out test voyages in the basin of the port and we dived there, although we couldn't see much in Wilhelmshaven. It's also called 'mudtown' and when you are two or three metres under the surface, the water is so dirty that you can't see anything. That's where we did our whole training with the boat, until finally all ten submarines arrived. Then these ten boats were put onto large trailers. There was a huge Büsing towing vehicle, which was typical of the kind used at the end of the war. The boats were loaded onto the rear and covered with tarpaulins as camouflage. When I think about it, this was also the time of the so-called *'Vergeltungs-Waffen'* ('Vengeance weapons'), the 'V1' and 'V2' missiles, which were often transported to the French and Dutch coast, so that our *Führer* could threaten England with them. If someone asked us, we said, 'Yes, these are those V1s and V2s we have on here.' Then we came to Ijmuiden, which is at the mouth of the Amsterdam sea canal, which stretches from Amsterdam to the North Sea. We set up camp behind the canal sluice gates and moored the boats there where it was a bit safer.

The flotilla was divided into four groups, each with a group leader (Kiep, Oblt.z.S. Wagner, Oblt.z.S. Paulsen and Oblt.z.S. Krüger who also doubled as deputy senior officer). Each group proceeded separately to Holland in trucks behind which they towed their Seehunds beneath their canvas shrouds. The groups drove via Groningen, Allersvoort and Amsterdam to their new base at Ijmuiden, travelling by night and lying to in woods during the day when Allied aircraft prowled the skies. Only days from Wilhelmshaven they were attacked by aircraft, which left several men of the flotilla dead in their wake. The first group arrived at their destination on 28 December, the remainder during the following three days. Rasch and Kiep were already at Ijmuiden when the crews began to arrive. Ijmuiden was a small suburb of the town of Velsen, which lay at the end of the North Sea Canal linking Amsterdam to the sea. The canal used a system of sluice gates and locks to provide the necessary flooding defence, a fact that the *Kriegsmarine* used to its advantage. The area also provided many small islands and riverbeds in which the Seehunds could be hidden from enemy aircraft if necessary. Initially the men of 312 K-Flotilla were housed in an unheated two-storey building near Rijkswaterstraat, though later they were moved to requisitioned private homes as Harald Sander recalled:

> They [the English] came and we were bombarded, although they only bombarded the entrance to the docks area where the S-boats were. They couldn't bombard us because the sluice gates would have been destroyed and Holland would have been flooded, so we were quite safe there. We 'drivers' were housed in private homes, which were close to Haarlem. Usually there were three or four 'families', as we called it, in one house. Two men (one submarine crew) always lived together and had to be really attuned to each other and for practical purposes made up a couple which functioned together perfectly. This actually worked quite well. We were locked in and had guards stationed around us and so on, the whole works . . . We had no idea what was in store for us and then we ran the boats down into the canal. Meanwhile I was still tinkering a little with my engine, trying to tune it up to go a bit faster, although on the other hand it can't go too fast or else it doesn't fire properly and so on. So those were the little games one played.[65]

Officers occupied small houses on Driehuizerkerkweg immediately south of the canal, while the enlisted men were quartered later in a villa on the eastern side of the railway line that led to Den Haag. The 100 or so shore support staff occupied terraced houses near the small lock gates on the canal and in a hotel in Velserbeck Park. The flotilla's operational staff was quartered and worked in an old mission house at Velsen's cemetery chapel, the quartermaster supply stores located both in the chapel and its adjacent crematorium.

The Seehunds themselves were left on their trailers some 300 metres from the South Lock under camouflage netting after their arrival in Ijmuiden, before being lifted into the water by dockside cranes at Hoogoven Pier on New Year's Eve. Six of the Seehunds had suffered damage to their periscopes while *en route* since the crews and ground staff had forgotten to remove them when passing beneath a low bridge in Amsterdam, and so these craft were unable to participate in the Seehunds' first operational sortie on New Year's Day 1945.

CHAPTER EIGHT

The Netherlands
Battles in the Scheldt

With the loss of France as a forward base the decision was taken on 22 September to base a Linsen flotilla in Holland for operations against Allied minesweepers and supply lines in the Scheldt. The first Linsens began to arrive at Groningen by train from Lübeck on 26 September.

As well as the harassment of Allied shipping at the eastern end of the English Channel, the advance base of southern Holland would also allow for 'Operation Kameraden' – the resupply of the defenders of Dunkirk by the *Kriegsmarine* – to be successfully launched. Initially it had been envisaged that this operation be carried out by small armed fishing vessels (*Kriegsfischerkutter*), however:

> . . . the group of armed fishing vessels that had been put into action for the supply of Dunkirk within the scope of Operation Kameraden had several times run aground after having passed Deurloo Gat. The operation was discontinued . . . the earliest possible date for a repetition promising success is the 10th of October.[66]

However, by that date the battle for the Scheldt estuary had begun and the gauntlet of forces to be run on the way to Dunkirk had increased significantly.

The Scheldt and its tributaries drain an area of about 21,860 km^2 that covers parts of northwest France, western Belgium and the southwest Netherlands. Catchments of numerous small streams compose the sprawling drainage basin, the smaller tributaries feeding larger bodies of water such as the rivers Leie, Dender and Rupel. After the failure of 'Operation Market Garden' at Arnhem in September 1944, Allied attention refocused on Antwerp and clearing its approaches so as to enable the front line to receive more immediate supply, Field Marshal Montgomery directing the British Second Army to break through into the Ruhr Valley. To facilitate the use of Antwerp to pro-vision the Second Army, the Scheldt estuary was to be cleared by the Canadian First Army. The capture of Antwerp was thought to be the solution to all Allied supply problems, as the port was expected to be capable of handling up to 40,000 tons of supplies a day. Once the dock was in Allied hands though, it remained useless without control of the approaching waterways. Antwerp was about 129km inland from the open sea on the River Scheldt. Between the port and the sea were the islands of Walcheren, North Beveland and South Beveland and ironically, this was the exact same area that the Germans had chosen to receive evacuated men from the Pas de Calais. Nearly 100,000 German soldiers embarked at Breskens in Holland and crossed to Vlissingen on Walcheren. From here they were meant to return to Germany, but then Hitler ordered Walcheren held and so the *Wehrmacht* was ordered to stand and fight.

Interestingly, German naval intelligence included, on 9 October, a summary of an article written for the London *Evening Standard* by the journalist James Stuart on the matter:

> The large port of Antwerp has been in our possession for one month, however, we cannot utilise it yet. The enemy batteries stationed on Walcheren Island are preventing the shipping in the Scheldt Mouth . . . The utilisation of the port of Antwerp will speed up the advance of the Allies. The port fell into our hands undamaged, and it is a tantalisation [*sic*] that one cannot utilise the grand facilities of the port of Antwerp.[67]

Thus, with public opinion in harmony with military necessity, the Allied seizure of the Scheldt estuary began. However, like so many plans before and since, the battle to clear the Scheldt took longer than expected, a tenacious defence mounted by General Gustav-Adolf von Zangen's Fifteenth Army making Allied progress torturously slow. The southern bank of the estuary around the towns of Breskens and Zeebrugge was flat, marshy country; much of it reclaimed polder land below sea level and easily flooded as a defensive measure. To the north of the estuary was South Beveland, a former island connected to the mainland by a narrow isthmus. Nearby was the heavily fortified island of Walcheren – which boasted several heavy coastal gun batteries matched by similar batteries on the mainland between Zeebrugge and Breskens – accessible from South Beveland by a single causeway that was again easily defended by determined troops.

On 16 October 1944 the Canadians took Woensdrecht, the town at the head of the isthmus of South Beveland and two weeks later a combined land and amphibious assault captured the strip of land. By the first week of November the south bank of the Scheldt had been cleared. Finally, the island of Walcheren was attacked from the air with precision bombing that breached the dykes and flooded most of the island. The island resembles a dish with steep natural sand dunes and man-made dykes forming the rim, holding back the North Sea from the polder interior. Allied planners were certain that the Germans would blow the dykes and thus force them to advance along well-defended embanked roads. By pre-empting this move, the Allies hoped to be able to use the floodwaters to their own advantage with commandos and amphibious vehicles. On 31 October the Canadians launched an attack across the causeway, eventually establishing a foothold on the island. Combined land and amphibious attacks followed, though the last German resistance did not end until 8 November. The port of Antwerp was reopened twenty days later after over 100 minesweepers had cleared the Scheldt approaches. It was into this port that Allied supply convoys now steamed, providing fresh and accessible targets for the weapons of the *K-Verbände*.

Combined with the Scheldt hunting ground the *K-Verbände* were also well placed to take the opportunity to support beleaguered German supply lines that trailed to Dunkirk, designated a fortress by Hitler and planning to hold out against the Allied advance. While the Scheldt battle was beginning a change in organisational structure was instigated for the now far-flung units of the *K-Verbände*. All *K-Verbände* and MEK units stationed between Dunkirk and Hanstholm, in Heligoland and the Frisian Islands were placed under the control of *Kommando Stab* Holland, headed by F.K. Werner Musenberg. Musenberg had commanded the experimental high-speed *U-180* for the latter half of 1942 until January 1944 when he was transferred to a staff position.[68] In turn Böhme's defunct *Kommando Stab* West was disbanded and he transferred first to Denmark and later onward to Italy, continuing his role as regional commander within the *K-Verbände*.

The first Linsen operation in Holland was planned for the night of 5 October as the land battle raged along the Scheldt. On that date the Linsens already in Groningen were moved to their forward base of Vlissingen. There they were to receive support from Oblt.MAdR Hans-Friedrich Prinzhorn's MEK 60. The original briefing was to have a formation of Linsens provide escort duty for an 'Operation Kameraden' Dunkirk supply convoy, while the remaining four groups of Linsens could attack Allied minesweepers operating off the

Flanders coastline. However, the mission degenerated swiftly when soon after 20.10hrs, as the escort group was leaving harbour, two were sunk in error by the German harbour defence patrol. The attack groups of Linsens sailed at around 23.00hrs though within three hours the weather had deteriorated, wind increasing to Force Five and this, combined with a heavy ground swell off the gently shelving seabed put the Linsens into great difficulties. By dawn, twenty-six had returned to Vlissingen and fourteen had been driven ashore and destroyed. That afternoon the Linsen base was attacked by Allied fighter-bombers, though the Germans sustained little damage.

Later that day the remaining boats of the flotilla were withdrawn to Rotterdam, two Linsens being lost to air attack on the way. Thus, within only 24 hours the strength of 214 K-Flotilla had been whittled down dramatically from sixty craft to just twenty-four. The flotilla in tatters, the remnants were shipped by road to Groningen on 7 October, where they were due to be entrained for Plön in Germany. The following day the sixty Linsens of 215 K-Flotilla were reported as two days short of battle readiness, moving to Groningen to replace the battered 214 K-Flotilla. There they were held at immediate notice for operational employment 'wherever targets should appear'. Arriving at Groningen after two days transit from Germany, the flotilla moved once more within another two days to Rotterdam. By 22 October they were in transit once more, this time to Vlissingen where twenty-eight Linsens arrived that same day, transported by transport barges (*Marine-fährpram*). The remainder of the flotilla was delayed, in part as one of the transport barges grounded while carrying seven of the Linsens.

The fresh flotilla was instantly put into action. In the days since the instigation of 'Operation Kameraden', Dönitz had shifted priority from the supply of Dunkirk to the maintenance of a barrage of vessels blocking the Scheldt and keeping local elements of the *Wehrmacht* supplied with ammunition. The commander of Fortress Dunkirk had enquired as to the possibility of using midget submarines for his own supply missions, but this had been refused by SKL as 'impossible', the onus placed on the use of Linsens instead – and only then if petrol was made available from Dunkirk for the small craft for their return journey. Twenty-four Linsens still left Vlissingen for Dunkirk on the night of 22 October, four others headed for Kadzand and the Breskens bridgehead with gun spares urgently required by the beleaguered German defenders. However, the combined Linsens were badly scattered by gunfire from Allied batteries west of Vlissingen, fourteen returning to port and the remainder suffering an unknown fate.

By daybreak on 26 October 215 K-Flotilla had been dispersed; twelve were engaged on an attempted supply run to Dunkirk having departed during the previous night, twelve more were at Vlissingen, nine at Kidderburg and fifteen at Rotterdam. That night, at 21.30hrs, Vlissingen's dozen Linsens departed port for an attack against Allied disembarkation berths at South Beveland, which were keeping Canadian forces supplied. However, all twelve grounded on a sand-bank near Terneuzen and the operation was aborted. The crews waited patiently through the night as they watched Allied supply ships move in and out of the Scheldt. All of the Linsens returned the following morning, unscathed from their ordeal and another attempt was planned for the following night. This time they were accompanied by four MEK-*Verbindungsboote* (commando craft). During the attack, four explosive Linsens were released, one of which was claimed to have hit the disembarkation jetty and exploded, damaging two 300-ton lighters that were unloading. Another hit a 600 ton lighter that was under tow, but failed to explode. The remaining two explosive boats overshot and hit the outer mole. The four commando craft strafed the area with machine-gun fire before retreating into the darkness. Three control and two explosive Linsens returned to Vlissingen, another stranded at South Beveland and two explosive boats were abandoned with engine trouble.

With the Vlissingen boats decimated by this operation, plans were made to move the fifteen remaining Linsens at Rotterdam to Vlissingen in order to facilitate another Dunkirk supply mission. However, the small boats that departed under their own power were delayed by bad weather near Dordrecht and forced to transfer aboard some Dutch motor vessels to complete their voyage. The possibility of making another run to Dunkirk using them was by this stage beginning to fade. Unless the weather broke and allowed the Linsens to take to the sea once more, the *K-Verbände* would be unable to operate again before the planned German withdrawal abandoned Vlissingen to the Allies. Indeed the deteriorating German situation on Walcheren was beginning to make the use of Linsens less and less viable. If the *K-Verbände* were to complete 'Operation Kameraden' then it would have to be by using submarines.

The inclement weather continued to prevent Linsen operations against Scheldt shipping until 30 October when eight Linsens were moved from Dordrecht to Veere in Walcheren, though they were repeatedly attacked by Allied fighter-bombers *en route*. On 24 October the Linsen unit that had suffered at the hands of British tanks during the withdrawal from France arrived in Groningen after refitting in Lübeck (Schartau). It was here that they met with Bibers that had also withdrawn from Normandy. The midget submarines had at first transferred to Jutland before being diverted to Groningen. The end of October also marked the end of Vlissingen as a Linsen base. A final sortie by six Linsens in the West Scheldt resulted in claims of a 2,000-ton ammunition ship, searchlight barge and anti-aircraft lighter sunk, though there are no Allied records of this. The remains of the flotilla then evacuated Vlissingen, the unit's equipment travelling by commandeered Dutch barges while the crews travelled in their Linsens.

By the beginning of November the *K-Verbände* strength within the Scheldt region was ninety-six Linsens (reinforcements of sixty new boats having arrived on 31 October) and the thirty Bibers of 261 K-Flotilla, a further fifty-nine Bibers being on their way from Denmark. Many of the new Linsens were to be based at Zierkzee and thus departed Dordrecht for this new base on the night of 2 November. However, due to what the SKL described as the 'enemy situation', none arrived. Six reached Zijpe, five grounded on a sandbank nearby, nine returned to Dordrecht and four went missing. The remainder were moved almost immediately thereafter to Hellevoetsluis at the head of the Waal/Maas estuary, considered the sole remaining advance base near the Scheldt suitable for them.

K-Verbände operations then experienced a hiatus, another fresh Linsen flotilla arriving in Den Helder on 4 November. Weeks passed in inactivity, as the Germans appeared unable to discern any usable pattern of Allied shipping within the Scheldt, though Dönitz pledged to Hitler the commitment of greater numbers of *K-Verbände* units in that region during early November. Walcheren remained the key position for interdiction of Antwerp supply convoys and Heye was therefore placed under pressure to support troops holding the island by any means possible. On 7 November Heye reported to Dönitz that he considered the only hope for successful operations lay in the use of individual missions by specially selected crews, while the bulk of his forces were kept in reserve to face what he predicted could be an Allied landing in northern Holland. In light of his recent pledge, however, Dönitz disagreed, placing particularly strong emphasis on the deployment of the new Bibers in Holland.

An advanced base for the Bibers of 261 K-Flotilla was prepared at Poortershaven, a small harbour on the Nieuwe Waterweg where the Oranjekanal meets the Maas Canal, west of Rotterdam between Maasluis and Hoek van Holland. The shipyard there was bounded

north and east by the Wilhelmina Harbour, south by the Nieuwe
Maas. The main flotilla headquarters remained in Rotterdam. At
Poortershaven, near Maasluis, some of the Bibers were accommodated in concrete shelters originally built for S-boats while the remainder were left in the water under camouflage netting. The base provided
an ideal working environment both because of its proximity to the
combat zone at sea and the provision of dockside cranes for moving
the craft to and from the water. However, the S-boat facilities had
already provided a tempting target for the RAF, Lancasters bombing
the port with 12,000lb Tallboys on 3 February 1944, wreaking havoc
amongst the dockyard installations. By the time that the Bibers arrived
to make use of the port fresh installations had been prepared.

Allied naval intelligence was extremely well informed of the development of *K-Verbände* operations. In a report dated 6 November 1944
written by H Clancy (British Naval Intelligence) the *K-Verbände* was
surmised as having been:

> . . . set up late in 1943 when it became apparent that the Allies might
> invade the Continent; and probably with the further object of bridging
> the gap between the failure of the 1943 U-boat offensive and the start
> of the new U-boat offensive late in 1944.
>
> The German organisation was founded by members of the SS
> counter-espionage, which had formerly played a role similar to that of
> British Naval 30 Assault Unit. The Navy took over part control early
> in 1944. The struggle with the SS for full control culminated in the
> appointment of Vizeadmiral Heye to command the unit in May 1944
> . . . When Heye took over the unit changed its name from *Marine
> Einsatz Abteilung* (Naval Assault Unit) to *K-Verbände* (Small Battle
> Units) and became an independent command directly responsible to
> Dönitz . . .
>
> In the future, Small Battle Units will probably endeavour to harass
> Allied shipping and communications in the Low Countries, and to
> follow the advance of Allied armies. Explosive motorboats and midget
> U-boats are probably available for operation in the Dutch Islands, and
> further attacks on bridges may be made by swimming saboteurs.
>
> Attacks by one-man torpedoes, explosive motorboats, midget U-
> boats and swimming saboteurs will probably also continue on the East
> and West coasts of the Italian Peninsula and the coasts of southern
> France and Dalmatia. At the same time there is evidence, graded B2,
> that flotillas of one-man torpedoes are now located in Northern
> Denmark, and C3 reports state that these craft have been sent to
> Southern Norway . . .

CONCLUSION: The Germans are expanding the training and scope of the Small Battle Units and probably intend to employ this organisation extensively to attack Allied inshore shipping and communications, both in the North Sea and the Mediterranean as the Allies advance in both theatres.[69]

By 15 November the Linsens were distributed between three bases: thirty-six at Den Helder, thirty-six at Scheveningen and twenty-four at Hellevoetsluis. The Bibers meanwhile were based at Poortershaven, though there were fifty-nine more of two flotillas still in Groningen awaiting transfer to an operational base. The problem of finding a forward base for the short-range Linsen was solved after a reconnaissance of the region revealed the suitability of using the port at Ouddorp for this purpose. Linsens were immediately ferried there by Dutch barges from Hellevoetsluis.

The pause in combat operations ended on the night of 21 November when Linsens raided into the Hollandsch Diep with the intention of destroying quayside installations at both Willemstad and Moerdijk. Despite the complete absence of Allied patrol craft to interfere with the mission, only the installations at Moerdijk were destroyed due to mechanical faults with the other Linsen party. Musenberg enthusiastically seized the opportunity presented by such a poorly defended Allied coastline and appealed for permission to step up raids against the area in order to compel Allied redeployment of forces from elsewhere to counter the new threat. Unfortunately for Musenberg, local *Wehrmacht* authorities objected on the grounds that they themselves intended to step up their own raids along the south coast of Hollandsch Diep. Undeterred, Musenberg and the local naval command reported to Dönitz on 26 November that there were ample opportunities for offensive action in the Scheldt. They advised that Linsens could possibly be modified to carry BM250 mines and could definitely be used for the delivery of commando units as well as their original explosive motorboat purpose. Bibers were also to be used for minelaying, a forward base at the Hook of Holland proposed for them. However, SKL demurred somewhat, correctly stating that the Bibers were subject to the vagaries of weather and that even if the entire *K-Verbände* force within the region were deployed within the navigationally difficult waters of the Scheldt, though they might inflict casualties on enemy shipping they could not be expected to bring traffic to a complete halt nor effectively block the waterway.

Meanwhile, the Linsens continued to sail. Twelve were moved to Burgsluis from Hellevoetsluis during the first week of December, lying in readiness for attacks on targets 'as soon as they were reported'. Heye requested reconnaissance of the Scheldt area on 4 December in search of such targets of opportunity, but he was given short shrift by Dönitz, who considered that the dire predicament of German forces in the region meant that the Linsens could not wait for reconnaissance and were to be despatched into action immediately, the pilots instructed to seek out their own targets. Dönitz at this point ordered the Molch units from Borkum and Heligoland to the Netherlands to support the offensive. However, before the Linsens could begin their task their forward staging area at Burgsluis was heavily bombed and the small Linsen presence nearly completely annihilated.

By 11 December the *K-Verbände* presence in Holland was disposed as follows:

> Sixty Linsens at Groningen, freshly arrived to the regional reserve.
> Thirty-six Linsens at Den Helder.
> Twenty-four Linsens at Scheveningen.
> Twelve Linsens at Hellevoetsluis.
> Twelve Linsens at Dordrecht.
> Thirty Bibers at Poortershaven (261 K-Flotilla).
> Fifty-nine Bibers at Groningen (262 and 266 K-Flotillas).

As Dönitz had instructed, thirty Molchs of 412 K-Flotilla were despatched first to Assen from their base on Borkum and from there onwards to Hellevoetsluis. A further sixty Molchs of 413 K-Flotilla were sent to Zwolle from Heligoland and Groningen.

The following day, 12 December, twenty-seven extra Linsens, slightly modified to improve their sea-worthiness and manned by hand-picked crews arrived at Groningen as well. They were immediately despatched to Hellevoetsluis in preparation for attacks on Allied convoy traffic in the Scheldt, towed to their new base by tugs of the Rhine Flotilla. Hopes were high for the new elite group, though their promise soon faded as twenty-one set out for their first mission, losing five to either engine trouble or grounding before the remainder aborted in thick fog. The dispirited remnants of this unit were returned to Germany for overhaul.

In December 1944, after Allied forces had taken the Scheldt and Antwerp was made operational, the Bibers based in the Netherlands began service. They had been allocated three patrol boats of the Rhine Flotilla and a group of R-boat minesweepers to act as tugs for operational use. The Bibers, only able to operate in a maximum of wind strength 4, were provided with advanced weather forecasts by Germany's meteorological service, augmented by weather reports from U-boats still active in the eastern Atlantic. A *Wehrmacht* radio listening station on the island of Schouwen in turn provided valuable intelligence of the imminent arrival of Allied convoy traffic headed for Antwerp.

Originally the maiden operation had been planned for 19 December, the Bibers at Poortershaven being divided into two groups to lessen the threat of losses by Allied interference. The plan was for an initial group of twelve, led by *Leutnant* (Ing.) Blessmann, to sail from Hellevoetsluis while another group of sixteen would sail simultaneously from the Hook of Holland to provide the second force. Both groups were to target general Allied shipping within the Scheldt. However thick fog forced a postponement.

On 20 December the first twelve departed Poortershaven for their forward base at Hellevoetsluis under tow by tugs. Disaster almost immediately overtook them when two of the small submarines were sunk by the wake of their towing river patrol boats of the Rhine Flotilla, although the two young pilots, *Bootsmaat* Nientiet and *Oberbootsmaat* Schmidt, were rescued from the icy water and returned to join a second group of Bibers departing later. The remaining ten proceeded to Hellevoetsluis where their vessels were concealed beneath camouflage netting and the pilots accommodated in private homes. Bartels arrived soon after the Bibers to pass on instructions for the upcoming mission including a rough sketch of their operational area. Each Biber would be equipped with one mine and one torpedo, the former to be laid in Allied supply ship routes as far into the Scheldt estuary as possible, the latter saved for any targets of convenience. The pilots were instructed to land on any German-held island after their operation was completed and telephone Bartels in Amsterdam to report their status, *Wehrmacht* troops on the islands having been warned of the possible arrival of bedraggled Biber pilots. Ultimately the Bibers were instructed to return to the Hook of Holland.

A second group of Bibers departed Poortershaven at 16.08hrs on 21 December, three R-boats towing three Bibers each while a fourth acted as guard boat. Leaving harbour, the small flotilla headed south at the Hook of Holland and proceeded to a position off Voorne. Here the weather inflicted great discomfort on the nine Bibers, all opting to abort their mission except for *Steuermannsmaat* Stock, who slipped his tow and went into action. He was never seen again. The remainder

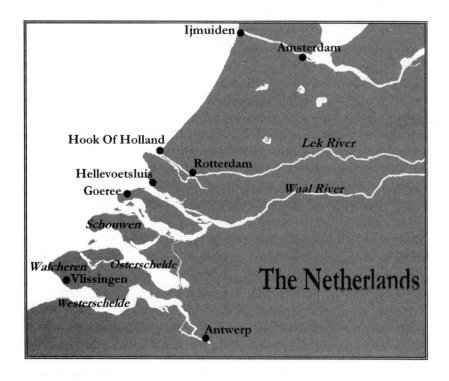

Ijmuiden
Amsterdam
Hook Of Holland
Lek River
Rotterdam
Hellevoetsluis
Goeree
Waal River
Schouwen
Walcheren *Osterschelde*
•Vlissingen
The Netherlands
Westerschelde
Antwerp

turned back though three of them were subsequently lost; *Ober-gefreiter* Pryzkling's foundered and sank, *Bootsmaat* Hadering's struck a mine off the Hook of Holland and *Bootsmaat* Resin's sank upon reaching Poortershaven. It was an inauspicious start to operations.

At 17.30hrs the following day, 22 December, the same group of Bibers that had aborted their mission the previous day sortied once again. Five R-boats, four towing two Bibers each and the last towing one in a bid to reduce loss caused by too many Bibers in the wake of each minesweeper, left Poortershaven and again turned south at the Hook of Holland. However, once more failure loomed when the group were sighted off Voorne by British MTBs and twice attacked while the submarines were still under tow. At the second attack at 20.00hrs, the R-boats opted to slip their charges free and enter the Hook. Almost instantly four Bibers were sunk as the R-boats retreated from the enemy, one Biber sinking while slipping its tow line, another unable to cast off and scuttled, and the final two abandoned due to mechanical defects. Thus only five Bibers managed to head into action from this group. Of those, *Oberfähnrich* Langsdorff and Tank and *Obergefreiter* Kramer disappeared, *Oberfähnrich*

Kärnmer was sunk and killed and the body of *Oberbootsmaat* Schmidt – who had been part of the first group before his Biber foundered and he later sailed in this second group – was recovered off Dunkirk on 29 December.

While the destruction of Langsdorff's group was being completed, the original group of ten Bibers – those that had transferred from Maasluis – had also commenced their outward journey, departing Hellevoetsluis at 17.00hrs in tow of units of the Rhine Flotilla. They were slipped loose from their tugs off Schouwen at 21.30hrs and headed into action. One tug and Biber had been sunk *en route* by mines off the West Schouwen Bank, another Biber badly damaged by mines off West Schouwen and returned to base, so it was eight that headed into action from this first group.

Leutnant (Ing.) Blessmann left his tug and sailed surfaced at 3 knots into his operational zone, laying his mine between Breskens and Vlissingen. Blessmann was an experienced Biber pilot. He had first arrived at Lübeck in September 1944 where he had studied a Biber for a week as it lay in the repair workshops, before being sent with thirty other new recruits to the accommodation ship *Deneb* that lay in Lübeck Bay. He and five others who had shown aptitude for the novel weaponry were selected as instructors, training the remaining men for two weeks to be coxswains. Blessmann was able to use his skill as a pilot to reach his target and successfully mine the shipping channel. However, it was upon his return journey that Blessmann ran foul of the enemy.

At 08.00hrs *HMML1465* was secured to a buoy on the south side of the Scheldt entrance keeping an anti-submarine vigil when its sonar operator reported a suspicious noise to port. Of short duration, the operator guessed it to be a small submarine blowing its tanks. Almost straight away the starboard lookout, Seaman Stanley Lilburn Cordell, sighted a 'suspicious object', which suddenly appeared and was moving eastwards. The captain slipped his mooring and immediately closed up to Action Stations and opened the throttle fully to close the object at maximum speed. The object was soon confirmed as a periscope, and heavy fire from a Vickers machine gun and a 20mm Oerlikon laced toward the target. Barber ordered a depth charge prepared but as his crew raced to ready the charge, the Biber partially surfaced, revealing her bows, periscope and conning tower before a single man was seen to bale out of his stricken submarine, which promptly sank. Blessmann was pulled from the water, stripped and searched before being given hot food and dry clothes.

Barber's crew soon sighted a second periscope about 400 yards to the northwest, the motor launch racing towards it as it submerged, dropping a single depth charge over its presumed location, but losing contact. Unfortunately for the young British lieutenant his day proceeded to go downhill after his initially promising start as *ML1465* later ran aground on a sandbank and lost its Asdic dome, having to remain stranded until the tide rose once again.

Twenty-year-old *Mechanikershauptgefreiter* Karl Mandel had also made his way into the Scheldt estuary when he realised at 02.00hrs on 23 December that the compass that he had been relying on was faulty. Losing his bearings he groped his way around on the surface until striking a buoy. Intending to bottom his Biber and wait for daylight in order to fix his position, he was dismayed to discover that the collision with the buoy had holed his craft which leaked badly when attempting to submerge. Pinned to the surface he quickly laid his mine nearby and determined to retreat from the vicinity of so much Allied patrol activity. However, his luck had deserted him.

Following the sinking of Blessmann's Biber by Allied coastal forces were alerted to the presence of enemy midget submarines in the area. A small squadron of motor launches and minesweepers centred on HMS *Tudno*, comprising *ML915*, *ML221*, *BYMS2015* and *BYMS2188* instigated anti-submarine search patterns during that morning after receipt of the warning, travelling at 13 knots in order to present a difficult target to potential attackers. At 10.30hrs a periscope was sighted near NF15 buoy, the British force increasing speed and beginning an immediate attack. A brief loss of sonar contact on the newly acquired target was followed by strong traces of the submerged German, whose craft was barely moving. One depth charge was released from Lieutenant (RNVR) R H Faulkner's *ML915*, set to explode at 50 feet in what was only seven fathoms of water, swiftly followed by a second charge over the target. As the disturbed water settled contact was lost with the Biber, though six minutes after the first attack the British MTBs sighted a man in the water waving his arms to be rescued. *ML221* closed the solitary figure, a dazed Mandel pulled from the water and taken prisoner. He was suffering from shock and exposure as the British attempted a brief interrogation of their captive. A map and notebook found on him provided information about his mission, though Mandel swore that his was the only craft operating in that area, lamenting his faulty compass which he revealed had been blown off its mounting by the first depth charge. Only two hours later *ML915* was again in action against a suspected Biber, two depth charges being dropped on an evading target, which promptly disappeared. No remains were found, though lookouts reported a black object blown from the water during one of the depth charge detonations.

The destruction of the attackers continued throughout the day. Three British motor minesweepers reported engaging a midget submarine east of NF15 buoy. At first the senior officer of the three-ship sweeping group believed the sighted object to be an Oropesa float that had become detached, though soon lookouts confirmed that it was a small grey conning tower. All three ships pulverising the visible conning tower with heavy machine guns, the glass seen to shatter under the heavy bullets before the bow of the Biber lifted clear of the water in its death throes. Levelling out, the stern raised and the small German craft sank bow first before the attackers could ram it. British motor launches criss-crossed the area during the day, carrying out sporadic depth charge attacks against possible Biber targets, some charges failing to detonate as they buried in thick silt before reaching their detonation depth. Despite no further confirmed kills there were several reports of probable damage claimed and perhaps this explains the Biber crews that were never seen again.

Another Biber present in the region achieved the sole success attributed to the operation. *Bootsmaat* Schulze had departed Hellevoetsluis with the first group, his Biber towed with that belonging to *Funkmaat* Hinzmann. Slipped from their tug at 20.32hrs on 22 December, Schulze lost contact with the other Bibers and made his way toward the sea lane between Vlissingen and the Belgian coast. Drifting with the current he sighted two masts, closing the potential target and attacking what transpired to be a Panamanian freighter. Estimating his target as between 6,000 and 8,000 tons it was in fact the 4,702-ton MV *Alan A Dale*, torpedoed at 16.25hrs on 23 December 1944, five miles ESE of Vlissingen. The ship had sailed from New York on 29 November bound for Antwerp via Halifax, loaded with ammunition, food, vehicles and mail. She was making 7.6 knots in 26 feet of water, with eleven lookouts scanning the smooth and calm sea for potential dangers. The weather was good as the Panamanian proceeded in convoy – the sixth ship in the starboard column. The single torpedo fired by Schulze struck the freighter on her starboard side and the ship was eventually abandoned at 08.30hrs the next morning after all attempts to save her were called off. All sixty-five crew survived the attack and the burning vessel was beached as the severe fire that followed completely gutted it, the vessel declared a total loss by the Allies and later towed out and sunk in the Westerschelde.[70]

Schulze was elated by his successful attack, though his joy was short-lived. During his return journey away from the area his compass also failed, the young pilot navigating by the sun and stars until he sighted land. Beaching the small submarine, which was later carried away by the tide, Schulze wandered inland where he soon discovered himself to be behind Allied lines, surrendering the following morning at West Kapelle.

The previous day, 23 December, eleven more Bibers (six of 262 K-Flotilla and five from 261), were readied for an operation in the Scheldt estuary. Some of the Bibers were this time equipped with two torpedoes, others armed with one torpedo and one mine, their orders to penetrate as far into the Scheldt as possible in order to lay their mines, carrying out torpedo attacks on any targets of opportunity along the way. The pilots were informed that although free to attack any given target, if possible they should wait for convoy traffic to and from Antwerp, which was scheduled to cross off Vlissingen between 13.00hrs and 14.00hrs as the tide was flooding. This would make a perfect area for minelaying and lying in wait for torpedo targets. Accounts differ as to why, but once again two Bibers were prevented from taking part, either through mechanical deficiencies or, as stated in Allied post-war analysis, one ran aground on West Schouwen at Hamstede and another swamped and sank. Of the remaining nine, none would return, though two pilots were later taken prisoner. Towed to the area between Voorne and Goeree, they were slipped from the R-boats' tow lines when almost directly opposite the imposing square red-brick lighthouse on the north-west corner of Goeree. An hour after heading almost due west they turned and entered the Scheldt.

Twenty-four-year-old *Funkmaat* Friedrich Abele's Biber (261 K-Flotilla), carrying two torpedoes, was plagued by defective steering gear once it had reached the operational area. As the hapless German attempted to steer his unmanageable craft he was sighted by a lookout aboard *ML1402*, which was proceeding east into the Scheldt one mile from NF12 buoy as escort for HMS *Blisworth* and *MFV1029*. An object was sighted by the British crew to starboard at 500 yards distance, soon identified as a surfaced midget submarine. Action Stations were immediately called as speed was increased to full and a ramming course set. As the launch raced toward its target the conning tower hatch was seen to open and a man's head appeared, disappearing briefly before returning to throw a rubber dinghy overboard and swiftly abandoning ship.

Abele had decided to abandon his useless craft, water pouring through the open hatch as the Biber lay stern-down in the water. The British slowed, holding their fire as they watched the curious events unfold. Smoke began to belch from the open conning tower and *ML1402* made a circular sweep around the small craft as a hasty sketch was made of it for the after action report, the number 73 and the 'German cross' clearly visible on the grey-painted conning tower. Abele was pulled from the water and after convincing the British that his Biber was now empty and liable to explode, along with its still-intact weaponry, *ML1402* eased away and opened fire with all weapons to avoid any potential danger to an approaching convoy. The Biber was badly holed by the gunfire and rapidly sank. The young British lieutenant's report sheds interesting light on the state of his captive, his possessions and intelligence gleaned about the Biber.

The prisoner . . . was searched for weapons, then taken below, stripped and given warm clothing. Preliminary questioning showed him to be an NCO aged 24 from Kiberachriss (Württemburg). He had not had a meal since midnight 23rd.

Abele was subdued and obedient, apparently not frightened. Of good physique he was well fed and was understood to have spent some years in Norway. His morale was good and gunfire had no upsetting effect. He was given a hot meal. He and his effects were transferred to HMS *Cattistock* . . . for passage to the UK.

List of belongings:
1 identity card
1 wallet
1 square black bulls eye torch
1 pocket knife
4 pistol cartridges
2 propelling pencils
1 fountain pen
1 small pink hair comb
1 identity disc
1 Netherlands note
7 Netherlands coins
9 drawing pins (black)
1 small note book
4 8-amp fuses in containers
10 black button-like discs
1 metal T-shaped tool

3 metal buttons
1 pair trousers
1 tunic jacket
1 blue sweater
1 forage cap
1 pair leather boots
1 pair socks
2 vests
1 pants
1 pair short gaiters
1 paper slip containing a broken *white tablet* [original emphasis – author] was found in the note book cover
2 pieces of cardboard

It is suggested that the T-shaped metal tool, which the prisoner took great care of, was affixed to a seacock and, like a depth charge key, could not be removed until the cock had been opened and that his retention of it was his proof of attempted destruction.[71]

The other survivor, 262 K-Flotilla's *Fähnrich* Karl Heinz Hoffmann, had been armed with one mine and one torpedo for the mission. He discharged his torpedo, missing a lone merchant ship that preceded the expected convoy. Owing to what he later described simply as 'difficulties', Hoffmann departed the Scheldt Estuary and laid his mine off Zeebrugge before his Biber was intercepted and sunk by *ML1402* near NF11 buoy.

On Christmas Eve nine Bibers were to have sailed but a breakdown of the torpedo transport wagon meant that only three were able to be armed and released for action, leaving port at 23.45hrs. None would return. Nine Linsens had also sailed some hours earlier; three control boats each with two explosive craft. The familiar spectre of engine trouble forced a return of six of them, the last group reaching Zeebrugge where they attempted an attack. One of the explosive boats struck a submerged wreck and sank, the remaining one missed a freighter estimated at 9,000 tons. The control boat returned to its base with the occupants half-frozen and the boat so heavily iced that it was almost unnavigable.

Christmas Day brought the Bibers no respite. The reserve flotilla in Groningen, 266 K-Flotilla, was ordered to move forward to Rotterdam to replace the heavy losses already suffered, while another flotilla stationed in Norden began its transfer to The Netherlands and into reserve. It was an auspicious date for other units of the *K-Verbände* –

the first six operational Seehunds already travelling by road for Ijmuiden and action. At the front line, six coxswains of 262 K-Flotilla left Rotterdam by truck bound for Hellevoetsluis. Arriving at 17.30hrs the six were given orders for their upcoming mission by Kaptlt. Schmidt and *Leutnant* Isenbach, *Obersteuermann* Birck providing navigational instructions. Their instructions were typically specific for the young pilots, evidenced by findings from Allied POW interrogations:

> After being slipped by their tugs off the Goeree lighthouse, the Bibers were to proceed for three hours on 230°, two hours on 220°, one hour on 170° and one and a half hours on 90°, which should have brought them off Vlissingen at 09.30hrs on 26 December. At high water between 11.00hrs and 12.30hrs they were to attack shipping off Vlissingen. They were also informed of convoys crossing between 13.00hrs and 14.00hrs which would be good targets.[72]

The six departed Hellevoetsluis at midnight, towed as always to the Goeree lighthouse now familiar to the R-boat and river craft crews. After two hours under tow the Bibers slipped their lines and began to follow the instructions provided by Birck, hoping that his tide calculations were indeed correct. However, *Matrosengefreiter* Stolp found himself off course and somewhere east of the port of Zeebrugge by 09.30hrs on Boxing Day. With heavy seas battering his small U-boat and visibility of only 200m Stolp was unable to fix his position with any landmarks on the featureless coast. Altering course to 90° to close the shoreline Stolp found himself confronted with a distant ship that he estimated at between 3,000 and 4,000 tons, the wreck of another freighter directly ahead of him. However as he pondered following the distant steamer he also became aware of engine noise ahead of him – two British 'Yard' class minesweepers closing fast. Stolp threw his Biber into a 180° turn and began frantically zig-zagging. With no time to turn back and launch a spoiling attack on the minesweepers, Stolp kept his Biber surfaced, opened the hatch and stood on the small green leather bucket seat to surrender to his attackers.

In fact there were three minesweepers bearing down on Stolp – *BYMS2213, 2141* and *2221*. They had been engaged on sweeping the shipping channel near NF17 buoy when the last ship sighted a periscope of another Biber to his port side. Almost simultaneously the First Lieutenant aboard leading sweeper *BYMS2213* spotted Stolp's periscope only about 15° off his ship's bow. The image soon hardened into the small grey conning tower of the Biber and Lieutenant L S

Hardy RNVR switched off his sweep and ordered full speed ahead. Unable to bring guns to bear he directed his helmsman, 2nd Hand A H Creighton, to ram.

> The submarine turned away from us and began zig-zagging, but when we were about one cable from her the conning tower opened and a German was seen frantically waving his arms in the air. However, we carried on and struck her just forward of the conning tower. The ship lifted and the submarine passed under the bow but reappeared on its side ahead of the S.A. towed box which was carried away on the starboard side. It passed astern and rapidly sank at 09.35hrs.[73]

Stolp was thrown clear by the impact and as his attacker slowed to a halt he grasped the tail line of the LL sweep that trailed behind the ship. Sub-Lieutenant R J Lord RNVR manned the minesweeper's dinghy and rowed out toward the clearly shocked German who had momentarily disappeared from view after releasing his grip on the sweep. Lord soon located him and Stolp was hauled aboard and taken back to the British ship where he was given dry clothing and later handed over to Dutch soldiers at Terneuzen.

While Stolp had been under attack, *BYMS2141* and *2221* chased down the initial periscope sighting. Lieutenant J Jobson RNR commanded the former, switching off the electrical LL sweep as he pursued the fleeing Biber, *BYMS2221* commanded by Lieutenant Napper RNVR following. A thick haze that hung low over the water had obscured the Biber from sight and the two minesweepers groped through the murk in search of their quarry. Radioed warnings were issued that German midgets were operational in the area, shipping in the nearby lower Honte anchorage immediately alerted to the potential threat. The Biber was soon sighted once again and attempted to evade its attackers, keeping them directly astern and between the British and the bright low-lying sun, making observation difficult for the minesweepers; difficult – but not impossible. Jobson's ship struck the Biber a glancing blow with the starboard bow, the Biber sliding down the length of the ship and being struck obliquely again by the other minesweeper. Despite the battering, the Biber twisted away and continued to run surfaced, attempting to hide in the sea haze. Aboard *BYMS 2141* Leading Seaman Rushton was ordered to open fire with the ship's port 20mm cannon, his shots hitting the conning tower in a welter of sparks and smoke. Jobson decided to attempt to snag it with his trailing sweep, but unbeknownst to him his enemy had already been vanquished.

I circled to foul him with my sweep . . . and caught him about 200 yards astern in the double cable of the LL sweep. The position now seemed favourable to attempt to capture the sub. During recovery of the sweep it was hauled close enough to the ship to secure a wire on it for towing. Serious damage caused by the 20mm was observed on the conning tower and the member of the crew, at the controls, who was the only man actually seen, had been killed.

By this time the sub had taken water through gunfire damage and was well down by the stern; the bow was being held up by the towing wire. In a few minutes the sub filled with water, heeled over, parted tow and sank immediately in position 51° 25' 42"N, 3° 34' 38"E at 10.20hrs.[74]

Elsewhere the running battle between the Bibers and Royal Navy continued into the night of 26 December. At 19.35hrs, sonar aboard the destroyer HMS *Curzon*, travelling in company with two Coastal Forces units on 'anti-E-boat patrol number 16', reported contact with a possible submarine. The sonar operator, Able Seaman W Phillips, classified the object as being 'half the size of a buoy' as it passed across the destroyer's bow heading from starboard to port. Immediately the destroyer gathered speed and prepared a five depth-charge attack. One of the weapons detonated fractionally early, rendering the radar, sonar and all radio transmitters temporarily inoperative. After twenty minutes they had been repaired, though contact was never regained. As HMS *Curzon* resumed its anti-E-boat patrol, it passed once again over the attack site, noting a small streak of diesel oil drifting down tide. As the Secretary of the Admiralty, Admiral Tovey, later wrote in an attachment to *Curzon*'s skipper's report:

> It is probable that the quick and resolute action taken on a hydrophone effect report by HMS *Curzon* at least damped the enthusiasm of a midget U-boat if it did not actually destroy it.[75]

However, Tovey's praise did not extend to two other destroyers that engaged another suspected midget submarine. HMS *Hambledon* and *Riou* were on similar patrol duty when two torpedoes were fired at them at half-hour intervals. Evading both threats, the destroyers frantically probed the area with sonar to locate their assailant, though they found nothing in a profusion of underwater echoes, many of which were the result of vigorous minesweeping in the area. Tovey considered the destroyers' response more in keeping with searching for a U-boat as opposed to the minute examination required to locate a midget submarine.

A final Biber mission for 1944 was scheduled for 27 December. Fourteen Bibers were prepared for departure within the Voorneschen Canal at Hellevoetsluis, manoeuvring into position with their tugs under a cloud of drifting fog. However, as the SKL War Diary reports, a brief urgent message was flashed to Berlin at 16.30hrs from the commander of the Rhine Flotilla.

> Approximately 16.00hrs two Biber torpedoes detonated, harbour fire at harbour Hellevoetsluis. 'HR01' sunk, 'HR03' severely damaged, Personnel lost unknown as yet.

Two torpedoes had been accidentally fired into the lock gates by one of the waiting Bibers. Of the fourteen assembled submarines, eleven were sunk as waves swamped their open conning towers, the remaining three hanging by their mooring lines as water emptied from the tidal lock basin due to damage to the gates. One man from the Bibers' 262 K-Flotilla was killed in the ensuing explosions, three more immediately posted as missing. The towing craft of the Rhine Flotilla had suffered more grievously. As well as one ship sunk and another damaged there were five killed aboard *HR01* which had been hit in the stern by one torpedo.[76] Amongst the assorted casualties was the ship's commander *Obersteuermann* Richarz who suffered a fractured skull. *HR01* went down next to the east bank of the Ost-Voorne canal. *HR03* was severely damaged by an explosion at its stern that wrecked much of the equipment aboard, the ship bursting into flames and sinking at the west bank of the canal, though it was later salved and repaired. Fortunately there were no casualties aboard the latter ship. The blast was so severe that the house occupied by 262 K-Flotilla's chief was rendered uninhabitable and vacated soon afterwards and the Voorneschen Canal and the lock gates were temporarily closed for shipping.

An investigation was begun almost immediately, concluding that ice forming on the Bibers as they moved behind their towing craft had triggered two torpedoes. However, hearsay from several veterans has indicated that it was more a case of tragic *'spielerei'* – 'playing about' – by some of the young pilots. Eventually the sunken Bibers were recovered, overhauled and put back into operational readiness. A brief account of the disaster was included in Cajus Bekker's book *Swastika At Sea* published only years after the war had ended.

> The boats are lying at Hellevoetsluis, the 'ground staff' making their final check-up, the pilots being briefed. Suddenly loud warning shouts are heard outside the room in which the last instructions are being

given. Some of the men are on their way to the door when a violent explosion shatters the little harbour basin behind the lock. The house threatens to cave in, raining on to the heads of the Biber pilots. 'Air raid!' someone yells.

The men tumble out through the doors and windows to seek safety in the open. In a matter of seconds another detonation follows. There is a wild commotion in the little harbour basin. A houseboat moored in front of the lock has apparently been hit – timber is flying through the air. A flood wave a yard high tosses the midget U-boats about like shuttlecocks, flinging them against the harbour wall. Most of them disappear underwater, and altogether the casualties and damage are considerable.

'But the aircraft – where are the aircraft?' It is also remarkable that the AA guns have not fired a shot. Finally it turns out there has been no air raid. One of those who had been outside by the boats enlightens his comrades:

'Some idiot must have mistaken the compressed air valve which fires the torpedoes for something else. It suddenly started hissing and before we could raise a finger the torpedo shot out like greased lightning and began careering madly about – it first struck the wall over there, then it turned and headed for the lock, bounced off again and exploded there on the bank . . .'

'Lucky it didn't go off when it hit the lock gates!' The arming mechanism had not run out soon enough for that. That was why the torpedo ricocheted a couple of times before exploding. 'And the second explosion?'

'The flood wave smashed all the boats into one another. Then another torpedo got loose and hit the houseboat over there.'[77]

The three Bibers that remained intact later sailed from the devastated canal basin and into action. None of them returned, though one made a dramatic appearance in the English Channel. On 29 December the *Algerine* class minesweeper HMS *Ready* sighted a drifting object near NF3 buoy off the North Foreland. Closing the unknown contact it was soon seen to be the conning tower of a stationary Biber, the black number 90 clearly visible on its conning tower. One of the ship's boats was launched to investigate whether the Biber could be recovered, whereupon the British sailors discovered the operator still sitting in his small cockpit, dead at the controls. A towline was secured to the stricken craft and *Ready* proceeded to tow it to Dover, passing the tow over to HMT *Brassey* once within the Downs. Unfortunately *Brassey* was compelled to stay moored in the Downs due to thick fog and was only able to approach the harbour the following morning.

Lieutenant J V Steele RNVR had been despatched to Dover on 30 December from his home in Surrey where he was on leave. His task was to oversee the preservation of the new prize. Steele had received orders to have the Biber beached at the harbour's western end near the hulk of the destroyer *Cordington*. However, *Brassey*'s captain failed to agree with the plan as his charge was rapidly taking on water. Steele had borrowed a small motor launch to rendezvous with the incoming trawler.

> By this time *Brassey* had entered the harbour by the eastern entrance, and having done so was apparently undecided as to the next move, and accordingly was turning 360° to starboard and had reduced speed. As this turn completed, the tow passed within about 100 feet of my launch, and I then saw that quite clearly the submarine was sinking and sinking quickly. Outside the harbour all the foredeck and conning tower was visible, but now only the forepeak and the top of the conning tower were in sight. By this time I was nearly alongside *Brassey* and seeing the tow disappearing under slack tow rope. I hailed him and advised him to get underway again and to make for the beach. Unfortunately, he had decided upon another course, and down went his anchor. Appreciating that the submarine was rapidly following the anchor, he weighed again and got under way, but too late, for just as the tow rope took the strain, the submarine sank by the stern and disappeared. This was at 09.25 on Saturday, 30 December.[78]

There then followed a communication breakdown that resulted in *Brassey* continuing to tow, the rope parting soon afterward. Fortunately the Biber was not completely lost without trace as, seeing what was about to happen, Steele had thrown a marker buoy in at the approximate location of the wreck. By a combination of echo sounder, Asdic, bottom sweeping and frequent diver investigations by Royal Navy divers from HMS *Vernon*, the Biber was located ten days later and dragged ashore, the last short distance being heaved free of the clinging silt by a Scammel truck's electric winch.

Steele immediately began work on the single torpedo still aboard the Biber on its port side. The boat had bottomed listing about 50° to starboard and Steele was able to render the exposed torpedo safe, released it from its mounting bracket and then ordered it hauled free of the beach on sheets of iron. Next he turned his attention to the Biber itself.

> I then tried to open the conning tower hatch in order to pump out the submarine, but no amount of persuasion would shift the clamps inside. However, the water, or rather, the dilute solution of sulphuric acid inside [from the flooded batteries – author's note], had softened the

Plexiglas scuttle in the hatch, so I broke this and was then able to reach the clamps. Quite a lot of water ran out until the body of the occupant jammed the flow . . . The next move was to remove the body of the 'pilot', so we, Lt.Cmdr. Powell and I donned Salvus gear as a precaution against gas and other 'decomposition products' and a violent struggle took place to get the body out – a highly distasteful business. It was most interesting to observe the reaction of the ratings, who had spent most of their service doing excellent work but in shore establishments, as against those who were only ashore because their previous close contact with the Hun had left them maimed for life.[79]

There remains one curious note in Steele's report. He states that:

One thing that did come to light was a bottle hidden under the seat, and inside was a document in English, which, romantic as it read, appeared to have some bearing upon the capture of the submarine, and possibly the explanation of why the pilot had met his end.

Despite this intriguing matter which I have not been able to shed further light on, a later post mortem on the decomposing body revealed that the pilot had died from carbon monoxide poisoning.

The Biber was the first of its type that the Allies had captured intact and they swiftly threw it into trials to assess the craft's strengths and weaknesses. Their conclusions were less than favourable, though not fully realised until April 1945 by which time the Biber threat had been successfully countered at sea. Nevertheless the British experience with the machine is of great interest. On 7 March four Soviet naval officers toured Chatham Dockyard on a day trip from London, accompanied by Royal Navy officers. The four Russians spent their first day watching electric motor trials in the basin after a false start caused by the Biber leaking upon hitting the water and requiring maintenance. Thereafter the Biber's temperamental petrol engine failed to operate and the Soviets saw no further running tests. The defects kept the Biber land-bound until 29 March whereupon trials were resumed. However the course of things to follow was less than encouraging as evidenced by a report written by Captain P Q Roberts of the 12th Submarine Flotilla.

During reassembly . . . the Bakelite top of the distributor was badly crushed and broke in five pieces. An Officer was immediately despatched to Chatham to collect the distributor cover from the craft recently completed there, an attempt was made to repair the broken cover, and a fruitless search was made to find a cover from any other source which could be adapted to this craft. The distributor cover arrived at noon on Monday 2nd April and was successfully fitted. During completion trials, however, a serious leak was discovered on the circulating water system with the result that the craft had again to be partially stripped down so that the leaking pipe could be renewed.

The Biber was eventually completed ready for running early in the morning of the 3rd of April . . . and the craft proceeded to carry out trials off HMS *Curlew*, arriving there at 09.00.

Trials were commenced . . . at 09.19, but on completion of run 1, some twenty minutes later, the engine stopped. All efforts to get the engine going again failed and the trouble was finally traced to the ignition system . . . An attempt was made to beach on the falling tide so that when she dried out the ignition system could be examined through a hand hole on the pressure hull.

This proved impracticable, however, due to the unfavourable nature of the bottom and eventually the stern of the craft was hoisted far enough out of the water by using the minesweeping gallows on the tender attached to the Innellan Range. Moisture was found in the distributor cap . . . Further examination showed a considerable amount of liquid in the base of the distributor. This could not be removed so an attempt was made to dry it out by borrowing an electric hair drier from the Wrens' Mess at Innellan. This had no effect, however, and it was found that the liquid was lubricating oil . . . The making good of this defect was beyond the immediate resources available, so it was decided to carry out as many trials as possible on the main motor . . .'[80]

Ten surfaced runs and two submerged runs were completed before the battery was considered to be 80 per cent discharged and the trials halted. Eventually the distributor problem was remedied, but upon return to the water an electrical connection on the main fuse panel blew when the craft was put to full motor speed. Next, after repair once more, the Biber suffered a seized clutch requiring the craft to be broken in two to remedy the fault, after which the engine began pinking and backfiring and stopped altogether, followed by trimming problems preventing more motor trials as a blown cooling pump sprayed water throughout the hull and causing it to sink stern first. Roberts surmised the experience of the Biber trials by stating that:

There is no doubt that the Biber is a lay-out and production of very low calibre and must be intended as a 'one-shot' weapon. It is proving . . . quite unable to stand up to prolonged running in spite of the tremendous amount of maintenance and replacement work which has been carried out on it.[81]

For the British the final insult was an explosion of petrol vapour that had accumulated within the craft during further trials after yet another engine breakdown had been repaired. As the ignition was pressed a 'violent explosion' blew from the stern and a large flame shot from the conning tower charring the clothing of the test pilot Lt.Comm. A C Halliday, burning his face and head and scorching Able Seaman J B Hastings who was standing next to the Biber. Both men were treated in hospital for their burns and quickly returned to duty. In light of the danger to his test crew, Roberts cancelled all further trials.

It was no wonder that armed with such a weapon the young and often-inexperienced German pilots suffered such appalling casualties, many of which remain unexplained as the craft simply disappeared at sea. By the end of 1944 the balance sheet for the Bibers was in severe debit. Thirty-one had been lost – only eight of which were claimed by Allied forces – for the return of one merchant ship destroyed. Only twenty serviceable Bibers remained in the Rotterdam area as a result of the explosion at Hellevoetsluis, though 1945 would see them continue to sail as the *K-Verbände* received its new weapon in the front line – the Seehund.

On 28 December K.z.S. Werner Musenberg advised that, due to the difficulties and time taken in getting the Bibers to their forward bases, lack of solid information regarding Allied shipping movements and the disappointing results obtained thus far, all Biber operations be suspended until experience had been gained in action using the Seehund. In Berlin, though, SKL again demurred, baldly stating that the dire situation on the Western Front demanded all available Bibers to be thrown into action against supply shipping in the Scheldt. Furthermore, the Seehunds were destined for operations elsewhere and their experience would have no real effect on Biber missions. Musenberg's reply acquiesced to SKL's wishes, though his wording could be construed as slightly disparaging, stating that it was impossible to judge the effectiveness of the latest *K-Verbände* sortie as none of the crews had returned yet. However, he continued, from an unspecified information source he concluded that results appeared to have been satisfactory and he intended to continue operations with every available means.

Dönitz attempted to ease the burden placed on his young crews as he ordered Musenberg and Heye to co-ordinate their activities with the *Führer der Schnellboote*, providing S-boat escorts for the outgoing *K-Verbände* sorties as it seemed that the Allies were using destroyers and MTBs against the midgets in the Scheldt. By deploying the S-boats in strength it was hoped to drive Allied coastal forces from the region, though it was a forlorn hope at best as the increasingly targeted S-boats fought their own battle for survival against overwhelming odds.

On New Year's Eve fifteen Bibers of 266 K-Flotilla arrived at Rotterdam, thirty Molchs from 413 K-Flotilla also arriving in Assen from Heligoland that same day. German troops faced the final bitter months of war with whatever energy they could muster; Hitler's forces had tried their last bid for success in the Ardennes and fierce fighting raged in the heavily forested area of Belgium. It was to be all or nothing for the *Wehrmacht*, including the men of the *K-Verbände*.

CHAPTER NINE

Twilight of the Gods

1945

On 1 January Dönitz and *Konteradmiral* Wagner visited Adolf Hitler at his *Adlerhorst* (Eagle Eyrie) Western Front headquarters at Ziegenberg near Bad Nauheim. There the dictator was ensconced with his commanders as the battle in the Ardennes raged. The idea that the beleaguered *Wehrmacht* and Waffen SS divisions could defeat the Allied troops that ranged against them was a flight of fancy that would ultimately doom the German forces in the west after the destruction of units they could ill-afford to lose. However, Dönitz had news of another difficult operation to impart to his commander-in-chief.

> 1 January – 1500: The C-in-C navy, informs the Führer that six Biber midget submarines will be carried by submarines to Kola Bay and will then proceed on their own against the battleship which has been located there, and against other worthwhile targets.[82]

On 17 August 1944 the 32,500-ton Soviet battleship *Arkhangelsk* had departed the UK in company with the thirty-three merchant ships of convoy JW59. The battleship was the British HMS *Royal Sovereign* (of the same class as the famously doomed HMS *Royal Oak*) which had been loaned to the Red Navy earlier in the year to help with the Arctic convoys. President Roosevelt had tacitly agreed to share one-third of the recently surrendered Italian fleet with Stalin, though Winston Churchill and his aides were alarmed at the deal, fearing that it would harm future co-operation from their new Italian allies. A compromise was eventually brokered that involved the transfer of the 1916-built British battleship, recently refitted in the United States, to the Soviets along with the loan of several British submarines and an American cruiser, later augmented with Italian submarines and destroyers.[83]

Thus on 23 August, *U-711* launched torpedoes against what it took to be a cruiser in company with the convoy, reporting both the

Arkhangelsk and the destroyer *Zharkij* (ex-HMS *Brighton*) hit after
torpedo runs of over eight minutes, though post-war reckoning doubts
that they were actually successful torpedo attacks.[84] However,
German U-boats in the Arctic now considered that they had a potentially disabled battleship anchored in the Kola Inlet where the great
vessel waited at moorings often used by British warships on the Arctic
convoy run. Two further attempts to attack the *Arkhangelsk* failed in
the face of anti-torpedo nets, leading to an appeal from *FdU Nord*
Reinhard 'Teddy' Suhren to SKL asking for:

> . . . action by small battle units in the Kola Gulf to obtain results
> against the ship of the line *Arkhangelsk* in Wajenga Bay where it has
> been seen many times. It would be possible to transport the small
> combat units (Bibers) to this theatre of operations by U-boat. A
> response is respectfully requested.[85]

After a brief deliberation by the naval staff, the plan was agreed and
six Bibers were to be transported into action by three U-boats to
attack the *Arkhangelsk* under the codename 'Operation Caesar'.
Trials were hurriedly completed in the Baltic to prove the viability of
carrying the small Bibers and the operation officially sanctioned.

There was already a Biber presence in Norway by this stage, the
thirty craft of 263 K-Flotilla having arrived in Kristiansand South on
9 October as part of the growing *K-Verbände* presence in the region
as the prospect of an Allied invasion of Norway haunted Hitler's
thoughts. But it was the new crews of 265 K-Flotilla, fresh from the
training grounds and commanded by Oblt.z.S. Fahje, that would be
tasked with the mission. The flotilla was moved into position at
Harstadt shortly afterward.

Three U-boats were assigned from Narvik's 13th U-Flotilla, *U-295*,
U-716 and *U-739*, each planned to carry two Bibers apiece mounted
in cradles on the upper deck. Two officers on Suhren's FdU *Nordmeer*
staff, Kaptlt. Hansjürgen Zetzsche and Kaptlt. Reinhart Reche
(Suhren's operations officer) both recommended that a small bay
north of Harstadt would present the ideal area in which to train for
the operation. However, Zetzsche later wrote:

> Reche and I weren't very confident in the chances of achieving results with
> this action, since we knew that the young volunteers steering their piloted
> torpedoes would really not have much chance of survival in the ice.

The trials held in the Baltic at carrying two Bibers on the upper casing
of a Type VIIC U-boat in the same manner that Italian and Japanese

midgets had been transported found the theory to be feasible, though the Germans failed to learn one vital aspect of such transportation from their allies. The Italians in particular had always carried their SLCs in weatherproof canisters on the submarine's top deck. Not only would this protect the fragile craft from the elements but would also provide some measure of insulation from the heavy vibration caused by running diesel engines. As would later become apparent, it was to be a critical oversight.

The schedule for the attack depended on the state of moon and tide in relation to the hours of darkness available and the operation was eventually planned for the night of 8 January. Several accounts state that German naval patrols captured two 'local fishermen' in late December who revealed much valuable information for the prospective operation. However, it appears that it was the Type VIIC U-boat *U-995* that took aboard two Russian sailors instead.

> The coastal area of Murmansk remained *U-995*'s patrol area until the end of the war. At Christmas 'Alex' and 'Ivan' unexpectedly came aboard: the engineer of a destroyed Russian cutter and the only survivor of an armed trawler who could be rescued from the freezing cold water.[86]

The two Russians later provided details of the formidable defences that included ASW patrols and a net and boom that protected the Kola Inlet on each side of Salny Island. The Bibers were planned to slip from the loosened chocks aboard the Type VIICs as they submerged gently beneath them, and sail 64km to the anchorage, twelve hours being allowed for the transit voyage from drop-off to the Kola Inlet. Once the attack had been completed the six Bibers were to retreat to a rendezvous point seaward of Sjet Navolok. There the Bibers were to submerge and make contact with their transport U-boats via a short-range transmitter employed for the operation. Once communications were established between the midgets and their 'parent craft', the Bibers would surface, scuttle and the pilots picked up for the return voyage to Harstadt. A second rendezvous point was arranged should any Bibers not make the first one in time and pilots were instructed that if all else failed they should make for Persfjord where they should scuttle their craft and head for Sweden overland.

The three Type VIIs departed Harstadt with their Bibers mounted on the casings on 5 January, running surfaced most of the way. Almost predictably the thumping diesels took their toll on the fragile midgets as did the severe weather conditions of the Arctic waters. Two of them were found to have leaking petrol lines within a few hours, though the U-boats' engineers rectified these. However, after further periodic inspections and following the submersion of all three U-boats as they navigated by periscope during the brief hours of Arctic sunlight, the remaining Bibers were also found to have leaks of varying severity, including ruptures in the stern glands that had allowed water to enter the machinery spaces in several of the Bibers, rendering them unusable. As the midgets' conditions deteriorated the U-boat commanders reported their predicament to Suhren. Zetzsche later wrote:

> On the whole, the commander of FdU *Nordmeer* was relieved and happy when the commanders of the U-boats sent their messages to indicate the damage caused by the storm [*sic*] . . .
> *Kapitän* [*sic*] Reche completely stopped the operation and gave the order to the U-boats to return immediately.[87]

The brief foray was over and all three U-boats were back in Harstadt by 8 January. Ironically had they succeeded in reaching the Kola Inlet the Bibers would have found the waters empty – the convoy had sailed and the *Arkhangelsk* herself had put to sea and was safely patrolling the White Sea. Vague plans to attempt a similar operation with an improved Biber were laid which would tentatively take place in autumn 1945. The course of events would, of course, soon overtake this idea.

However, this mission was not the only debacle that had befallen the *K-Verbände* during the first week of 1945. New Year's Day finally saw the operational debut of the Seehund as 312 K-Flotilla was ordered to attack Allied convoy traffic off the Scheldt Estuary and Ostend Roads. The SKL War Diary recorded the mission parameters:

> K-Stab Nord: K-Flotilla 312: 17 [*sic*] Seehunds 17:00hrs out of Ijmuiden for operation against Antwerp convoy traffic in Ostend-Kwinte Bank Buoy region. Course via Hook of Holland 5nm off the coastline, then via East-Hinder, course for Ostend. Cruise speed 7 knots. Duration of undertaking from three to five days. Next operation with eight boats on 3 January.

Dönitz had informed Hitler of the prospective mission during their conference on 1 January, confidently stating:

> Assuming that out of the 80 Seehund midget submarines scheduled to operate per month, only 50 are able to attack, then one hundred torpedoes will be fired at the enemy. If 20 per cent of the torpedoes hit their targets, then about 100,000 tons will be sunk.[88]

He was soon to be proved wrong.

All eighteen available boats of the 312 K-Flotilla, known as the 1st Seehund Flotilla, were ordered to assemble in the lock at Ijmuiden by 14.00hrs. As the waters of the lock could only hold a maximum of nine Seehunds at a time they were divided into two groups, each Seehund slipping from harbour at roughly five-minute intervals from the others. Once past the harbour mole the Seehunds were ordered to steer 290° true for 10 minutes before altering course to 214° and awaiting the sighting of the Hardwijk light at what was estimated by the mission planners would be approximately 17.50hrs. This course would take the Seehunds parallel to the Dutch coast and about five miles offshore. By 21.20hrs the Hook of Holland light should be visible abeam, at which point they were to alter course to the southwest and pass the end of the Schouwen Bank into the Hinder Channel. With three more navigational waypoints set in their instructions (involving sounding to determine the depth below keel), the Seehunds were reckoned to be in position within their operational area off the Kwinte Buoy by 07.05hrs and within the Allied convoy lane. The attackers would continue towards the Ostend Roads, lying submerged during daylight and awaiting inbound traffic. Their detailed written instructions including the following briefing:

> Enemy possibly at anchor outside boom. After nightfall proceed surfaced to Kwinte Buoy. *Attack* traffic bound for Ostend and Antwerp. After exhaustion of offensive power return night of 4/5th . . .
>
> Enemy Defences: Outward and homeward bound, and in operational area, MGBs and SGBs are chiefly to be expected.
>
> Along the line Kwinte Bank buoy – Ostend, probably several patrol boats (trawlers).
>
> Danger from air: everywhere.[89]

Recognition signals and flares had been given to all of the Seehund crews and German coastal troops warned of the operation in the event that the Seehund attempted to land elsewhere other than their homeport.

The first Seehund out of the lock at 15.00hrs was *U-5318*, piloted by *Oberfähnrich* Hertlein, *Maschinenmaat* Heinze his engineer. Hertlein and Heinze proceeded as planned to Bligh Bank where they bottomed their Seehund at 30m in order to determine their exact position. Reckoning that Kwinte Bank lay not far to the southeast they proceeded to follow their navigational instructions surfaced as dawn spread in the eastern sky. At 10.00hrs as *U-5318* continued on its way between

Ostend and Blankenberghe, Hertlein sighted an escort vessel that he immediately decided to attack. By this time their instructions had specifically ordered them to remain submerged and await darkness before attacking and it was with great difficulty that Heinze finally cooled his coxswain's fighting ardour and persuaded him to indeed submerge and wait for nightfall. As soon as the boat's nose tilted downward to the shallow seabed the main compass failed, something that Heinze later reckoned would have been caused by a magnetic sweep being towed behind the escort ship they had sighted.

U-5318 remained submerged at a depth of only 10m until mid-afternoon on 2 January whereupon Hertlein and Heinze set course for due north, sighting a buoy at 17.00hrs and, unsure of their position, surfacing to examine it in detail. As Hertlein identified it as NF12 and began scouring the chart for it, Heinze reported a solitary freighter approaching. Immediately Hertlein opted to attack, deciding to remain surfaced. However, as the Seehund manoeuvred into a firing position another freighter and two destroyers hove into view, the warships immediately opening fire. Unbeknownst to the two Germans they had stumbled on elements of convoy ATM26 bound from the Thames to Antwerp and lookouts aboard HMS *Cowdray* had sighted what they at first thought was a spar buoy, but, as they later reported: '. . . the "spar" quickly scuttled down the conning tower hatch and the submarine dived.'

As the British gave chase the target 'porpoised' and broke the surface, coming under fire from the destroyer's bow-chaser pom-pom. The British gunnery was excellent and hits were immediately scored on *U-5318* and water began to flood the shattered interior. Both Hertlein and Heinze leapt from their small seats and dived overboard as the Seehund sank rapidly beneath them, *Cowdray* having no chance to salvage the craft before they rescued the shocked Germans. The first encounter between a Seehund and the enemy had ended and two of the *K-Verbände* men were prisoners of war. It was a portent of the grim fate that would overtake the majority of the eighteen Seehunds that had sailed from Ijmuiden.

HMS *Ekins* later that day sighted another Seehund north of Ostend, swiftly destroying it with well-placed depth charges. A British MTB found another drifting abandoned, while seven were beached while attempting to return to German lines. Of the latter nearly all of the crews reached home, though one of them was gravely wounded, possibly by Allied aircraft attack. L.z.S. Fuchs and his engineer *Maschinenobergefreiter* Egon Wollny may have been attacked and then grounded their badly-damaged Seehund. Apparently Wollny was so severely wounded that he asked Fuchs to shoot him with his pistol, which Fuchs reluctantly did to ease the man's suffering. According to the historian Klaus Mattes, Fuchs may well have shot himself in the head as well, though *Wehrmacht* soldiers rescued the badly wounded man from an S-boat wreck that he had sheltered on. He was treated for his wounds and later transferred to Apeldoorn where he was hospitalised and underwent immediate surgery. Fuchs was rendered blind by his head injuries and was scheduled to later face a military enquiry for the tragic events of his mission. This author does not know the results of this enquiry, or court martial if indeed there was one.

L.z.S. Ernst Wagner aboard *U-5311* had fired two torpedoes at an enemy destroyer and missed, though he and his engineer Hans-Günter Wegner later reached Ijmuiden on foot. L.z.S. Winfried Scharge and *Maschinenmaat* Rösch had also attempted to attack an enemy ship, though the torpedo missed. As they began their return their diesel began to misfire, the Seehund eventually forced ashore near Scheveningen and the two men rescued by men of a *Luftwaffe* flak battery. *Leutnant zur See* Pander and *Maschinenmaat* Baumgärtl reported that they had only lost their Seehund, *U-5309*, after weathering at least seventy-six depth charges in a sustained attack. They had been confined in the vicinity of NF8 buoy for twelve hours as the small submarine was battered by the exploding charges dropped by British MGBs, but *U-5309* was so small that it was tossed aside. Finally the boat crept away, the hammering having rendered the diesel and compasses useless and the crew eventually scuttling the boat near the Hook of Holland, later rescued by a German armed trawler. Likewise L.z.S. Markworth and his LI L.(Ing.) Spallek aboard *U-5024* whose conning tower was adorned by the word 'Nico' painted upon it, were savagely bombarded with depth charges and then badly damaged by air attack. The Seehund was run aground near Goeree lighthouse and its crew later returned by friendly troops to Ijmuiden. *Leutnant zur See* Kallmorgen and his LI *Leutnant* (Ing.) Vogel also grounded their Seehund south of Katwijk, returning to Ijmuiden on foot.

Oberfähnrich Korbinian Pettenkofer and *Maschinenmaat* Werner Schulz of *U-5305* returned to Ijmuiden after the unnerving experience of being captured by a British soldier and then liberated by one of their own *Wehrmacht* detachments as the frontline fluctuated wildly. Schulz in his memoirs recalls having found Pettenkofer as a 'go-getter' but somehow rather 'boastful'. Their shared experience stretched their already uneasy relationship almost to breaking point. After departing

Ijmuiden their Seehund was attacked by an enemy aircraft, diving to escape the bomb that followed them under as they raced away in only 15m of water. Hours later as they proceeded surfaced towards the Hook of Holland Pettenkofer sighted what he identified as a darkened tanker to starboard and launched both torpedoes toward the enemy ship. Almost immediately, Pettenkofer shouted for Schulz to take the boat hard to port and dive to 20m as the sound of military propellers penetrated the thick layers of salinity. As the depth charges began to explode around the small boat, Schulz asked if they had succeeded in their attack, though he, retrospectively perhaps, was less than enthusiastic about the potential destruction.

'My God' shouted Pettenkoffer 'we haven't hit it'. He smashed his hand against the hull plates. 'Damned shit, god-damned shit! It was all for nothing!'

'They were people' I thought 'if we had actually hit the tanker I wouldn't have wanted to experience the detonation'.[90]

The boat crept away to the north as the enemy hunted in vain for them, the sounds of explosions gradually receding. The two men ate bread and ham, consuming some of their caffeine-laced drinks and Schoka-Cola as they sailed away from the scene. Finally they surfaced to begin the home run on the diesel, though their trouble was far from over. The seas had mounted considerably and the small Seehund found itself tossed uncomfortably about as Schulz struggled to start the engine. No matter what he tried it would not start, the Seehund unable to gain steerage way and left at the weather's mercy. They were left with little choice other than to run on the electric motor, hoping to reach the coast before their batteries were completely drained. They faced the uncomfortable prospect of landing behind enemy lines.

'Have we actually got a white flag aboard?'

'Rubbish', he angrily reacted. He didn't want to admit it but we would be aground soon. The *Oberfähnrich* Pettenkofer, commander of the small Seehund type U-boat, identification EJH, spoke now quite pathetically: 'I will stay here to the bitter end.'

Complacently he sat down in his chair. He must have heard that in a film. But rather quickly the boy inside him collapsed. I could imagine myself in his position. He had been unsuccessful.[91]

The Seehund inched towards the coastline, slowed by the ebbing tide. As the coast of Voorne hove gradually into view the two men prepared to abandon ship, setting scuttling charges as they jumped overboard and swam for shore. Behind them the Seehund exploded as they dragged themselves ashore to face whatever lay in wait. It was not what they were expecting though as their first encounter was with a signpost that bore the grinning skull and crossbones and vivid German lettering – 'Achtung! Minen!' They had unwittingly landed amidst a German defensive minefield, shivering in their soaked leathers as they inched single file across the lethal stretch of sand. Shortly after clearing the area they encountered soldiers, the British patrol swiftly capturing them and locking them in a deserted house after providing them with corned beef sandwiches. Pettenkofer was quiet and withdrawn, seemingly haunted by his failure, until the sound of machine-gun fire and an approaching armoured vehicle heralded another change in their circumstances, as a German NCO dismounted and asked them who and what they were. Hours later, Schulz and Pettenkofer, dressed in dry *Wehrmacht* uniforms, were reunited with their flotilla by members of a *Luftwaffe* flak battery.

They had been luckier than other Seehund crews that were forced ashore. On 3 January, the handing over of two bedraggled Seehund crewmen by local civilians surprised British troops at Domberg on Walcheren Island. L.z.S. Andersen and his engineer *Maschinenmaat* Haidacher had left Ijmuiden in *U-5327* at 17.00hrs on 1 January, arriving in its operational zone near Kwinte buoy the following morning, spending the next two days alternately lying on the shallow seabed at 11m or surfacing to search for targets. Eventually the dispirited men decided to head for home during the early hours of 3 January. During the night their automatic steering unit malfunctioned and at 03.00hrs the harsh grating of their Seehund running ashore near Domberg shook them. Stranded high and dry the two men abandoned *U-5327* and set their scuttling charges as they ran from the scene. Unfortunately for them there was no explosion and local Dutch civilians soon captured them. The British subsequently recovered the Seehund and its torpedoes, though the interior was badly flooded after tidal inundation and full of thick glutinous sand. Lieutenant Coulan of the Royal Engineers was charged with the craft's recovery, while Lieutenant Waters RNVR was to recover the torpedoes, the latter using a chisel and hammer to remove the corroded pistols in order to disarm them. In between gales and driving snowstorms the men and their work parties eventually dragged the Seehund shoreward to ease their recovery work, which was completed in early February.

Only two Seehunds returned intact to Ijmuiden, L.z.S. Sturzenberger and *Bootsmaat* Herold's *U-5035* and L.z.S. Hullmann and Lt

(Ing.) Hinrichsen's *U-5013*. Four remain unaccounted for from the operation to this day, presumed lost in the severe weather. Days after the mission the body of coxswain *Obersteuermann* Martin Dräger washed ashore near Zouteland, the cause of his boat's loss unknown.

As well as Dräger and his engineer *Maschinenobergefreiter* Kauper, the flotilla had lost four other crews: L.z.S. Dieter Scharfenort and his engineer *Maschinenmaat* Rapp, L.z.S. Adolf Dörr and *Maschinenmaat* Erwin Frommhold, L.z.S. Wolfgang von Ebener and *Maschinenmaat* Truske and Oblt.z.S. Heinz Paulsen and his engineer *Oberfähnrich* Gerhard Huth. The last boat unaccounted for was *U-5312* the fate of which only became clear on 5 January.

The crew of *U-5312*, L.z.S. Löbbermann and Oblt. (Ing.) Plappert began the operation with great promise. The last of the Seehunds to leave Ijmuiden at 17.30hrs on 1 January, *U-5312* reached what the crew thought was the area north of Ostend by 16.00hrs on 2 January, dodging enemy MGB patrols as they eased into the battle area. About one and a half hours later Löbbermann sighted a red light astern of a merchant ship outbound from Antwerp. However, the Seehund's large turning circle made it too late to enable the boat to be positioned for an attack. It was while attempting to follow the merchant ship that Löbbermann saw a destroyer, apparently motionless about 90m dead ahead. He realised that they must have been sighted and fired a torpedo, regardless of the fact that the destroyer was too close for safety. HMS *Cattistock* opened fire at almost the same moment, pompom fire being seen to strike the conning tower of *U-5312*, the low structure adorned with the boat's symbol of a shield with a toadstool in its centre. As the British pressed home their attack the small boat frantically submerged. Zig-zagging at full speed in only 8m of water, Löbbermann and Plappert were shaken by sporadic light charges dropped from their attacker, though they gradually faded astern and the Seehund was slowed, resting on the bottom for an hour as the two Germans regained their composure.

Surfacing that evening Löbbermann was surprised to see two lights that marked the entrance to Zeebrugge harbour, putting him considerably east of his previously supposed position. *U-5312* headed west, patrolling surfaced until midnight when it was forced to submerge in increasingly heavy seas. There were no sounds to disturb the German crew save for the shifting sand beneath them, engine noise and the expected convoy traffic conspicuous by its absence. At 08.00hrs on 3 January Löbbermann surfaced his boat, sighting only some distant MGBs, heading the Seehund toward Kwinte Buoy in search of more tempting targets. Once alongside the buoy the Seehund submerged again until the following morning.

Once more battered by heavy seas, U-5312 headed back toward Ostend and on to Blankenberghe during 4 January, until, with worsening conditions, Löbbermann opted to head for home via Kwinte Bank. In mid-afternoon that day Löbbermann sighted several light warships and at least one merchant ship inbound to the Scheldt and decided to launch a final attack. By this stage the conditions within the Seehund were rapidly deteriorating. Water was entering the craft from an unidentified leak that had sprung in the severe weather and the boat was stern heavy, the stern bilge pump apparently blocked. In this state of trim the boat was difficult to get to submerge, the bilges only able to be pumped if the forward part could be lowered and the forward pump used, though connection to this pump ceased to function. Despite the dire state of his boat a single torpedo was launched, roughly aimed and with no discernible result. Unarmed, the Seehund staggered onwards as the targets sailed blissfully unaware of their presence.

U-5312 finally managed to submerge where the crew attempted unsuccessfully to repair the pumps, but water continued to rise within the boat until it reached their calves. They eventually discovered the leak was in the air intake valve whose float did not close properly. Periodically they surfaced until reaching what they believed was the Kwinte Buoy where they submerged and worked again on their list of defects. They were finally successful in repairing all but the stern pump, managing to pump water from the Seehund as it lay at 20m.

At about midnight on 4 January Löbbermann opted to withdraw from the area lest they encounter more convoy traffic, hoping to charge the depleted batteries while running surfaced. However, a fault in the fuel supply caused the diesels to fail forcing an hour and a half of repair before they could be restarted. During this period of time owing to water splashing over the diesel air intake and closing the valve the diesel was mainly dependent on interior air, which resulted in a drop in pressure to 400 millibars below atmospheric. For half an hour it was impossible for Löbbermann to open the hatch due to the pressure differential, until finally he managed to leak some air into the craft and equalise. Conditions inside the Seehund were appalling by this stage as the weary operators sat in bilges reeking of diesel, stale seawater and human waste. The batteries were now exhausted and the Seehund drifted towards shore. Löbbermann reckoned their position to be off Schwouen and as water reached their calves again land was sighted at about ten miles distance. Three tall chimneys were visible, leading Löbbermann to believe that they were near Hellevoetsluis.

As *U-5312* drifted ever closer to shore the two Germans were dismayed to see a line of Allied patrol vessels, the realisation that they were nowhere near the German lines aboard a sinking submarine finally putting an end to their plans to return home. Appreciating their dire predicament they decided to seek Allied rescue and Löbbermann fired two flares into the air as the Seehund sank lower into the water. Löbbermann huddled on the outside casing, shutting the hatch to avoid Plappert being swamped inside the Seehund, until ss *Samarina* began to head in their direction. On Löbbermann's instructions Plappert then eased himself out of the Seehund and the pair of them abandoned ship after setting scuttling charges aboard *U-5312*. The British ship rescued both men, *U-5312* sinking quickly as water flooded through the open hatch.

It was an inauspicious start for the Seehunds, their sole success the sinking of the 324-ton Royal Navy trawler HMT *Hayburn Wyke*, torpedoed by Group Leader Oblt.z.S. Heinz Paulsen and his engineer *Oberfähnrich* Gerhard Huth before they too were lost at sea. The flotilla had lost sixteen of its eighteen boats and eighteen of its men. Heye was shocked by the dismal failure, he and Rasch called to a conference with Dönitz to discuss the operation.

In turn Dönitz reported to Hitler on 18 January, including a synopsis on the experiences of the first Seehund operation, together with the first disturbing acknowledgement of the dangers faced by the *K-Verbände*:

> An unexpected storm interfered with the success of the first operation by Seehund midget submarines. However, valuable experience was gained and the boats continue to operate. Because of the long distances involved, other small battle weapons can be used only as suicide weapons, and then only if the weather is suitable, as they would otherwise not even reach the area of operations. Despite these limitations, all efforts will be continued to interfere with enemy supply traffic to Antwerp.[92]

Elsewhere, Dönitz was more forthright in his views on the Seehund failure. He reasoned that they could only operate dependent on weather conditions and since they were evidently unable to sail in packs, they should be despatched independently like ordinary U-boats, or at least no more than four to any single group. The flotilla structure, like that of U-boat flotillas, remained an organisational and logistical entity only. When an attack was planned any available seaworthy craft would be used. The Seehund crews were given orders that they were to remain surfaced after sighting enemy aircraft, unless they considered that they had been spotted themselves. Dönitz was also gratified at the apparent resilience of the small craft while under sustained depth charge attack as evidenced by two of the survivors' reports. The weather remained a key component to operational success. It was not only the seaworthiness of the Seehunds, but also the fact that in calm seas the coxswain could stand on the outer casing and thus increase his visible horizon dramatically. If closed down he was reliant on the small Plexiglas dome or periscope and their limited radii of vision.

Despite the tragic results of the first Seehund operation, morale remained relatively steady within the flotilla.

> Goodness, how old were we then? It was 1945 and I was 22, or not even quite 22 since I was born in May. One tried to make something from almost nothing. Many people still ask me these days, 'Why did you do it? Why did you get into that boat?' and so on. I have to be honest and say that sometimes it was the boat itself. It's the same as when I ride in a motorboat these days and have fun with it. In those days for us boys it was simply a lot of fun to take the boat out. The seriousness behind it all was just accepted, or we were not really aware of it. There was no fear at all. We took the boat out and we were not afraid. That is the way we were raised. 'Go and do it', – this had been drummed into us as children and boys. France and England and the others were the enemy and we had to conquer the enemy and so forth. That was the attitude we had on the boat. The important thing was to do our job well during a manoeuvre and of course to make sure that nothing happened to you. That wasn't easy on those boats . . . This wasn't necessarily because of enemy action, but mostly due to human error. Some couldn't handle the boats properly and it was very difficult. They were so small and fat and then it was underwater. We didn't have any assistance like they do these days with all the electronics. That didn't exist.[93]

As SKL had previously noted in its War Diary, eight Seehunds comprised the next planned mission, scheduled for 3 January. However, the disaster that had befallen 90 per cent of the flotilla that had deployed only two days previously, combined with increasingly volatile weather conditions, forced a cancellation of the intended sortie. However, there were other misfortunes that would befall 312 K-Flotilla before they deployed operationally again. On both 4 and 5 January two Seehunds were involved in accidents. The first capsized and sank within the harbour basin immediately before the lock gate, the second accidentally discharged a torpedo which sank a moored barge and damaged a harbour defence vessel in the North Sea Canal. However, it was not just human error that plagued the Seehunds; an attempted sailing by eight Seehunds on the night of 6 January was again foiled by bad weather, all boats forced to return to harbour, some with diesel problems compounding the frustration.

The next *K-Verbände* operation was not mounted until 9 January when six Linsens slipped from Hellevoetsluis to attack shipping in the Scheldt. By this stage three S-boats (*S130*, *S167* and *S168* from the 9th S-Flotilla) had been modified to carry and launch Linsens and trials within the Maas waterway were progressing on their use in operations. Each S-boat could carry one control boat as well as its two explosive boats that it handled. Small davits had been placed on the S-boat's aft deck, the mine rails having been removed. The Linsens themselves sat aboard small floats with wooden skids. Once in a suitable release position, the Linsen and its float were hoisted outboard of the S-boat and lowered to the sea. The floats were subsequently taken back aboard once the Linsen had slipped off. Each launching took approximately one and a half minutes to complete. However, until perfected, the Linsens were compelled to rely on their old towing methods and the small craft still suffered enormously at the hands of the elements. In heavy swell the Linsens sortied, though forced to return by the foul weather and terrible visibility, one of them being lost.

It was not until 10 January that the Seehunds again went into action. Five sailed from Ijmuiden for the Dumpton Buoy area off the Kentish coast near Margate. This buoy marked a transit point for shipping that traversed the English Channel from the Thames Estuary to the Scheldt. Leaving port between 18.30hrs and 19.30hrs the Seehunds proceeded on a direct course for their prospective hunting ground. Once again mechanical problems began to plague the small group, *U-5311* being forced to abort its mission that same evening after developing problems with the trimming system and automatic steering unit, and a further two Seehunds the following day, one of which, *U-5035*, was attacked by aircraft off the Hook of Holland and later depth-charged by two British MGBs. Whittled down to two Seehunds, the attacking force continued towards the British coast, both of them soon in sight of the enemy and potential targets.

The first, crewed by the flotilla's Senior Officer, Oblt.z.S. Jürgen Kiep and his engineer Oblt. (Ing.) Heinz Palaschewski, battered through a Force 7 wind (rated as a 'near-gale' force) on the Beaufort scale, shuddering through the turbulent sea amidst frequent snow squalls. There was little chance of reaching the Dumpton area but the Germans' perseverance was rewarded at 04.15hrs on 12 January when they sighted a convoy of three ships off the Kentish Knock, claiming one of about 3,000 tons successfully torpedoed. German *B-Dienst* (radio listening service) operators intercepted a British radio telegram about the sinking of an unidentified vessel that corroborated Kiep's claim.[94] Expending both torpedoes in the attack, Kiep turned for home though the severe weather forced them underwater and unable to recharge the boat's batteries as water flooded through the diesel vent when surfaced. If too deep the crew faced the possible jeopardy of damaged batteries and chlorine gas. The Seehund eventually arrived at Ijmuiden with her battery cells virtually exhausted – and little by way of diesel remaining either.

The other boat, *U-5042*, had surfaced to find itself in only 8m of water off the North Foreland, where Oblt.z.S. Krüger (Deputy Senior Officer of 312 K-Flotilla) sighted two small ships. However, attempts to close the target and launch an attack failed as water frequently crashed through the diesel exhaust valve threatening to swamp the Seehund. Again, this problem made them unable to recharge batteries and to compound matters the overworked bilge pumps became choked with aluminium paint flakes from the boat's interior. Desperately the crew headed for the nearest German-held coastline, reaching the sandy beaches near Zandvoort and grounding the stricken submarine to prevent it sinking. Krüger and his LI Lt(Ing.) Hellmuth Bahlmann, both seasoned seamen, later reported that they had become violently ill from seasickness, illustrating the atrocious conditions they had suffered. Though the mission had achieved little, only two boats even reaching their operational area, Kiep and Palaschewski were rewarded for their success with the Iron Cross First Class, finally providing a cause of celebration for the flotilla.

The first Molchs arrived for combat in the Netherlands on 10 January. Twelve Molchs had been brought to Hellevoetsluis from Rotterdam to begin operations against convoy traffic in the Scheldt Estuary. They were towed via the Vlissingen–Breskens narrows by small ships of the Rhine Flotilla. However, bad weather forced a postponement of the planned mission as the Molchs were virtually uncontrollable, the craft returning to Hellevoetsluis. For the next two days the pilots and their support crews watched as the weather continued to deteriorate, until on 12 January the Molchs were ordered to return to Rotterdam to be laid up. Even this journey was problematic, three of the tugs grounding in a blinding snowstorm, sinking one Molch and badly damaging six others. On 12 January three Linsen units were transferred from Den Helder to Rotterdam, though operations planned for Linsens were cancelled for three consecutive days beginning on 11 January due to fog, rain and damage sustained by several of the small boats during an air attack as they readied themselves in the lock at Hellevoetsluis.

Meanwhile the Seehunds were also being reinforced. The 2nd Seehund Flotilla (beginning life as 313 K-Flotilla) had begun forming during January, Kaptlt. Borm appointed Senior Officer. The ten crews proceeded in two parties to Wilhelmshaven from Neustadt's *Neukoppel*, the coxswains led by Oblt.z.S. Ross in one group, engineers under an *Obermaschinist* in another. They were quartered in the Roon barracks as they regrouped, their Seehunds again lying in the West Werft undergoing final preparation for operational use. After three days in Wilhelmshaven the flotilla headed by road for Ijmuiden, arriving on 15 January where they bolstered the remaining men and seven surviving boats of the 1st Seehund Flotilla, the Seehunds temporarily out of service with mechanical faults. Thirty more Seehunds were due to arrive over the remainder of the month as prospective crews continued to train in Germany.

That same day Dönitz again stressed to his Naval Staff in Berlin the urgency of attacking convoy traffic bound for Antwerp. He stated that the *K-Verbände* had met with little success due to its reliance on clement weather to allow the small craft to operate properly. Dönitz appealed for the use of destroyers and torpedo boats in the Scheldt region, but there were few available and those that were would face such opposition that their deployment would be little short of suicidal. To strengthen the relationship between the S-boats and the *K-Verbände* and their operational co-operation F.K. Musenberg was moved to accommodation within S-boat headquarters. Dönitz appealed for bolder measures in the fight within the Scheldt and against the convoy traffic that trailed from the Thames and Heye's *K-Verbände* were to be in the vanguard again. An official communiqué listed the *K-Verbände*'s disposition in Holland on 20 January as reckoned to be:

26 Seehunds in Ijmuiden.
27 Linsens in Hellevoetsluis.
33 Linsens in Scheveningen.

27 Linsens in Den Helder.
30 Molchs in Rotterdam.
60 Molchs in Amersfoot.
60 Molchs in Zeist.
17 Molchs in transit from Heligoland.

The Biber numbers were not stated.

During the evening of 20 January 1945 Lt (Ing.) Hinrichsen reported to Rasch that twelve Seehunds were available for operational use from the two flotillas. However, this appraisal was soon found to be wildly optimistic. In actuality only six were ready, though Rasch and Kiep continued to plan for the original twelve as technicians carried out frantic repairs. Their plan called for three groups of four Seehunds each: one group off Great Yarmouth; one near Dumpton Buoy off North Foreland and the last near buoys used by Allied destroyers lying astride the convoy route from the Thames Estuary to Belgium.

At 12.00hrs the following day ten Seehunds had been made ready and after the pilots had spent the intervening hours studying tide tables and charts, Rasch inexplicably announced what amounted to quite radical changes in final dispositions of the attackers, reshuffling which boat headed for which destination. Four boats were to be despatched to Dumpton Buoy, due to depart at 15.30hrs; three directed to the convoy route, their departure planned for 17.00hrs and three others to Great Yarmouth, their departure period beginning at 18.00hrs. Though several men had spent the last few hours studying the wrong charts, there was little time for checking the correct tables and charts as all Seehunds were to be ready by 14.00hrs. The meteorological service had given a forecast of fine weather and light seas so Rasch had decided to rush the crews into action despite their lack of preparedness rather than risk losing the window of opportunity in what had been a string of stormy weeks.

As the first group bound for Dumpton Buoy slipped from harbour Oblt.z.S. Wagner was the first of many forced to abort with technical problems as his engine lost lubricating oil and threatened to seize up. *U-5033* and *U-5368* both aborted with diesel engine and ventilation defects, *U-5339* losing the use of both onboard compasses while outbound and also forced to abandon its voyage. *U-5334* suffered a catastrophic failure of the bilge pumps, main compass and trimming system as well as almost constant air alarms while another Seehund terminated its journey for more embarrassing reasons, after colliding with a buoy outside the harbour caused damage to the small submarine. The last of the group to abandon its mission was L.z.S. von Dettmer whose engineer was so incapacitated by seasickness that the Seehund was put aground 10km south of Ijmuiden and abandoned, later being blown up after recovery proved impossible.

Two of the remaining three Seehunds managed to patrol and return to Ijmuiden, though neither had sighted anything worth attacking, bringing their torpedoes back with them. The final Seehund that had sailed from Ijmuiden was the only one that would not return home. *Leutnant zur See* von Neefe und Obischau and his engineer *Maschinenmaat* Scheidinger were new to Holland, among the men of 2nd Seehund Flotilla that had recently arrived from Germany. They slipped from harbour on schedule and proceeded to the south west running surfaced at 6.5 knots. During the night the first problem occurred when the magnetic compass failed, but the Seehund continued, diving at 08.00hrs and proceeding for six hours submerged, before surfacing to recharge for an hour. Their designated hunting area was near Dumpton Buoy and at 22.00hrs von Neefe sighted a light some 15 miles off North Foreland. One and a half hours later he attempted an attack, firing one torpedo at what he took to be an anchored steamer. With no discernible results, *U-5303* retreated, heading back out to sea for one and a half hours. At this point the boat suffered more mechanical problems as the automatic steering system failed. Unwilling to proceed, Von Neefe decided to bottom his boat during mid-morning on 23 January, awaiting sunset. Surfacing at about 20.00hrs von Neefe guided the boat towards land once more, navigating by using the moon. Again, after only about an hour or so, he decided to bottom the boat, *U-5303* sinking to the seabed, all the while being gently pushed northwards by the half-knot current.

At 08.00hrs the following day *U-5303* surfaced and after an hour Von Neefe sighted what he took to be a 400–500-ton merchant vessel heading on a southwesterly course, though he had little idea of his own heading. It was in fact a Harwich trawler, which had in turn sighted the Seehund off South Barnhard Buoy despite Von Neefe submerging to avoid detection. The trawler radioed its sighting and when von Neefe surfaced once more after twenty minutes slow submerged running he sighted a ship approaching at a distance of about 200m on the starboard beam. The young commander submerged at once as the propellers passed directly overhead, followed by a first pattern of four depth charges as *ML153* attacked. Twenty charges were dropped in total on *U-5303* as the latter lay at only 12m depth on the seabed. Amazingly, the resilient craft suffered almost no damage save for the trimming pump being broken from its mounting and the FK38 compass coming unshipped. The motor launch prowled above and plastered the area with depth charges, reporting the Seehund as probably sunk later that day.

However *U-5303* was not dead yet. Von Neefe and Scheidinger remained pinned to the seabed until they were certain their attacker had departed. Shaken, though unhurt, the crewmen decided to surface at 19.00hrs and begin their return to Ijmuiden. *U-5303* was pointed roughly to the southeast and headed surfaced for where the Germans hoped their homeport was. At 01.00hrs on 25 January the Seehund came to a shuddering halt as the keel bit into the thick glutinous sand of South Scroby Shoal off Great Yarmouth. The two men waited for high water and frantically tried to free their stuck Seehund, but it refused to budge. After another day of trying, they abandoned their vessel, deciding to blow it up and attempt to surrender. The two men set their scuttling fuse and waded ashore on to the nearest sandbank, firing distress flares as they did so. They were spotted almost immediately by the Trinity House Vessel *Beacon* as well as a nearby air-sea-rescue launch *RAF HSL2507* that was in transit from Grimsby to Ramsgate. The shallow-draught *Beacon* was able to approach the sandbank and rescue the two Germans, lowering a tender with Coxswain Arthur 'Jock' Slater and another *Beacon* crewman aboard. As the small tender approached, the two Germans ran to the far side of the sandbank as the charges aboard *U-5303* detonated. The two dispirited and exhausted Germans waded out to the small tender and were pulled aboard, though their discomfort was not over as they huddled in the small boat while Slater attempted to nurse the boat's diesel back to life after it had stalled. Von Neefe und Obischau and Scheidinger were taken aboard the *Beacon* and in turn transferred to the RAF launch which took them onwards to Ramsgate. Notified by the Red Cross of the capture, the rescue was apparently later broadcast by Berlin radio.

Heye was again disappointed by the lack of success for his men. After talking with his Seehund units he issued a memorandum dated 22 January in which he stated that the Seehunds obviously had to be deployed against the Thames–Scheldt convoy traffic, but that their first difficulty lay in actually finding this route. To this end they required some conspicuous navigational point by which they could recognise their positions. Thus only the Kwinte Bank and Dumpton areas offered any immediate prospect. Pack tactics had been discarded in the face of concentrated Allied defences and in future Seehunds would sail in four groups; two for the Kwinte buoy and two for the Dumpton buoy. One group would remain in contact with each of the buoys, while the remaining two would spread themselves east and west along the convoy route. Subsequent Seehund sailings would be timed to allow continuous occupation of these positions. However, this last proposal was altered some days later so that the largest number of available boats could sail simultaneously, allowing for the expected Seehunds that aborted with technical difficulties.

Furthermore, it was decided to establish a Seehund base in Rotterdam, with accommodation for 700 men and berths for at least thirty boats. The shelters and berths at Poortershaven were to be completely abandoned as they had been discovered by Allied aircraft and were routinely bombed. For the first time, Heye also reported difficulty in recruiting men for the *K-Verbände*. The recruitment of officer cadets that were undergoing U-boat training had failed to meet demand and Heye planned to establish a new training camp under the command of K.K. Heinrich Hoffmann and intensify recruiting efforts.

In the Netherlands the bad weather and ice continued to delay further Seehund sailings. Three control Linsens and their explosive boats sortied from Hellevoetsluis an hour before midnight on 24 January, the only three not frozen-in by the thick ice. Two of the control Linsens returned the following morning after having destroyed their explosive boats through a lack of fuel. The third, impeded by snowstorms, did not return until that evening, also having destroyed the explosive boats. They had sighted nothing.

Biber and Molch trials were scheduled in January to attempt to provide answers to their ineffectiveness within the Scheldt area. The principal question to be answered was whether the fully equipped midgets were capable of reaching the areas to which they were to be directed. The Biber trials did not take place until 26 January when four boats put out from the Hook of Holland to proceed along the coast to Den Helder, each carrying one torpedo and one mine. Two reached their destination, though the remainder were forced to divert to Ijmuiden. Nonetheless, the results were considered satisfactory and Bibers put once again on operational readiness.

The Molchs, however, were less than acceptable to Heye. He reported to Dönitz that the Molch could not be used in the Scheldt because the intense cold reduced their battery performance by as much as 30 per cent, lessening their range to a little over 80km. Heye considered the range inadequate for operations and recommended that the 180 of them that were present in the Western theatre be moved to the Mediterranean. However, Dönitz and his staff disagreed. The

range of 88.5km that had been achieved was considered sufficient as
long as the craft were towed as far as the Goeree lighthouse. Dönitz
was also pleased at the successful testing of launching Linsens from S-
boats, Heye concurring with his superior that this method could be
used on the Thames convoy route as soon as the weather moderated.

CHAPTER TEN

Midgets and Commandos
Final operations in The Mediterranean and Adriatic seas

The beginning of 1945 found little respite for the *K-Verbände* in the Mediterranean theatre. The Marder units had withdrawn almost completely from battle, leaving assault boats, Linsens and frogmen to carry the war on. Air raids continued to plague the *K-Verbände*, eleven one-man assault boats being destroyed during a raid on San Remo on 8 January. The following evening five two-man assault boats set out to attack expected Allied destroyers. Radio messages between Allied warships in the Ligurian Sea were intercepted by German stations at San Remo and near Bolzano and passed to MOK Süd who in turn alerted the *K-Verbände* of such potential targets. For the men of 611 K-Flotilla things were even more direct. The flotilla had a direct communications link with the Harbour Commander, K.K. Heinrich Forster, at San Remo who in turn connected with the radar stations at Bordighera and Cap Arma. The five boats made contact with the enemy at 22.15hrs, two of them attacking at point blank-range but still not hitting their targets, one torpedo missing and the other jamming in its tube. However, despite the heavy defensive fire, all five boats returned to San Remo.

Despite the provision of relatively up-to-date intelligence and the undoubted fighting ardour of the men themselves, 611 K-Flotilla registered little success from San Remo. During the entire time it was stationed there it launched approximately forty missions against enemy warships. The sole victory was claimed on 17 April 1945 when the French destroyer *Trombe* was successfully torpedoed but not sunk by an Italian member of the flotilla, *Pilota* Sergio Denti.

Alongside their anti-shipping activity, the flotilla was also involved in the landing of agents and armed reconnaissance missions, a contingent of thirty men of Kaptlt. Krummhaar's MEK80 stationed in San Remo from the beginning of 1945. On the night of 17 January two

SMAs were ordered to attempt a reconnaissance of Nice harbour, each boat carrying a rubber dinghy and three MEK80 frogmen. Twenty-four hours earlier their mission had been aborted, but by midnight on this second attempt they had reached a point 6km south of Nice. As they were readying rubber dinghies for the frogmen, Allied patrol vessels surprised the two boats, sinking one of them and capturing two of its crew.

The first true agent landing by the flotilla was attempted on 20 February on the French Riviera coast. However, the two boats tasked with the mission turned back due to extensive coastal illumination rendering it impossible to approach. Despite this initial setback the flotilla continued to be used for landing agents, so much so that Böhme offered during March 1945 six MTMs of the flotilla to be stationed permanently on Italy's eastern coast at Venice purely for the use of MEK71 and its trained saboteurs. In total, by 25 April, twenty-eight agents had been successfully landed by the flotilla, mostly along the French Riviera and often in conjunction with the men of MEK80.[95]

Krummhaar's MEK80 had failed during their second attempted mission behind enemy lines at the end of January 1945. Landed by assault boat between Monaco and Menton the small landing party accidentally triggered some beach mines and were hastily withdrawn under fire. During February and March two missions with 611 K-Flotilla were carried out in conjunction with *Oberstleutnant* Engelmann of the Italian-based *Abwehr (Mil. Amt. Führungsstelle Italien)*. On both occasions three Frenchmen were landed and later successfully extracted, once between Monaco and Menton and once near St Juan. Kaptlt. Krummhaar's luck finally expired in March 1945 when he was captured by Italian partisans whilst *en route* from Milan to Genoa. Fortunate to survive the encounter, he was later handed over to the Allied authorities.

On 7 February 1945 L.z.S. Heckner took charge of 611 K-Flotilla operations in San Remo and Kaptlt. Wilhelm Ullrich, the unit's commander up until then, moved to La Spezia with forty men in order to establish a new base of operations there. Five new SMAs and eleven MTMs were brought by road and landing craft from Sesto Calende as Ullrich was kept in readiness for an expected Allied landing that never transpired. Eventually, with Allied pressure increasing on the German front, Ullrich was ordered to withdraw to Genoa on 27 March, taking seven MTMs and four SMAs, the remainder left as a rearguard in La Spezia. Eventually Ullrich was also moved on, this time to a staff position with *Kommando Stab Süd* at Levico, the far-flung components of 611 K-Flotilla being taken over by Oblt.z.S. Frenzemeyer.

On the Adriatic front, men of MEK71 and supporting transport flotillas carried out the vast majority of *K-Verbände* operations. The entire Axis naval presence within the Adriatic was a mish-mash of assorted units, among them were four small Italian midget submarines, *CB14*, *CB15*, *CB16* and *CB17* and three Italian transport submarines, *Grongo*, *Morena* and *Sparide*, nearly ready for launching, earmarked for use either by or in support of the *K-Verbände*. While *Kriegsmarine* control was to be exerted over all of these U-boat units, the latter were to be crewed completely by Germans. However, an air raid on Pola dockyard on 4 September destroyed the transport submarines and their prospective crews returned to Germany to be retrained for future Seehund operations.

The VI K-Division that had formed out of the remains of *Einsatzstab Haun* had moved to Pola on the Croatian Istrian Peninsula at the beginning of December 1944 and been placed under the command of Kaptlt. Witt, Böhme's deputy commander. Witt was simultaneously the commander of 612 K-Flotilla, one of five formations administered by VI K-Division, the remainder being 613 and 411 K-Flotillas, MEK71 and the Italian CBU Flotilla commanded by Lieutenant Siervo.

Like most intermediate commands, VI K-Division could not act independently and was required to submit operational plans to *Kommando Stab Süd* by wireless or teleprinter. Each projected plan was designated a code word which would be radioed back to the Division headquarters if it had been accepted. Witt was fortunate to also have a close working relationship with 1 S-boat Division based at Pola and controlled by MOK *Süd*.

The divisional headquarters in the former Italian submarine school 'Monumenti' in Pola was bombed by Allied aircraft during February 1945, the buildings being almost completely destroyed and fifteen men killed after a direct hit on a shelter. Sharing the town was the 612 K-Flotilla following the evacuation of their advance base at Cigale on 18 February due to advancing Allied troops and they too lost valuable assault boats and Linsens during the air attacks. Subsequently, the flotilla 'farmed out' its boats, moving six to Vasana and the remainder with their fuel and equipment to the island of Brioni. A sister unit, 613 K-Flotilla, had formed during January 1945 at Fiume from men provided by Lehrkommando 600 on List. Oblt.z.S. Gerhardt's new flotilla numbered nearly 150 men and at first could muster only some makeshift assault boats of dubious Italian manufacture. Found to be barely seaworthy they were replaced in April by twelve new MTMs and five new SMAs from Sesto Calende, the whole flotilla moving to

Porto Rose near Trieste. These assault boats would soon be put to a wide variety of uses, primarily relating to island-hopping commando raids alongside what was probably the most active *K-Verbände* unit within the Adriatic – MEK71.

This fully motorised *Kommando* had formed at the beginning of 1944 with an initial strength of twenty-five men armed with light automatic weapons. After the unit's normal six-week training period it had been despatched to Aix north of Marseilles where it commandeered several French Chris Craft motor boats for further exercises. The unit comprised an almost independent command in Aix, though directly subordinate to Admiral Paul Wewer, Commanding Admiral of the French South Coast (*Kommandierender Admiral der franzoisische Südküste*). By June 1944 MEK71 numbered thirty men and had added three more seaworthy craft to its equipment, French motor boats named *Popol*, *Qwepy* and *Frigane*.

Following the Allied landings in southern France MEK71 remained largely uncommitted, though they mounted a single agent-drop on Corsica for the *Abwehr*. During May 1944 the MEK's commander, Oblt.MAdR Horst Walters, had been introduced to Major Werner of the *Abwehr* at Aix and requested to lay his unit's facilities at their disposal, the *Abwehr* wishing to land agents on Corsica. It was not until July that they actually were tasked with the mission, transporting two Corsicans to the island's west coast aboard *Popol*. The agents, who possessed no W/T gear, had been ordered to stay on the island for at least three days before *Popol* would return to take them off. Five days later *Popol* returned with Walters aboard, the two agents seen safely ashore through binoculars. As the boat nosed towards the coastline the two men abruptly fled and heavy fire arced towards the boat, wounding the radio operator as *Popol* turned tail and escaped to return to St Tropez.

MEK71 next acted as bodyguard to Admiral Ernst Scheurlin – Admiral Wewer's successor – during the German general withdrawal, before posted to Frieburg where it was temporarily disbanded. In September the unit reassembled at Mommark in Denmark. This time it numbered seventy-two men; twenty truck drivers, twelve wireless operators and forty seamen, all trained for combat duties. The unit was again fully motorised with an establishment of three heavy trucks, two Kubelwagens, three W/T trucks, three armoured personnel carriers and four motorcycles. They were also given five explosive Linsens on trailers for future use.

During late September and early October they were relocated to Pola and moved into the same submarine school shared by VI K-Division. It was here that twelve frogmen from Lehrkommando 700, under *Stabsfeldwebel* Mietzschke, were added to the already formidable complement. Three SMA boats were placed at the disposal of the men of MEK71 by 213 K-Flotilla, replacing the MEK's Linsens. The situation within the Adriatic was one of complete enemy air and naval dominance, though judged by the Germans to be largely by day as the British tended to retreat into harbour at night as there was no requirement for convoy protection during the hours of darkness. With Lussin the farthest island on the Dalmatian coast still held by German forces the stage was set for commando troops to thrive amidst the scattered islands that fringed Croatia's coastline.

This was also where another branch of the *K-Verbände* truly came into its own with Dr Konrad Voppel and a small band of researchers in Germany poring over texts, charts, articles and whatever snippets of information they could find to provide the best geographical information to aid in commando raids. Voppel had been curator of Leipzig's Geographical Museum and armed with 30,000 volumes, 250,000 charts and at least 50,000 photographs, he and his team were on call for Heye to provide whatever information they could on a given location – topography, water depths and so forth, all prepared in the finest detail. Designated 'Kosmos', the small group relayed their required information to Heye who in turn passed it to the necessary unit, MEK71 among the recipients best placed to use it to their advantage.

MEK71 lost fourteen men during October, four of them frogmen, who were transferred to Weissenburg in Bavaria where they were to operate against bridges on the Danube. *Oberfähnrich* Schulz led the men back to Germany, his small group joined in December by sixteen more commanded by *Leutnant* Tegethoff, the whole unit leaving MEK71 and becoming *'Kommando Wineto'*. Those that remained in Pola began operations during December.

According to British Admiralty records the first recorded *K-Verbände* commando raid within the Adriatic was carried out on the night of 15 September 1944 when the S-boats *S45* and *S71* carrying assault boats and six frogmen (including Von Wurzian who had devised the operational plan), set out to attack Ancona Harbour. The mission failed as one of the assault boats capsized upon launching, 29km from Ancona and the operation was apparently abandoned. A second attempt three nights later was also aborted due to 'Allied searchlight and radar activity'.[96] Whether it was indeed MEK71 that actually attempted these missions remains unclear in German records.

A further commando operation directed against Sibenik also took place during October, one escorting assault boat lost. Further losses to 612 K-Flotilla were suffered when Allied light naval forces sank two assault boats on escort duty in the Split area on 27 October.

During November the assault boats continued to be used for attacks on harbours within the Dalmatian islands, carrying the frogmen to their targets and in turn being transported aboard S-boats to within striking distance. They were also employed for reconnaissance missions and involved in rescuing survivors of the hospital ship *SS Tübingen* (formerly the French liner *Gouverneur General Tirman*) which was sunk near Pola on 18 November. On 19 November, as the assault boats were still engaged on their rescue mission, their headquarters at Cigale were attacked by Allied fighter-bombers, the flotilla retaliating that night by transporting men of MEK71 in an attack on Selve and Gruizza in which a lighthouse was destroyed.

During December the tempo of raiding by MEK71, supported by the assault boats and S-boats of 1st S-boat Division, was increased. Their targets ranged from signals stations, store houses, shipping, road and rail bridges, petrol dumps, electricity and water stations and radar stations and ranged all along the Dalmatian coast including areas held by British troops and Tito's Yugoslavian Communist partisans on the Croatian islands of Olib, Silba, Melada (Molat), Ist and Dugi Otok. An attempted attack on an aerodrome on the island of Vis was abandoned after two requisitioned Italian motorboats foundered when lowered from their S-boat transports off the island's coast. On the night of 11 February S-boats carrying assault boats, MEK71 commandos and frogmen set out from Cigale to raid Split harbour on the Croatian mainland. The commandos landed successfully by assault boat, though the frogmen abandoned their task due to their transport suffering damage. Damage was inflicted on an LCF and the cruiser HMS *Delhi* that lay alongside. However, during the withdrawal five one-man assault boats and an unspecified number of commandos became cut off and stranded on the island of Lacieta, where they apparently remained until the war's end as all attempts to rescue them were frustrated by Allied MGBs.

During March an attack on Ancona's fuel stores, bridges and supply dumps was aborted due to thick fog blanketing the target area. MEK71 was then reinforced by the arrival of *Leutnant* Schmidt who would lead the next raid on the Italian coastline near Senigállia during April. Due to the increasing tempo of Allied air attacks against Pola, MEK71 moved to Valbandon, north of the city, the bulk of the unit

then moving on to Treviso, leaving a rearguard of twelve men, reinforced by twelve more that returned from Treviso led by Schmidt. It
was this rearguard that launched the attack on the Italian coastline
during April 1945. The assault was carried out in two waves, each
comprising two MTM boats on loan from 213 K-Flotilla. The net
result of this attack was the destruction of an Allied petrol dump, the
severing of the petrol pipeline in three places, a road bridge destroyed,
railway trucks damaged and disruption to electricity cabling. The K-
Verbände commandos were as successful as their more celebrated
Allied counterparts, though their history remains one seldom told.

Another aspect of the operations of MEK71 was the dropping of
Abwehr agents behind enemy lines and these missions dominated
April 1945. The Kommando maintained a group of six MTM boats
at Venice on behalf of 'Kommando Eulenspiegel' – Hauptmann
Pfannenstiel (alias Lux) of the Abwehr and his agents. During March
1945 Böhme ordered Walters to report to Kommando Stab Süd for a
meeting in which Pfannenstiel was also present. Once again the
Abwehr were to have elements of MEK71 placed at its disposal, this
time the six MTMs that had been initially provided from the strength
of 612 K-Flotilla.

Their first mission did not take place until the beginning of April
when three Italians were to be landed in the area of Corsini to observe
shipping movements in the port. However a navigational error by
Oberfähnrich Becker on assignment from the 612 K-Flotilla landed
them at the mouth of the River Po and the dispirited Italians soon
returned empty handed. Six Italians were taken on 9 April to replicate
the mission, this time Obergefreiter Büttner of MEK71 leading the
three MTMs to successfully land the agents as planned. Four of the
Italians returned via collapsible dinghies on 13 April with the news
that three or four enemy ships were present in the harbour. MEK71
remained at Treviso until 24 April 1945 when Böhme's Kommando
Stab Süd ordered it to Vigo di Fassa. There they would remain until
the final German surrender in May 1945.

The evacuation of German troops from Lussin and Cherso was
aided by the K-Verbände, but one of the final mentions of their activities relates to an Allied air attack on Brioni on 24 April. In a raid that
lasted from 07.30hrs to 18.00hrs the accommodation buildings were
levelled, three assault boats sunk and others damaged and serious
casualties were inflicted on K-Verbände personnel.

The end of the K-Verbände's war in the Adriatic remains a obscure,
piecemeal affair from German records. MEK90 was known to have

been active within Montenegro and Albania during the early months of 1945 though nothing is known of its exact involvement in operations. A W/T message to KdK was picked up by Böhme's *Kommando Stab Süd* in March 1945 appealing for vehicles to aid the evacuation of MEK90 from Yugoslavia, though a final message from Agram stated that they had managed to organise evacuation by rail. Reports followed that the unit had reached Germany by mid-March 1945 but there it disappears. Sporadic movements of other troops were recorded as raiding continued until almost the final days of the conflict. The same is true of *K-Verbände* units based on the west coast of Italy.

West coast *K-Verbände* operations during the final months of the war appear to have consisted of little more than attempts to raid the harbour of Livorno and nearby Allied anchorages. On 16 January thirty-three Linsens had set out from La Spezia to attack shipping off Livorno, Marine di Pisa and Viaraggio. The assault on Marine di Pisa failed absolutely, while no ships were found in either of the other roadsteads. The Linsens sailed into the harbours themselves, with what was reported as some success though the Germans lacked the ability to confirm this due to a dearth of aerial reconnaissance.

Logistics had become increasingly difficult for the *K-Verbände* in Italy and Dalmatia during the end of 1944 and beginning of 1945. Motor transport had always faced fuel shortages in the region, for example the petrol used to transport thirty MTM boats from Sesto Calende to Lehrkommando 600 had to be provided from Germany using the increasingly hard-pressed and vulnerable railroad system. Though naval petrol stocks had been ample until the end of January 1945, the situation then began to deteriorate rapidly. The first restrictions on *K-Verbände* use were introduced at the end of that month following the exhaustion of naval reserves and continual interdiction of rail transport between Germany and Italy. The local flotillas used their operational reserves and were then forced to trim their scale of operations, routine runs of all boats curtailed unless on Böhme's express orders. This hamstrung the operational units considerably and also greatly hampered their ability to remain at combat readiness; the training programme for 611 K-Flotilla halted completely. With this inactivity K.K. Hugo Gerdts departed his role as *Einsatzleiter* of 611 K-Flotilla on 6 January 1945 when the post became redundant. The four MAS boats that he had held control over were passed to the charge of Oblt.z.S. Hecker, the new Liaison Officer with the remnants of *Decima Mas*, though the boats were never committed to action – doomed to inactivity by their exorbitant petrol consumption. Each flotilla maintained an absolute final reserve of fuel (*Sperr-Bestand*) that could only be used on Böhme's direct orders or in the case of invasion. These were finally exhausted while carrying out the final *K-Verbände* operations of *Kommando Stab Süd* on 23 April 1945.

On 21 April all *K-Verbände* units were ordered to withdraw from the Ligurian coast and prepare to place all available personnel at the disposal of Naval Commander Liguria (*Seekommandant italinische Reviera*), K.z.S. Max Berninghaus to be placed into ground units for fighting the advance of Allied troops on land. Böhme later recounted to Allied interrogators that he felt 'reluctant' to order the destruction of all the remaining *K-Verbände* equipment without allowing it to put up one last fight against the Allies at sea. Accordingly, he issued an immediate order for the remaining elements under his command to launch a do-or-die attack of total commitment– '*Totaleinsatz*'.

This final mission was compiled by eleven boats of 611 K-Flotilla that had been based in Genova under the command of Oblt.z.S. Frenzemeyer and moved to Portofino and joined forces with five boats under *Leutnant* Bühnemann. This combined force of twelve one-man assault boats and four two-man assault boats moved south during the night of 23 April and attacked Livorno harbour. They pressed home their attack with great determination – only two boats surviving but no Allied casualties recorded. Frenzmeyer was aboard one of the two that returned to Portofino where he scuttled his boat. The remaining twenty boats of 611 K-Flotilla that were still in San Remo were thought to have also launched an attack in the direction of Menton and San Juan supported by six Marders of 364 K-Flotilla. One heavy enemy unit was claimed sunk though German casualties remain unknown. With this final effort the *K-Verbände* had virtually ceased to exist within the Mediterranean.

The fifty men of MEK80 that had been tasked with guarding the supply depot at Meina clashed with partisans in the closing days of the war, a battered remnant of ten men surviving to reach Vigo di Fassa on 28 April 1945 where they subsequently surrendered. K.K. (Ing.) Burckhardt's *Gruppe Nachschub* transport column was another *K-Verbände* unit involved in the desperate rearguard action of the *Wehrmacht* in the Mediterranean theatre. On 25 April partisans attacked their headquarters and transport park at Sesto Calende. Burckhardt and his surviving men escaped the vicious battle and headed towards Milan where they too would eventually surrender at the war's end.

In Venice, Kummer finally managed to persuade KdK to allow himself and his anti-aircraft crews to leave the island of San Giorgio.

The deserted training ground of Lehrkommando 700 on the island had come under repeated attack by Allied aircraft and Kummer had lost men from his unit, kept there despite there being nothing to protect. His request for transfer for his unit was eventually granted in April 1945 and the camp dissolved that month as forty of Kummer's men were sent to Innsbruck to guard a consignment of entrained Linsens that would never reach List. Kummer and a rearguard of five men moved to Vigo di Fassa on 28 April 1945 where they awaited the final surrender.

One of the most interesting – though least-used – *K-Verbände* units within the Italian theatre faded from history during the confused fighting in Yugoslavia. At the end of January 1945, the *K-Verbände* personnel office at Kappeln had passed forty new recruits to *Maiale Gruppe Lehmann* which was at that time still based in Venice and busying themselves with overhauling their battered Italian chariots. These new men were despatched to Valdagno for swim training in the same baths that had been used by Lehrkommado 700, Lehmann, Wirth (now a *Leutnant*) and the eight original recruits undertaking the training of the new men. Even there, however, the low water temperature of 12°C hampered training. At the end of March they transferred back to Venice, though only four of the new chariots had arrived as promised, these possessing such severe constructional faults that they were unusable.

It was a disappointing end to *Maiale Gruppe Lehmann*'s initial Italian posting, the whole detachment travelling in mid-March to the Ruhr Valley and attachment to *Kommando Sioux*, a makeshift *K-Verbände* battlegroup commanded by Kaptlt. Bartels and not known to have been operationally deployed. There, Lehmann's group were supposed to mount an attack against Allied-held Remagen Bridge over the Rhine, though the idea eventually came to nothing. By this stage the *Gruppe* was composed of two officers, six *Oberfähnrich* and *Oberfeldwebeln*, one *Fähnrich*, ten *Obermaaten* and *Maaten*, seventeen enlisted men as well as a medical *Fähnrich*. Lehmann and his men entrained once more for Italy, arriving in Venice and basing themselves on the Island San Andrea at the beginning of April 1945. There they waited in inactivity until the German surrender whereupon they destroyed their equipment and attempted to reach Sistiana aboard a surrendering *Marinefährpramm* (naval transport barge).

Among the *K-Verbände* units that were gathering in Sistiana were also *Gruppe* Dexling; L.z.S. Dexling and six frogmen who had been posted from Lehrkommando 700 on Sylt to Pola, which had been designated a 'Fortress' by Hitler during December.[97] Controlled directly by *Kommando Stab Süd*, they were loosely attached to 612 K-Flotilla but saw no action in their planned role as raiders against Ancona and the Dalmatian islands. They were eventually incorporated into VI K-Division at Sistiana and prepared to adapt to an infantry war. The *ad hoc* composition of the ground force that VI K-Division had become also included the remains of 411, 612 and 613 K-Flotillas. Their naval equipment was destroyed at Sistiana after which they fought as infantry against the 2nd New Zealand Armoured Division and Tito's forces. Driven rapidly into retreat the battered survivors became embroiled in the savage street fighting in Trieste, eventually surrendering to the Yugoslavian Communists at the end of the battle.

CHAPTER ELEVEN

Conventional War

Seehunds in the Thames Estuary

By 29 January 1945 the ice at Ijmuiden had melted enough for the Seehunds to return to action. Likewise in Hellevoetsluis, the Bibers were no longer trapped in port by the thick winter ice and they too were made ready to sail. Ten Seehunds put out through the small lock at Ijmuiden in two groups; one bound for the Dumpton–Margate area and the other for the South Falls. The Seehunds were ordered to break off operations if the weather deteriorated from the southwest, though all ten successfully sailed. The first to return, *U-5342*, entered port that evening, *Obersteuermann* Böcher and *Obermaschinist* Fröbel breaking off their journey with clutch failure after only three hours at sea.

Over the following days seven of the Seehunds returned with various mechanical problems or because of the increasingly heavy seas. Some had reached the approximate area of their intended operations, though they had been forced to abort. *Leutnant zur See* Henry Kretschmer was one of those that returned, bringing *U-5041* into port after being battered by the elements. His engineer, *Maschinenmaat* Karl Radel, had become violently seasick and reached port in a state of almost complete exhaustion.

Only two of the Seehunds successfully patrolled their target areas, L.z.S. Stürzenberger and *Obermaschinist* Herold aboard *U-5335* sighting three steamers and two escorts in convoy, but they were unable to gain a firing position. They soon broke off the mission in mounting seas, reaching Ijmuiden on 31 January. Oblt.z.S. Ross and his LI Oberlt (Ing.) Vennemann reported the sole success after torpedoing an estimated 3,000-ton collier near Dumpton Buoy in Margate Roads on 30 January. The two Germans were elated, though the British reported their steamer sunk by mines. It was the third sinking made by a Seehund since they had been put into service, aggregating an estimated 6,324 tons.

The same day that the Seehunds had sailed, fifteen Bibers set out from the Hook of Holland, having arrived there from Rotterdam the previous day. However, disaster overtook them almost immediately as three were sunk by hitting patches of ice which in places were 20cm thick. Five more returned with damage caused by the ice and another was beached near Hellevoetsluis after spending 64 hours at sea hunting in vain for the sight of any potential targets. The remaining six failed to return at all, their fate unknown.

January ended on this grim note for the *K-Verbände*, though Heye remained optimistic about the Seehunds at least. In a review of their operations Heye wrote on 4 February that despite their operating in severe weather conditions and meeting little success, they had unquestionably been of great value in eliminating teething problems with the small U-boats and for the training of their crews – at least those that had survived. He also expressed faith in better results once weather conditions moderated.

On 3 February the commander of the Seehunds in Ijmuiden was changed. Kaptlt. Rasch was rotated back to Germany to oversee the operation of Lehrkommando 300 in *Neukoppel*. His replacement was the celebrated U-boat veteran F.K. Albrecht Brandi, who became the chief of 312 K-Flotilla and later 5 K-Division. By now the threat of the midget submarines was being taken very seriously in British military thinking and on 3 February thirty-six Lancasters of 5 Group attacked concrete shelters at Ijmuiden (9 Squadron) and Poortershaven (617 Squadron) with Tallboy bombs. It was believed by the British that these pens were sheltering the midget submarines and in clear weather the RAF claimed hits on both targets without loss to themselves. Their appraisal had been correct: the S-boat bunkers in the Haringhaven received three direct hits though there was no damage to the Seehunds of which there were four operational and twenty-seven non-operational currently in the port. The bunker was never fully completed after work had begun on it, only ten pens being finished out of a planned eighteen, the Allied bombing achieving little despite its accuracy. On the other hand, the Molch depot was hit with greater result by Spitfires of 2nd Tactical Air Force who were engaged on a general attack against the railway system in the town of Amersfoort. Though no Molchs themselves were damaged the depot was virtually destroyed. Lancasters also attacked the Biber depot at Poortershaven and once again though no submarines were hit, damage to dockside installations prevented any more operations in February. The British were soon back again against the *K-Verbände* when fifteen Lancasters of 617 Squadron dropped

Tallboys again on the pens at Ijmuiden without loss to themselves on 8 February. Of equally great concern was the RAF battering of rail communications between Germany and Holland that threatened to seriously disrupt the supply of Seehunds to the forward area. On 11 February consideration was given to transporting them via road through Zuiderseedamm and employing them within the inner Scheldt. This would negate the effect of bad weather as the inner reaches were relatively sheltered from the harsh elements of the North Sea and plans were developed to attempt a trial Seehund operation within the Scheldt.

In the meantime operations continued against the convoys trailing from England. Eight boats sailed on 5 February; *U-5368*, *U-5033* and *U-5326* all returning defective, *U-5339* stranding north of the Hook of Holland, *U-5311* stranding 14km north of Ijmuiden and *U-5329*, *U-5348* and *U-5344* returning without success and with varying degrees of depth charge damage. On the evening of 10 February eight Seehunds sailed, *U-5335* forced back to harbour to repair a defect in its steering gear, though it was able to depart the following day. The dockside at Ijmuiden was scarred and still smoking from the attack by nine 8th Air Force B-17 bombers that had carried out the first of what they termed 'Disney' missions using Royal Navy rocket-boosted concrete-piercing bombs against the pens at Ijmuiden. Three more Seehunds – *U-5363*, *U-5337* and that belonging to L.z.S. Polakowsi – were forced to return on 11 February with mechanical faults and *U-5330* the following day, having sighted Allied ships but achieved nothing. *U-5339* entered Vlieland on the evening of 12 February; *U-5345* into Ijmuiden and *U-5347* grounded on Texel 30km north of the port on the morning of 13 February after suffering severe damage in an air attack. Only *U-5349* failed to return from the operation.

A further five departed Ijmuiden at 17.00hrs on 12 February, despatched to the North Foreland. Again two – *U-5332* and *U-5342* – aborted with mechanical difficulties. *Oberfähnrich* Streck and *Maschinenmaat* Niehaus aboard *U-5345* reached their operational area, but were detected and subjected to a barrage of depth charges that the *Kriegsmarine* men counted as numbering 259 detonations before the attackers left the scene. With the boat badly damaged and crew shaken by their ordeal they limped towards Ijmuiden, eventually beaching their boat at the inner mole of the harbour. The fourth Seehund, L.z.S. Götz-Godwin Ziepult and *Maschinenmaat* Reck's *U-5361*, returned on 17 February after claiming to have torpedoed a 5,000-ton merchant ship off North Foreland two days previously. The ship concerned was the Dutch tanker *Liseta* from convoy TAM80, badly damaged by a torpedo hit although able to reach port without sinking. However, the Seehund was not the only attacker to claim the hit, the Type VIIC U-boat *U-245* also claiming to have torpedoed the Dutchman. Nonetheless, it was a victorious crew that reached Ijmuiden. The last of the five, *U-5356*, never returned.

On 14 February, while many of the Seehunds were still on station, it was decided to slip their leash more and extend operations to any-where within their range, which included inside the Thames and as far as the Humber estuaries. Hitherto these areas had been off limits for the Seehunds. It was also ordered to stop any *K-Verbände* mine laying along the Thames-Antwerp convoy route to allow conven-tional U-boats to begin patrolling there as part of their last-ditch inshore campaign in British waters.

In the meantime a number of Molchs had been moved from Amersfoort to Scheveningen to be used in the Scheldt estuary. Their use was planned for the night of 12 February, but the deteriorating weather forced a postponement. During the night of 14 February two Linsen units were moved from Hellevoetsluis to Zeriksee on Schouwen to operate against Walcheren as the *K-Verbände* intensified its Scheldt attacks once more. As part of this stepping-up, the trial of the Seehunds in the Scheldt began on 16 February.

Four Seehunds sailed from Ijmuiden for the West Scheldt that morning, five Linsen units also sailing for the region that night. It would be the baptism of fire for the two-man midgets within the con-fined waterway and one that was ultimately unsuccessful. There was no word from the Seehunds until 20.00hrs on 18 February when *U-5363* beached 15km north of Ijmuiden after experiencing no success at all. Another, *U-5332*, also beached itself, this time 3 kilometres north of the port at the same hour the following day. L.z.S. Wolter had fired two torpedoes after sighting an enemy convoy of several large landing craft but had missed after being kept at bay by the escort screen and unable to launch an attack at a close enough range. The remaining two boats, *U-5041* and *U-5337*, did not return, though *Maschinenmaat* Karl Radel of *U-5041* drifted ashore on the island of Voorne in a rubber dinghy, dying before he could relate his experi-ences. His coxswain L.z.S. Henry Kretschmer had been captured after a successful depth-charge attack by *HMML901* on 22 February. The British motor launch was severely damaged during the battle with *U-5041* in which a depth charge set off a sympathetic explosion of the midget's torpedoes, damaging the ship's wheelhouse. Five out of six rounds fired from the motor launch hit the Seehund and Kretschmer was soon pulled from the sea, Radel drifting away unseen in the early morning darkness. It was to be the last time that Seehunds were deployed within the Scheldt itself, that zone of control left to the equally unsuccessful Linsens, Bibers and Molchs. The Linsens that had deployed into the western Scheldt on the same day as the Seehunds had achieved no success either. Only two units reached the target area where they found nothing, the rest turning back in thick fog losing two of their number.

Bad weather once more frustrated plans for three Seehunds to sail for the Dumpton area on 19 February, though they were able to put to sea the following day. One returned with engine trouble which took 24 hours before it was rectified and the craft put out once more. Three more put to sea that same day, destined for the Elbow buoy in the South Falls off North Foreland, another single Seehund making for the same area on 23 February. *U-5097* returned after a frustrating journey dogged by bad weather and poor visibility. After reaching the area that they considered to be the shipping lane from southeast England to the Scheldt estuary they were surprised by two British MGBs that raced out of a fog bank with machine guns blazing. Crash-diving to the seabed at a depth of only 30m, the two Germans were then subjected to a fierce depth charge bombardment, able to see the flash of the exploding Torpex through the Plexiglas dome. After nearly 24 hours, *U-5097*'s attackers dispersed and the Seehund was able to creep away toward Ijmuiden, severely damaged. The boat was leaking from the area of the electric motor and its compass had been destroyed, so they were unable to remain submerged, the captain, Wachsmuth, navigating by the constellations of the Great Bear and the Small Bear when they became briefly visible through the cloud. By daylight he used the horizon from which he considered the strongest morning light to emanate, unable to actually see the sun due to the daytime fog. As *U-5097* headed for the Dutch coast Wachsmuth was suddenly confronted by a stone wall looming from out of the fog and rapidly threw the boat to port to avoid hitting it. However, in hindsight it appears that the vision was an hallucination brought on by the Pervitin pills that the two Germans were consuming to stay awake. The wall vanished as quickly as it had arrived.

They eventually made landfall as fuel and battery were almost exhausted, though with no idea of their location. In fact they had grounded the Seehund at Egmond aan Zee, 16km north of Ijmuiden and there they blew it up. Wachsmuth and his LI remained unsure of their location until a *Wehrmacht* soldier appeared. The newcomer was Mongolian and nervously escorted the pair off the beach and into a bunker occupied by *Luftwaffe* Flak troops. They still had to convince their rescuers that they were not Allied commandos before eventually contacting Brandi by telephone and being returned to Ijmuiden.

U-5342, on its first operational sortie, did not return; the two crewmen listed as missing presumed killed on 1 March 1945. The last crew of the trio, also new to action, did make a successful return to Ijmuiden, though Fröhnert and Beltrami had achieved nothing.

L.z.S. Winfried Ragnow's *U-5367* was one of the four-boat group that had departed on 21 February. Ragnow later recounted his departure from Ijmuiden, a scene repeated for all departing Seehunds.

On 21 February my boat was the first of the flotilla to be cleared for patrol. A fortifying breakfast, specially catered – 'klinker-free' diet (as our 'sled' had nothing like a WC). F.K. Brandi gave our operational briefing 08.00hrs. We learned one more time all the important details about the operations area; currents, weather forecasts, enemy locations and convoy routes for the Thames–Scheldt supply lines, security, defence, air dispositions and so on. Weather wasn't especially good, but it was supposed to be better in the Thames. Best wishes, a handshake and I was dismissed. Equipment taken by truck to the harbour where the LI is on hand and just as tense as I am about the mission. *KUB367* (*U-5367*) lies at the pier. This time we have sharp torpedoes under her belly (each Eel had 300kg Trinitrotoluol in the head). We smoked a last cigarette, said goodbye to our comrades and support personnel. And then we went. Past the lock gates and outer mole. Windy – sea state 3 – breakers washing over the boat. Trim dive test by the Ijmuiden navigation marker and then course southwest at 6 knots – on towards England![98]

Despite their stalwart beginning, the two men had no success on their arduous voyage. Alternately hunting surfaced and diving to avoid enemy destroyers, MGBs and aircraft – once making the unprecedented depth of 76m with no untoward problems with their boat – they unsuccessfully attempted to attack a destroyer before heading back towards Holland. They grounded their boat amidst the beach defences, huddling in a bunker and keeping warm with schnapps before found by a *Kriegsmarine* artillery unit and returned to Ijmuiden. Later, Brandi dispatched a group to find and recover their Seehund, but it had drifted off with the tide and presumably sunk. Ragnow and Paul Vogel were sent to Wilhelmshaven to collect a new boat; both men awarded the Iron Cross Second Class on 28 February, the first of their flotilla to receive the decoration.[99]

The three other Seehunds that had sailed as part of the group led by *U-5367* experienced mixed levels of success. L.z.S. Horst Gaffron and his engineer *Maschinenmaat* Huber fired both torpedoes at an enemy destroyer, reporting a hit though British records do not confirm this. L.z.S. Walter Habel and *Maschinenmaat* Karl Rettinghausen also reported success. Sailing toward England on their first mission, the boat ran surfaced towards the Thames. The trails of V2 rockets could be seen arcing overhead on their way toward London as the young crew sailed toward their enemy. At 09.00hrs they sighted an enemy destroyer and launched two torpedoes before breaking away as an MGB passed overhead dropping defensive depth charges for twelve hours. They claimed to have hit the destroyer that they identified as HMS '*Mecki*' – perhaps *Mackay* – though British records do not confirm this. However, the 1,625-ton tank landing ship *LST364* of convoy TAM87 was hit by a torpedo and sunk, the attack attributed to an unidentified Seehund. The 220-strong British crew, of whom twenty-four were burnt and wounded by the detonation, were taken off by the trawler HMT *Turquoise*. Seehunds were the only active German submarines in that area, though the identity of the successful attacker remains unknown to this day. The last of the group, L.z.S. Hermann and Omasch. Holst's *U-5365* ran aground while returning without encountering the enemy. Stranding in shallow water near the German artillery batteries on Katwijk, Hermann paddled ashore in a small rubber dinghy to report their predicament while Holst remained with the boat. Shortly thereafter a Dutch lifeboat from Ijmuiden arrived with a salvage command on board, the Seehund towed into Scheveningen shortly afterward.

The last sailing of February, L.z.S. Klaus Sparbrodt and *Maschinenmaat* Günter Jahnke's *U-5330*, which had put to sea on 23 February, was more definite in its result. This, the eleventh Seehund operation, was again targeting the Dumpton area, though it suffered its share of problems *en route*. They had barely reached Scheveningen when the diesel engine failed, forcing a premature return to Ijmuiden on electric motor. The problem was swiftly identified as a blocked oil pipe and soon rectified, the boat putting out once more for action. Attacked by Beaufighter 'J' of 254 Squadron as they cruised with battened hatch due to the choppy water, Sparbrodt crash-dived his boat and continued from the scene submerged while the hunter circled the area searching in vain for the Seehund.

By 22.00hrs we were nearing our patrol area. An hour later we were approaching a light-buoy, which told us that we had found the Dover route. Suddenly an unmistakable sound met our ears; the ignition of the engines of two motor gun boats lying in wait between the convoy route and the Goodwins. We dived immediately and lay there at 58 metres until 04.00hrs on 24 February. From then on we surfaced every hour to see how the situation was, but every time when we were at the top we heard the noise of the MGBs and we shot like a stone back into the 'cellar'. At 07.00hrs the end came and we heard the gunboats heading away, surfacing in time to see them travelling at high speed for Ramsgate.

The sea was mirror-like – sea state 0. We headed at half speed towards Dumpton Buoy that lay in the middle of our operations area . . . We hoped that here we could find a convoy and fire our torpedoes at some worthwhile targets . . . A slight haze hung low over the water and we patrolled up and down at low speed. A little after 10.00hrs in a thickened mist I saw what looked like a vessel lying stopped, and we were slowly getting closer to her. At 10.20hrs we dived and began our attack.

I could now see that the ship was a warship, the forepart clearly visible but the rest lost in mist. I saw a long and high forecastle, a menacing cannon, large bridge, mast and funnel that showed it was at least a corvette and worthy of an Eel.

At 10.27hrs, the LI reported port torpedo clear for firing. I studied the target through the periscope. Its bow was facing left, at about 80° from us, and I observed no change as a minute passed. This indicated that it and the Seehund were both set in the same direction by the gentle current.

Estimating the range at 600 metres, after that minute I ordered 'port torpedo – fire!' and Jahnke pulled the lever. We heard from the boat's hull a scream and roar as the Eel sped on its way. I started the stopwatch and put the rudder hard to starboard. I wanted to make a full circle and return to the same attacking position. 50, 60, 70 seconds went by and we heard nothing. The torpedo must have missed, but I was determined to get off a second shot.

Then at last, after 80 seconds following the shot, we heard a sharp crack through the water, but nothing more. This meant that the range had been 850 metres. I saw a column of water and smoke from the explosion rising midway between the bridge and funnel. I shouted, 'blow tanks' and within seconds we were on the surface and I called Jahnke to the tower. We saw the last of the ship as her bow lifted high and she quickly slid stern first into the sea.[100]

The two men quickly submerged, celebrating their attack with a meal of chicken and rice followed by some strawberries before ten depth charges from a tardy retaliation reminded them of their precarious situation. They lay on the seabed as the hunt faded away and headed from the scene. Later that night, according to several accounts, they fired their last torpedo at a sighted ship but apparently missed, heading back to Ijmuiden and a victorious welcome. After confirming the details of their attack with Brandi the two Seehund men were informed that they had sunk the 1,505-ton Free French destroyer *La Combattante*, corroborated by intercepted British radio transmissions. The 'Hunt' class destroyer had begun life as HMS *Haldon*, but had transferred to the Free French Navy in 1942. She had patrolled the English Channel from March 1943 onwards and joined the Normandy landing on 6 June 1944, later conveying General Charles de Gaulle for his first journey to liberated France on 14 June 1944. She took sixty-two men, including two British, down with her. Curiously a torpedo also hit the British Post Office cable-layer steamship *Alert* east of Ramsgate during the night of 24 February. The 941-ton ship sank so rapidly that it was unable to send a signal reporting its loss, and this has been attributed to *U-5330* as well. Could this have been the target that Sparbrodt believed he had missed?

There remain several sinkings often attributed to either mines or Seehund attacks that to this day remain unconfirmed as to what caused their sinking or indeed their exact identity. As well as the mysterious HMS *Mackay*, *LST364* and the cable layer *Alert*, a Seehund whose number remains unknown reported sinking a ship named SS *Rampant* from convoy TAC near buoy NF8 off Ostend in the early hours of 26 February according to the eminent historian Jürgen Rohwer. However, despite the other ships apparently rescuing forty-six crewmen, Lloyd's Register carries no such ship name. Additionally, on 26 February the 4,571-ton British steam tanker SS *Auretta* was in convoy TAM91 with twelve other merchants and five escorts *en route* to Antwerp in heavy seas when she was either torpedoed or hit a mine. Likewise the American steamer SS *Nashaba* was also lost from this convoy to either a mine or torpedo hit, one crewman and the pilot going with her to the seabed.

Harald Sander was engineer aboard one of the Seehunds that was active during February:

Some were actually inside the mouth of the Thames. So the two of us had to go down there. Well, I will never forget those two days and the conditions we experienced. We had a wind speed of 10 or 11 and the swell was correspondingly large . . . So anyway, we got there all right. The only thing was that then misfortune struck. The diesel air valve stopped working and every time we came up out of the water a wave washed into the boat. Our stern was getting lower and lower in the water and it was almost as though the rear of the boat couldn't get to the air at all but stayed submerged. At the time I asked my commander, 'How deep is it here?' 'Oh', he said, 'we are already quite far down. We are just about in that deep valley that runs from the North Sea through the channel in the direction of Biscay'. And he said, 'It must be a good fifty metres'. I said, 'Let it go down'.

At thirty metres the situation normally became quite serious with our boats, but we let it go down and we waited till we got to the sand and then we said, 'So, now we are down'. One has to consider that we had an atmospheric pressure per square centimetre of five and the thickness of the outer metal around the boat only had a strength of five millimetres. The boat ribs were placed thirty centimetres apart, so it was practically like fishbones . . . and the body of the boat only had minimal strength.

But it didn't crack. There was no noise from the boat. The only thing was that water came from astern into the front and we were both sitting in water. Well, the commander was seated a bit higher and I was a bit lower behind him, but we were both sitting in water. First we took a deep breath and then we said, 'Okay, what shall we do now?' and then we tried to surface the traditional way. The diesel engine cannot be started under water because it needs air, so we tried it with the electric motor. We put the hydroplane up at the front and then we started the electric motor and revved it up until the boat was high enough to have the nose poking out of the water, so that air came in and I could start the diesel engine. The diesel engine was then used to pump out the diving cells. We were so heavy that there wasn't much water in the diving cells anyway. I hadn't flooded them. The boat itself was heavy enough. A ship only floats if it has enough displacement to allow it to remain above the surface. Well, all right, this didn't work because we were too heavy. We couldn't pump either because our bilge pump only managed at a depth of 25 metres. It had 2½ times atmospheric pressure and this could be managed with the hand bilge pump. This was possible, although at a depth of 50 metres . . . We were both still fit and didn't want to abandon ship. Getting out was not that easy at a depth of 50 metres and it could have been dangerous. So we kept trying.

We had two compressed air tanks in the boat in case of emergency and I released compressed air into the first diving cell in the bow and in this way the boat rose at the front a little. Then I started the electric motor and the boat actually rose up with this pocket of air in the bow. If you can imagine that practically half of the boat was still submerged, then we began pumping. We were pleased that we were at least up on the surface. Then came the question, 'Are there ships up there?' Underwater you can hear a long way. You can hear the noise made by every screw. There was nothing. We had waited so long for night time, until it was dark. They didn't discover us and we began pumping eagerly in order to make the boat lighter so that we could continue on. We knew that the valve was broken. We were of course swaying close to the surface. The air quality inside wasn't very good which made us both very anxious and we exchanged comments, such as, 'Come on, do it, keep pumping', and so on. At some point afterwards, I don't know when, suddenly the commander said to me, 'Harry, I can't go on, I don't know what's happening, I'm getting out', and such things. He was panicking and thinking he wouldn't make it, but we had to, because if we didn't keep pumping we would have sunk again and been down on the bottom at 50 metres. For me it was . . . anyway, I don't know how I managed it. I yelled at him. I really told him what I thought. I said, 'If you don't, I will smack you between the eyes!'. He had to be brought out of his shock. So this was how it was. These days I get asked, 'How could you have done anything in that small boat?' The narrowness had an effect in that moment when neither of us were sane.

We managed our work all right but at any moment it could have all gone wrong. The English could have run us over if a boat had been there and if they had discovered us they could have chased us down to the bottom and so on. So I really had to pull myself together. The fact that I managed this is a great thing. I still say today, God had a big hand in it my whole time with the navy. In any case, to cut it short, we managed and we returned home, at least to Ijmuiden. We went on a bit and then we both pumped again and then we went on until we came to the locks. Then we told the lock keeper to adjust the crane after we were through and pick us up with the crane straight away so that we didn't fall again because the boat was only just floating. That was the best it could do. They weren't very pleased when we returned, but the main thing was that we were there. Both torpedoes were still attached, so they hadn't been wasted. It was all valuable material. But, yes, the boat was wrecked.[101]

During February there had been thirty-three Seehund missions, four of the Seehunds being lost in action. Despite these losses and the destruction of several machines that had been run aground, for the first time the month ended on an optimistic note for the Seehund crews as victories appeared to be on the increase.

Linsen operations had been delayed by bad weather in the latter half of February though three units departed Hellevoetsluis on the night of

21 February in search of targets within the Scheldt. Two of the units turned back with engine problems, while the third searched in vain, forced to scuttle one boat due to lack of fuel. Molchs too had begun operations in the Scheldt that same night. Ten were towed to the Scheldt and four others setting out from Hellevoetsluis under their own battery power. This operation marked the beginning of an almost suicidal undertaking – *Totaleinsatz*, or, 'total commitment'. *K-Verbände* planners only envisioned the possibility of a maximum of four boats returning. Nevertheless, at least two-thirds of the Molch crews volunteered on 22 February for what they were told was probably a one-way mission. As it transpired, eight Molchs returned, but claiming no results. *B-Dienst* listening service indicated that Allied forces off West Kapelle sank three and captured two men. Three further Molchs were destroyed at their depot at Assen and another three damaged by air attack on 21 February.

The general situation for the German armed forces was dire in the extreme as March dawned on an increasingly beleaguered *Wehrmacht*. In conference with Hitler on 26 February Dönitz had suggested that Seehund attacks be concentrated against the Thames area as aerial reconnaissance had shown large shipping concentrations there. The latest Seehunds possessed an increased combat radius due to the addition of external saddle tanks as standard fittings and he expected better results than achieved previously. He also stressed the necessity of maintaining Dutch ground for the *K-Verbände* if it was to be able to operate effectively. Indeed the SKL later pointed out that the maintenance of Dutch roads and railways was vital to *K-Verbände* operations, since it was only from the Netherlands that Seehunds could reach the Thames under their own power, let alone the Biber, Molch and Linsen operations. Requests to transfer some Seehunds to the Mediterranean were declined by Dönitz, at least until a strength of eighty machines was reached in Ijmuiden. Dönitz countered this proposal with an idea to ship a Marder unit to Rhodes, though the *Luftwaffe* representative at Führer headquarters, *Oberst-Leutnant* von Greiff, replied that an undertaking of that nature would only be justifiable if of extreme strategic significance due to the fuel requirements and the necessary reallocation of Ju290 transport aircraft. The idea was immediately abandoned and the *K-Verbände* fought on as before. The sole addition to their arsenal was a so-called 'Marder simulator' which comprised a Plexiglas Marder hood from which was suspended an explosive charge that would be exploded by ramming. It is unknown if they were ever deployed, but a shipment of them

Staff Officer Naval Intelligence: Oblt. Waldemar Heinemann
   Oblt. Graf Horst von Korthus
Navigation Officer: Lt. Götz Hunger
Staff Officer: Lt. Fritz Barthel
(Controlled two Marder Flotillas, one Biber flotilla, one tender at
   Kristiansand)

Kommando Stab Skagerrak
Formed 26 September 1944. Purely defensive role anticipating an
   Allied landing on Danish coast.
(Aarhus/Denmark)
K.z.S. Düwel 9/44–1/45
F1: Kaptlt. Kolbe
Adjutant: Oblt. Konrad Wenzel
Administrative Officer: Oblt. Hilliger
Leader Stützpunkt Heligoland: Kaptlt. Dr. Karl-Heinz Kinscher
(Commanded 365, 263, 264 and 461 K-Flotillas)
In January 1945 Wenzel and Düwel were detached for duty with the
Kommando Stab zbV and control of this region given directly to the
General Operations branch.

Kommando Stab zbV
Formed January 1945
Formed for operations in Allied-held waterways within Germany.
See also MEK zbV.
K.z.S. Düwel 1/45–5/45
F1: Oblt.z.S. Wenzel

1 *K-Verbände* Division (Narvik): Kaptlt Wolfgang Woerdemann
2 *K-Verbände* Division (Trondheim) Oblt.z.S. Schuirmann
3 *K-Verbände* Division (Bergen) K.K. Dr Silex
4 *K-Verbände* Division (Oslo): Kaptlt. Ludwig Vellguth – 3/45
4 *K-Verbände* Division (Holland): Kaptlt. Helmut Bastian 3/45–5/45
5 *K-Verbände* Division (Holland/Ijmuiden): F.K. Albrecht Brandi
   1/45–5/45
6 *K-Verbände* Division (Opicina/Pola) Kaptlt. Witt
(This was purely a headquarters unit established to facilitate co-ordination with Adriatic Naval Command and to bridge the considerable
distance between *Kommando Stab South* and *K-Verbände* units on the
Istrian Peninsula.)

Naval Recruitment (Lübeck): Kaptlt. Heinz Schomburg
1/44–10/44

Training and Deployment Abteilung (Lübeck)
Kaptlt.M.A. Buschkämper 5/44–7/44
K.K.M.A. Hans-Hinrich Damm 8/44–11/44
The supply service was established on 1 October 1944. Thus this training and deployment Abteilung was divided in November 1944, deployment and training attached to *Standorte Kappeln* while the MEK-training was transferred to the Danish region.

Training (Kappeln)
K.K. Heinrich Hoffmann 11/44–5/45

MEK-Training abteilung (Sonderborg and later Silkeborg)
K.K.M.A Hans-Hinrich Damm 11/44–12/44
K.K.M.A Buschkämper 4/45–5/45

Supply Service (Waren/Müritz)
Kaptlt.M.A. Heinrich Schlüter 10/44–4/45
One company of this supply department was transferred to Flensburg in March 1945. The remaining men of the unit were formed into the Naval Rifle Battalion 979 and fought around Mecklenburg in the final days of the war.

K-Base Helgoland
Kaptlt. Richard Becker 2/45–5/45

Security Detachments
The *K-Verbände* raised the *12 Sicherungsabteilung* with five groups (*Sonderkommandos*).
Sonderkommando Glatze
Sonderkommando Schomburg
Sonderkommando Seehund
Sonderkommando Zander
Sonderkommando Hydra
The 1st Hydra Flotilla (Oblt.z.S. Eicken) was formed in spring 1945, based first in Kolding then moving to Langballigau.

K-Regt (Mot)
Dönitz appealed to Field Marshal Keitel (C-in-C OKW) on 12 July for motor vehicles to be made available to Heye's *K-Verbände* from OKW stocks. Thus, the Admiral der *K-Verbände* formed in spring 1944 the 3rd Transport unit (*Kraftwageneinsatzabteilung*). In July 1944 he also formed 5th Transport unit.
3. Kraftwageneinsatzabteilung: K.K.(Ing.) Banditt (8/42)–10/44

bound for the frontline was definitely destroyed in an air attack on Rosenheim on 6 March.

Adverse weather forced a suspension of *K-Verbände* operations until 6 March when Seehunds and Bibers were once more cleared for action. For the Bibers it was also another day marked by disaster as they gathered ready to put to sea. In the crowded harbour basin at Hellevoetsluis, ten minutes before the Bibers were due to commence departure, a pilot accidentally released his torpedoes sinking fourteen Bibers in the resultant explosion and damaging another nine. Only eleven Bibers were left in a seaworthy state following this fresh accident, but they all sailed for the Scheldt that evening. None of them returned. One was captured by a British motor launch off Breskens on 7 March, another sunk by coastal artillery fire off Westkappelle the following day, four found abandoned ashore on the coastline at North Beveland, Knocke, Domberg and Zeebrugge. The remaining five vanished without trace. Undeterred, the assault against Scheldt shipping continued with six Linsens leaving Hellevoetsluis on the night of 10 March to attack the Veere anchorage on the northern Walcheren coast. Sighted by shore batteries they were driven away by heavy fire, leaving two boats grounded behind them.

The following night a combined massed operation was launched by using fifteen Bibers armed with torpedoes and mines, fourteen Molchs and twenty-seven Linsens, all targeting shipping in the West Scheldt. The results were predictably disastrous; thirteen Bibers, nine Molchs and sixteen Linsens lost for no result. Of the Biber casualties, the RAF's 119 Squadron off Schouwen sank two on 11 March.

During the afternoon F/LT Campbell took up the Anson on an air test cum /ASR flight (searching for an aircraft lost on 9 March) . . . Having a keen eye, he spotted something suspicious in the sea 10 miles east of Schouwen and on flying down to investigate identified the conning tower of a Biber. No R/T, no W/T, but remembering his early training, he switched his I.F.F. to Stud 3 trusting it would be picked up and understood but it wasn't. As the Anson was unarmed there was no possibility of attacking the midget, but a spot of 'beating up' was attempted without, however, shaking the Jerry sufficiently to make him do anything silly. After several attacks it was eventually given up as a bad job, and the aircraft was just making for home when lo and behold! Another little Biber made its appearance about a mile away. Campbell tried out the same tactics, and this time success greeted his efforts for the 'U-Boat Commander' (as the subsequent newspaper story dubbed him) evidently didn't like the feel of an aircraft roaring over him at twenty feet, and on the third dive pilot and observer glimpsed one large rump disappearing over the side of the U-boat. On the final return a figure was seen trying to struggle into a dinghy, the midget turning turtle and slowly disappearing beneath the waves. 'Killer' Campbell returned to make his report and Swordfish 'H' . . . immediately took off followed in a few minutes by 'R' . . . to search for the U-boat that was still at large.[102]

At 18.25hrs at position 51°48'N 03°31'E, Flying Officers Corble and O'Donnell aboard Swordfish 'F' sighted the Biber's cupola as it surfaced, and attacked with four depth-charge runs. The last exploded almost directly beneath the Biber which was enveloped in spray and disappearing, leaving just a thick oil slick on the disturbed surface of the sea. The second Swordfish then arrived and dropped four more depth charges on the oil streak to ensure the Biber's destruction.

The following day Swordfish 'E' of 119 Squadron encountered Linsens for the first time, sighting three and diving to release depth charges and strafe the Linsens below, disabling one which was seen to be 'lower in the water after the shoot up' and later still found floating abandoned on the swell. Further Swordfish encountered more Linsens, attacking and then calling for support from two Tempest fighter-bombers of 33 Squadron who destroyed the sighted Linsens with strafing, a single survivor seen floating in the wreckage.

The run of success enjoyed by 119 Squadron continued that day as two more Swordfish encountered Bibers, both subjected to depth charge and machine gun attacks rewarded by both Bibers sinking and in once case a small yellow life raft observed amongst the oil slicks, the other leaving only wreckage and oil behind. The jubilation felt by the Swordfish crews was reflected in their Squadron Log Book: 'Four Bibers in two days! Whizzo!' Two days later Swordfish 'D', engaged on a similar anti-Biber patrol, arrived on the scene of a single Linsen being circled by a Warwick and Beaufighter. Soon a Walrus flying boat of 276 Squadron arrived and landed beside the solitary German to pluck him from his disabled boat.

Four more Bibers were sunk by MGBs off Westkappelle, another four by shore batteries at Vlissingen and Breskens on 12 March. That same day a Spitfire attacked and sank a Biber off Walcheren and the following day HMS *Retalick* engaged another.

At 02.17hrs a midget submarine, Type Biber, was observed inclination 90 right dead ahead. Speed was increased to maximum and Pom-Pom opened fire. The submarine passed close down the starboard side and five charges, set for 50 feet, were fired. The submarine by then was very low in the water, and passed within ten feet of the starboard side at 02.27hrs. A five charge pattern, set for 50 feet, was fired. The charge from the starboard thrower was observed by myself to fall over the submarine. There was a particularly violent explosion and all trace disappeared. There was no doubt that the submarine had been hit repeatedly and was probably sinking before the last pattern was fired.[103]

Gunners aboard HMS *Retalick* swore that they had also seen another Biber nearby during the attack, so the ensuing search for a survivor was brief and unsuccessful.

The massacre of the Bibers, Linsens and Molchs would continue throughout March. Linsens had also been deployed against the Thames estuary for the first time on the night of 11 March, carried into action aboard the converted S-boats. Launched in the South Falls area at midnight against a TAM convoy that had been sighted at a distance of 18 miles, the attack was unsuccessful. The sole German reference to it was that three control Linsens, carrying the pilots of their expended explosive boats, grounded the following morning near the Goeree lighthouse, where they were destroyed and the men killed in an Allied air attack. Linsens were also sortied on the nights of 22 March and 26 March without any success.

During the night of 23 March, sixteen Bibers armed with mines and torpedoes left Hellevoetsluis for the Scheldt estuary once more. This time there were more survivors as seven managed to return though with no successes. Of the remainder one was found abandoned on Schouwen and another sunk by Beaufighters of 254 Squadron off Goeree. Beaufighters 'R' and 'G' of 254 Squadron engaged on anti-Seehund patrols sighted the Biber at 09.40hrs on 25 March, circling the surfaced craft that appeared to be stationary and listing slightly with the operator standing atop the hull next to the conning tower. Consideration was given to capturing the Biber and the two Beaufighters circled while awaiting notification of whether a motor launch was close enough to assist. Two hours after first contact the aircraft were instructed to sink the boat and attacked immediately.

'R' made two attacks and 'G' four attacks, one-man crew seen to jump overboard and enter dinghy. He was last seen paddling away with both feet making his way to the distant Dutch coast.[104]

HMS *Retalick* took a heavy toll on the Bibers deployed. The after action report submitted on 24 March recounts the ship's actions against the attacking midget submarines as the battle soon developed into chaos.

At 19.41 when in position 293° Westkapelle 9.75 miles, Course 030°, Speed 14 knots, a small radar echo was detected at 030° 2 miles . . . At 19.48 Asdic contact was obtained, two echoes being recorded on trace . . . before a five charge pattern set at 100 feet was fired . . .

Course was maintained at reduced speed . . . and a second attack made . . . At 20.02 a third and deliberate attack was made.

The area was illuminated and at 20.15 shouting and whistle blowing was heard and two men were clearly seen in the water. All the bridge personnel saw these two men, one of whom (subsequently recovered) was very active, the other bleeding from the mouth was much quieter. Their pale grey clothes and red or orange life-belts were unmistakable. An attempt to recover them was made when it was realised that this might invite disaster, and a calcium flare was dropped, FH3, *MTB493* being instructed to recover the survivors. He could only find one however, and after some time had elapsed at 21.14 *Fähnrich* Heinz Lehne was placed on board.

The prisoner was most emphatic that his was a one-man craft, nevertheless there were two men in the water. The plot shows some discrepancies as to the position and it may be that two midgets were close together, one attack being delivered on one and one attack on the other and both destroyed.

At 21.24 . . . a small radar echo was detected . . .

HMS *Retalick* engaged the third Biber with depth charges and cannon fire when an object was blown to the surface. Gunners reported the propeller of the midget submarine thrashing in the air as the Biber went down in a spume of churned water, *Retalick* herself violently shaken by an underwater explosion that was probably the midget's torpedoes. The third 'kill' rendered no trace and at 02.37hrs another radar echo was established. Racing to intercept the Biber was seen on the surface as snowflake was fired above it. Cannon fire peppered the Biber as it passed to starboard, hammered as well by a full depth-charge pattern. Two large oil patches were all that marked its obliteration.

Aboard *Retalick* there was understandable jubilation at the destruction of four Bibers. Lehne was brought aboard soon afterward for interrogation and to have his effects examined. Amongst the usual equipment found on him were:

Leave tickets, photograph folder, photographs (personal), newspaper obituary and cuttings.

His initial interrogation revealed to the British that he:

> . . . had served in submarines for six months. Was hit by the first pattern, and escaped after his submarine was holed, using escape apparatus: was the member of a mobile unit, and was out with several others proceeding independently.
>
> Most insistent that he was the only man in the submarine. He was no Nazi, but a German citizen and his duty was to his country. No one in his service had yet returned from an operation. It was a suicide job, he did not expect to return. He was partial to the English, but opposed the Russians.[105]

HMS *Retalick* had destroyed four of the six Bibers, the remainder disappearing without trace. Of the fifty-six Bibers and Molchs which sortied in March 1945, forty-two had been lost for no result.

The SKL were appalled by the results of these brave though doomed missions. They appealed for greater assistance from the *Luftwaffe* who were asked to bomb the docks and locks at Antwerp to delay Allied stores from being unloaded. The *K-Verbände* were obviously not having the desired affect on Allied supply lines with which the German Army struggled against on land. The German Naval Staff complained to OKW that counter-measures against the various midget services had been intensified, including the use of 'old biplane aircraft' which by virtue of their slow speed were capable of a more thorough search for targets below.

Fortunately for the men of the 1st and 2nd Seehund Flotilla, their two-man submarines fared better during the month of March. German records remain incomplete for this period, so the events can only be gradually pieced together. During March thirty-one Seehunds sailed, though two that put to sea on 13 March stranded outbound; one near Katwijk and the other near the Hook of Holland. Both crews were rescued, but their boats are not in the list that follows. The attackers mounted two distinct waves focussing on different regions, the first spanning from 6 to 19 March, the second 24 to 26 March.

> 6 March – five boats sailed for Margate Roads and the Elbow Buoy, four boats for Great Yarmouth area.
>
> 9 March – three boats sailed for Margate, one for Great Yarmouth.
>
> 11 March – two boats sailed, one for each of the above stations.

16 March – again one boat for each station.

19 March – two boats sailed for Great Yarmouth.

24 March – three boats sailed for the Thames–Scheldt convoy route, two for the British east coast north of the Thames.

25 March – one boat sailed for each of the above areas.

26 March – two boats sailed for the convoy route, one for the Thames.

Again Harald Sander was aboard one of the Seehunds that were active off the English coast. After his experiences during February, when his Seehund was wrecked, he had been allowed time to return to Germany before putting to sea once again.

Admiral Heye . . . said, 'Harald, go home to Berlin for eight days and then from there go back to Wilhelmshaven and get yourself a new boat'. Then I told him that I didn't really get on with my companion. 'Okay, find yourself a new commander. We still have some in training' . . . It wasn't easy coming to Berlin because the 'chain dogs' were in operation . . . Mr Himmler and Adolf had formed these troops that were a sort of military police force and they wore chains. Everyone running around in Berlin and elsewhere was gathered together by them as troops for the Berlin defence. This was already the end of February and the Russian troops were advancing on Berlin. I had a special pass of course, so that they couldn't recruit me. I had papers from Heye stating that I was in the 'K group' so they couldn't send me off towards Russia.

Then the scheme started again from the beginning. Pick up a boat in Wilhelmshaven, then run it in, then we travelled from there by train. The whole ten boats in the flotilla were loaded onto a train. We had the infantry there as guards and we travelled by night. By day we halted at the border in a siding under guard and then we continued on, arriving in Ijmuiden after the second night. And then we ran the boats in again. Down there at the Scheldt it was different now. The invasion was more advanced. Then I was given the job of going to Great Yarmouth with my comrade. If a line is drawn directly from east to west from Ijmuiden you come to the corner of England where the port and the city of Great Yarmouth are situated . . . In two days we chugged across, lying low by day and continuing by night, because the boat couldn't move fast . . . Then in Great Yarmouth we went to ground and the next day from a long way off we heard the sound of two ships and then we surfaced. There was a destroyer and a big commercial ship. At the time we estimated about ten or twelve thousand tonnes. It was behind the destroyer. Okay, it was a target and we wanted to try it out. We dived again until the destroyer had passed overhead and then we went down to sea bed level and my commander tried it out. I had to pull both the levers which were behind my chief engineer's seat in order to free the torpedoes – first one lever and then the other. There was no explosion.

Well after firing we dived straight away and stayed on the bottom and then we had to be quiet. We couldn't make a sound, no sound of metal, otherwise the English would start to attack immediately. Then came the sonar 'Asdic', as it is called . . . it sounded as though a handful of gravel was being thrown against the outside of the boat. There is this ticking noise, which comes at intervals. Then it was quiet for a while and then we heard the destroyer returning. The other boat, the freighter, of course, had kept moving and then the destroyer came looking for us.

That took a couple of hours. Either they changed position, or we changed position and when they changed position we moved as well, because it was sound against sound. And then when they were quiet and stopped moving they were looking for us, so we remained still. The whole thing went like that and they dropped about thirty depth charges on us. We weren't hit directly, otherwise I wouldn't be here, but they kept trying by dropping depth charges in our general position. They kept this up for a while and then afterwards we were so far away and we were really quite a small target. The boat is not quite one metre wide and with a length of twelve or thirteen metres it is not a big target to pinpoint. So we were in luck again and then we went home by night. We landed in Ijmuiden again and that was towards the end. It was already late March or early April of 1945. At that time the Canadians and the English were steadily advancing towards us.[106]

Of the nine boats that sailed on 6 March, Oblt.z.S. Ross, L.z.S. Gaffron, L.z.S. Göhler, L.z.S. Drexel and L.z.S. Markworth were all forced to return with technical faults. One other was sunk by *MTB675* 26 miles east of Ramsgate on 7 March.

Over the remainder of the month several more Seehunds were lost. The confusion of reported attacks and sinkings from Allied sources and a lack of German records that detail losses, returning boats and sailing dates mean that only estimates can be made of the scale of sinkings experienced by the Seehund units. It is thought that at least fifteen boats were lost, possibly more.

As well as the confirmed sinking made by *MTB675*, there are several other definite German losses. One Seehund was lost to a Beaufighter attack on 10 March near Goeree, another sunk the following day and

L.z.S. Newbauer taken prisoner. Two Seehunds were sunk by HMS *Torrington*; the first, *U-5377*, near Dumpton Buoy on the edge of Goodwin Sands on 11 March, the second, *U-5339*, 20 miles north of Dunkirk three days later. The hunt for this second Seehund caused considerable damage to *Torrington* herself, the engine and boiler rooms suffering from the concussion of depth charges set for 50 feet and exploding in shallow water. During the bombardment the wire rope lanyard that operated the starboard depth charge thrower parted following the first salvo. Its operator, Able Seaman Charles Horton, picked up a duffel coat and wrapped it around his head as he continued to fire the thrower by hand, burning his face and hands until the Seehund was destroyed.[107] *Leutnant zur See* Siegert and *Maschinenmaat* Heilhues of *U-5377* were both taken prisoner, picked up by *MTB621* and later transferred aboard *Torrington*. Five minesweepers reported sighting and attacking a Seehund on 13 March northeast of Felixstowe. *HMML466* attacked and sank a Seehund on 12 March in drifting fog, capturing the coxswain L.z.S. John but killing MascMt Teichmüller with machine gun fire. L.z.S. Hermann Böhme and his coxswain were also listed as killed by fighter-bomber attack on 12 March west of Schouwen. On 21 March enemy aircraft attacked L.z.S. Göhler and *Omasch*. Kassier as their boat sortied from Ijmuiden after the rectification of their technical problems – the boat was sunk and both men lost. Another Seehund of the first wave of attackers was sunk by *MTB394* 23 miles south-east of Great Yarmouth on 22 March, both crewmen rescued.

The second wave that had slipped from Ijmuiden between 24 and 26 March fared little better, losing one Seehund to Beaufighter attack at 14.40hrs on 25 March 20 miles north-west of the Hook of Holland, though misidentified by the attacking crew.

Aircraft 'Q'; F/O B.V. Ekbery, F/S Thomas on Anti-Seehund patrol. 14.40: 52°12'N, 03°45'E. Sighted wake dead ahead and identified as conning tower of a midget U-boat, believed to be a Biber. Aircraft attacked with cannon as U-boat was crash diving. Hits were probable but target was hidden by splashes. About three minutes after attack a patch of thin oil was seen, about 15ft in diameter in approximate target position.[108]

Another Seehund was lost to HMS *Puffin* off Lowestoft in the early morning of 26 March. The ship rammed a Seehund, the subsequent impact causing a torpedo to detonate, obliterating the Seehund and buckling the British ship's bows. HMS *Puffin* limped into Harwich where the damage to the ship was judged so severe that she was not repaired. In Jürgen Rohwer's book on U-boat successes he states that: 'HMS *Puffin* was obviously rammed by a surfacing midget, which had already been abandoned.'[109]

The same day that *Puffin* made her attack, the Royal Navy motor launch *ME1471* sank a Seehund, and perhaps the final German victim for March fell to *ML586* the following day west of Walcheren.

Their attempts were not without success though. On 10 March L.z.S. Lanz and Lt(Ing.) Gerhard Müller's *U-5364* recorded a successful torpedoing of a destroyer, though Allied records hold no mention of this. However, on 13 March the 2,878-ton Canadian steamer SS *Taber Park* taking coal from the Tyne to London was torpedoed by L.z.S. Maximilian Huber and Lt(Ing.) Siegfried Eckloff. The ship was travelling out of convoy and sank rapidly, killing four DEMS gunners and twenty-four crew out of a total of thirty-two people aboard. Two of the Seehunds operating within the Thames area claimed two ships sunk, Fröhnert and Beltrami claiming a steamer hit before they were subjected to a devastating depth charge bombardment that they narrowly managed to sneak away from and return bruised but intact to Ijmuiden. Kruger and Schmidt's *U-5064* also claimed a large steamer, estimated at 3,500 tons sunk in the Thames Estuary. Neither claim has been firmly corroborated by Allied sources.

On 21 March Hauschel and Hesel's *U-5366* torpedoed and sank the American Liberty ship SS *Charles D. McIver* southeast of Lowestoft. Enroute to Southend from Antwerp and then planned to head onward to New York, the Liberty ship was at first thought by Allied sources to have been mined, though the attack coincides with that reported by the crew of *U-5366*. On 22 March *ML466* was sunk by what has been suggested was a Seehund torpedo, though no surviving crew claimed the attack. More definite was the torpedoing by Küllmer and Raschke of the British steamer SS *Newlands* within the Thames Estuary. *Newlands* was hit with a shot fired from 320m, the Seehund escaping to return to Ijmuiden. The last sinking attributed to a Seehund for March was the successful torpedoing of the British coastal freighter SS *Jim* travelling from Goole to Dieppe.

The pressure on the Seehund crews was increasing during March as Germany tottered towards annihilation between the Russian and Western Allied forces. In Ijmuiden the USAAF returned to attack the concrete pens twice more; nine B-17s using 'Disney' rockets on 14 March, three more returning with the same payload a week later.

March had yielded some more hopeful results for the midget service though, with Seehund attacks taking their toll despite a total of fourteen men definitely killed on operations and at least the same number captured.

As well as attacks against the enemy's merchant shipping, the question of allocating Seehunds to the resupply of German defenders at Dunkirk – 'Operation Kameraden' – had been raised once more. This time Dönitz agreed and the opening supply run departed Ijmuiden on 27 March, Fröhnert and Beltrami the first of three crews assigned. The Seehund's weaponry had been removed and replaced with two empty canisters of the same dimensions as a torpedo. These so-called 'butter-torpedoes' were loaded with the intended cargo, which comprised urgently-required foodstuffs such as a fat ration for each of the defenders as well as weaponry such as anti-tank mines and anti-tank artillery ammunition. Beltrami later recalled their voyage:

> On 27 March we three supply Seehunds left Ijmuiden. We successfully travelled about two or three miles and made the obligatory trim test dive in salt water. But as soon as my tower hatch went under water I got a cold shower down the neck. We put the boat on the seabed to determine where the water was coming in and discovered two more places around the hatch that it was leaking from. I assumed that this was caused by damage that we had taken on an earlier mission when we were heavily depth charged by the enemy. The difficult mission that we had lined up ahead could not be accomplished with a boat unfit to dive. We decided that we had to return. When in the headquarters I reported to F.K. Brandi, complaining about the sloppy work done when repairing our boat.

The Seehund was worked on throughout the night and made ready to sail during the following afternoon. This time the test dive passed without problems and Fröhnert and Beltrami were able to begin their mission proper. They headed into the teeth of a severe weather front that forced them underwater for hours as they waited for the storm to subside. Once surfaced they ironically had to creep past enemy shipping traffic – normally a target they longed to see.

> We followed the coast and in the grey morning of the seventh day, we saw the silhouette of Ostend. There were many enemy ships in the harbour and we only had 'butter torpedoes' . . . We hugged the coast on to Dunkirk. There we were unable to enter the harbour as a minefield blocked our way forward. So we decided on a plan: I would climb

out and signal with a hand torch to notify the posts on shore that we were there. It was still sea state 4! If I should fall overboard then the LI was to head south toward the beach. So I did what I said: clambered out, shut the hatch and held on to the periscope and signalled. The boat dipped a little so I was sometimes up to my waist in the water. In due course a signal came back from the head of the Mole: 'Head 100 metres to the east, you are in a minefield! We will send a boat to guide you'. Open the hatch and back in the boat, the LI is very pleased. We head east . . .[110]

Once docked in Dunkirk soldiers took the two crewmen to the hospital where they were given a warm bath while their boat was unloaded. The Fortress Kommandant, Admiral Frisius, made time to personally congratulate them, Heye doing likewise via radio. On 9 April they departed Dunkirk under a glowering sky. Their 'torpedoes' had been reloaded, this time with outgoing mail and messages from the trapped soldiers. Following a brief brush with a Mosquito fighter-bomber – bullets hammering the sea where the boat had just dived – and the almost obligatory motor and engine problems the Seehund entered Ijmuiden on 11 April. With the idea proven, the pattern of this successful mission was to be repeated until the end of the war.

By the beginning of April 1945 the Allied isolation of German-held regions within the Netherlands was nearly complete. The problems of supply for the *K-Verbände* had become critical and consideration was given to withdrawing the Biber and Linsen forces and rebasing them at Emden to defend the Ems waterway. This idea was deemed logistically unworkable and rejected almost as quickly as it had been proposed, though further thought was given to moving Biber, Molch and Linsen units from Borkum to Emden instead. This too was judged impractical on transportation grounds and use of a single Linsen flotilla, which had already operated in support of the Army, was mooted instead.

Admiral Frisius in Dunkirk suggested that the *K-Verbände* units still in the Netherlands should move instead to Dunkirk from where they could continue operations against the Scheldt traffic. Frisius's idea was based on the fact that the Seehunds remained the only craft of sufficient range to reach their allocated combat area from German bases, though his proposal was ultimately rejected and the *K-Verbände* fought on in Holland.

The bad weather that had dogged Fröhnert and Beltrami on their way to Dunkirk remained in place until 5 April after which operations were resumed. The Seehunds immediately began sailing, directed against the Thames–Scheldt convoy routes as well as the supply lines that traversed the British coast east of the Thames and as far as Dungeness. Seehund strength on 8 April in Ijmuiden was recorded as twenty-nine, of which only perhaps half were operational on that day. Reinforcements were scheduled to arrive from Germany; eleven Seehunds heading from Neustadt on 18 April to Wilhelmshaven and ultimately Ijmuiden, shepherded as far as Brunsbüttel by the armed trawler *KFK445*. The Seehunds had originally been intended to relocate to Heligoland but increasingly heavy air raids had rendered the island virtually unusable. Four other Seehunds arrived in Ijmuiden from Wilhelmshaven on 20 April and three more by the beginning of the following month, bolstered by a further two from Heligoland.

In total thirty-six Seehunds put to sea on war patrols between 5 April and 28 April, the maximum effort achieved on 12 April when sixteen boats were at sea. Of the thirty-eight that sailed, eight returned prematurely with defects, fifteen returned safely, six were recorded as definitely lost by 28 April, three unaccounted for and four were still at sea on that date. Only three of them reported successful attacks.

The first, *U-5309*, crewed by L.z.S. Benediktus von Pander and Lt(Ing.) Martin Vogl claimed a 1,000-ton tanker hit north-north-west of Dunkirk on 9 April, the day before they returned to Ijmuiden. The American army tanker *Y17* had been hit and set ablaze by a torpedo in that approximate position while part of convoy TAC90. The 484-ton ship was one of the small tankers operated by the US Army. They were of a standardised design, similar in size and appearance to the Navy Yard oiler, though designated as 'Y' boats. These vessels were built for the Transportation Corps in two classes, a twin-screw version and a single-screw version, *Y17* belonging to the latter. Burning fiercely after the magnetic torpedo exploded beneath the hull, *Y17* was lost in less than thirty minutes after being hit.

Seehund *U-5363* attacked convoy TBC123 off Dungeness late on 9 April, the British Liberty ship ss *Samida* hit and sunk and the American Liberty ship ss *Soloman Juneau* damaged a little before midnight. Again, there is confusion over who actually hit the two ships, German *B-Dienst* listening service crediting the Type VIIC *U-245* engaged on Dönitz's inshore campaign with the attack, though her captain denies that he was responsible. The likelihood is that it was L.z.S. Harro Buttmann and *Omasch*. Artur Schmidt's Seehund that inflicted the damage, though the German midget was subsequently lost to an attack by *ML102* during the action and both crew killed.

Schmidt's corpse was recovered during August 1945 in fishing nets near Föhr Island, his remains interred in Wyk cemetery. At around the same time that *U-5363* was sunk by the British motor launch, Beaufighter 'W' of 254 Squadron accounted for another of the Seehunds destroyed during that month.

Markworth and Spallek's *U-5070* obtained a hit on an estimated 4,500-ton ship from convoy UC63B near Dungeness on 11 April, successfully torpedoing British ss *Port Wyndham* though the 8,480-ton Port Line ship survived the attack. Hit twice off the outer Lade Buoy at Dungeness the ship was holed forward, later being towed stern-first into Southampton where she was given temporary repairs prior to permanent work being completed by her builder. *U-5070* had little time to celebrate as an escorting destroyer, HMS *Vesper*, hammered them for several hours with depth charges before they managed to limp silently away.

L.z.S. Reimer Wilken and *Omasch*. Heinz Bauditz aboard *U-5368* made the third Seehund claim though in hindsight their target appraisal remains optimistic. They recorded two hits, the first against a corvette on 14 April that they fired at from a range of 800m, the second a 5,000-ton ship hit two days later at 18.30hrs from 1,000m. There is no Allied record of the former but on 16 April the 1,150-ton British Post Office cable layer ss *Monarch* was torpedoed near Orford Ness, this likely to have been Wilken's target. Nonetheless, it was a successful and aggressively handled patrol, *U-5368*'s two crew expending their boat's last reserves of diesel by 18 April, the incapacitated Seehund drifting ashore five days later near Katwijk.

In Ijmuiden there were also two further successes transmitted to Brandi's men by the *B-Dienst*. On 18 April two ships from convoy TAM142 were torpedoed half a mile from the South Falls buoy early that morning, the Norwegian freighter MS *Karmt* and British steamer ss *Frilleigh* subsequently sinking. However, the attribution to Seehund attack appears to be misplaced as *U-245* logged the attack in its own War Diary, making Seehund involvement unlikely.

The returning crews also reported three unsuccessful attacks during their patrols. The most dramatic narrow escape was undoubtedly suffered by *Oberfähnrich* Korbinian Penzkofer and *Obermaschinist* Werner Schulz's *U-5305* after an attempted attack on a destroyer in the South Falls area on 10 April. The port torpedo was readied to fire at the British warship, but failed to disengage, dragging the terrified crew through the water toward their enemy. As the Seehund shot underneath the ship the magnetic warhead failed to detonate and after a severe counter-attack from the startled British crew that involved a great deal of machine gun fire at the crazed midget that was apparently attempting to ram a British 'Hunt' class destroyer, *U-5305* was able to creep away from the scene and return to Holland. *U-5071* also recorded near disaster when they were attacked while homebound and still carrying their torpedoes. A splinter penetrated the warhead of one torpedo, though it failed to explode.

Aircraft continued to be a prime predator of the Seehunds, at least 1,000 of them being involved in anti-Seehund patrols, alongside 500 naval vessels. Mosquito 'H' of 254 Squadron, Wellington 'V' of 524 Squadron and Beaufighter 'M' of 236 Squadron combined to destroy a returning Seehund off the Hook of Holland on 12 April. The following day Barracuda 'L' of 810 Naval Air Squadron attacked another in the same area.

> Friday 13th: New patrols now being flown off the Dutch coast . . . S/Lt McCarthy made an attack on a midget some 14 miles off the Dutch coast. The attack was successful, two survivors coming to the surface! S/Lt Taylor made an attack on a disappearing contact, but no results were observed. S/Lt Bradbury made an attack on a midget during the last patrol. Nothing came to the surface. But it can be assumed to be a probable.[111]

Unbeknownst to the men of 5. K-Division the bloodbath was over for them as of 28 April. The final four Seehunds to run supplies into Dunkirk, *U-5365*, *U-5074*, *U-5090* and *U-5107*, were the last of their kind to be on active patrols. There they would see the end of the war, later destroyed by their own crews before Dunkirk eventually capitulated.

Chaos had overwhelmed the German military in Holland during April. As Dutch harbours and installations were prepared for both defence against ground assault and destruction in the face of possible German withdrawal, Georgian troops that were serving in the *Wehrmacht* on the island of Texel revolted on 8 April. It was two more weeks before German soldiers managed to subdue the rebellion, the same day that the locks at Ijmuiden were destroyed by demolition. Dutch resistance members reported German morale to the British as 'low', though not among 'younger elements' which may well have included the *K-Verbände*. Looting began to increase amidst the breakdown of military order, though Heye's men remained disciplined and loyal to the very end.

While the Seehunds had helped carry the war back into British home waters, the Bibers and Linsens had continued their desperate onslaught in the Scheldt, sixty Molchs being held in reserve in Amersfoort. In the early afternoon of 9 April, five Bibers armed with a mine and torpedo each had sailed for the Scheldt estuary. Two were forced to return within two days with mechanical defects, one striking a mine and sinking *en route*, while the remaining three were lost without apparent success, Beaufighter pilots of 236 Squadron and Swordfish of 119 Squadron reported attacking and hitting Bibers within the area.

For the Biber pilots the emphasis moved completely to mine laying and on 11 April two Bibers sailed from Zierikzee to lay their mines before Sandkreek. One accomplished its mission successfully while the other was lost. Swordfish of 119 Squadron probably accounted for the missing Biber, their logbook entry echoing what had become regular reports for Allied airmen as they harvested a grim tally of Biber kills.

April 12: Swordfish 'F' . . . Scrambled to search for Bibers reported approximately 40 miles north of base. At 15.10hrs two were sighted in position 0051°54'N 0003°17'E, one stationary on surface, the other just surfacing about 50 yards away. The first Biber apparently attempted to submerge but the conning tower was still visible when 'F' attacked with four depth charges. The stick fell between the two, the first one being blown out of the water and left stationary on the surface. The second was not seen again.[112]

At 06.30hrs on 21 April the penultimate Biber mission in Holland was launched with six leaving to lay mines in the silt of the Scheldt estuary. Only four of them returned.

On 26 April the final recorded Biber mission from Dutch territory took place when four left Poortershaven at 01.30hrs to lay mines again in the Scheldt estuary. One grounded while outbound and was forced to return with damage. American Thunderbolt fighters off the Hook of Holland attacked the remaining trio, two of them sunk in the battle. The sole survivor escaped the prowling aircraft and aborted his mission, returning to base. During April, the twenty-four remaining Bibers that were in the Rotterdam area had all taken part in missions. Of these, nineteen were lost with no sinkings or damage of enemy ships attributed to their missions. The defeat of the Bibers was complete.

The last active component of the *K-Verbände* in Holland – that of the Linsens – had also comprehensively failed in its missions during April. Weather conditions moderated enough by 11 April to allow a

211

resumption of their operations. Five units put out from Hellevoetsluis to attack shipping off Ostend during that evening. One unit reached the target area and unsuccessfully attacked an Allied patrol vessel. Of the remainder, one unit returned with mechanical problems, two failed to find the target area and another unit was lost in action. The same mission plan was repeated on the night of 12 April by seven units in total. Two of the control boats were also tasked with landing agents ashore in enemy-held territory, but the mission was scrubbed due to an unexpectedly heavy swell.

Five nights later two formations of Linsens set out once more. Two units were to attack enemy shipping in the Scheldt estuary again, while the remainder were destined to head for Dunkirk and continue their operations from there against the Thames–Scheldt convoy route as Frisius had suggested. The former returned with engine trouble while the fate of the latter remains unknown and conjectural.

At 21.30hrs on 20 April the last recorded Linsen operation began with four units slipping from Hellevoetsluis to attack Allied convoy traffic due around buoy NF8 at 02.10hrs and from there to sail onwards to Dunkirk at 04.00hrs. Two units aborted with engine trouble while the others were hammered by Allied naval vessels and aircraft west of Schouwen a little before midnight and obliterated. Once more the MTB control frigate HMS *Retalick* and its four accompanying MTBs were heavily involved in fighting the *K-Verbände*. The British report on the action paints a harrowing picture of the demise of the Linsen unit.

> An overcast night but owing to the moon behind the clouds, one of reasonable visibility.
>
> Both MTB units (FH3 and FH4 of two MTBs each) were established in position . . . Aircraft reporting at 22.26 a persistent contact . . . At 00.16, a small radar echo bearing 355°, 1.8 miles stationary and thought to be a midget submarine. Range closed at high speed and snowflake [illumination flares – author's note] used. Target (I) seen to be a small motorboat, which was engaged as it started to move. Immediate hits were seen, it burned fiercely and stopped.
>
> In the glare of the burning boat a second (II) was seen . . . this was pursued but contact was lost at 00.21 . . . At 00.33 EMB (III) was sighted after radar contact, pursued, engaged and seen to burn at 00.38.
>
> Seen through the smoke from III, IV was seen, pursued, being destroyed at 01.00. A survivor was recovered from the water. FH3 and FH4 were vectored to search for survivors and wreckage. Depth charges were dropped at 00.49.

HMS *Retalick* recorded the destruction of four Linsens and another probable before the battle ended. The British had suffered no casualties or damage and gathered together the few shocked survivors.

> The prisoners recovered were the leader, *Oberleutnant zur See* [Karl] Feigl and his coxswain [*Bootsmaat* Robert] Klein, both of whom were dead, having had the major portion of their heads shot off. Both [*Matrosenobergefreiter* Walter] Kettemann and [*Funkgefreiter* Günther] Mellethin, who were alive (Kettemann with his arm broken by gunfire) were in separate boats. They kept on enquiring for Schultz another member of the unit, whom one had seen in the water . . . Feigl had a chart and his orders on him.
>
> The prisoners stated that after the death of their leader . . . they were thrown into confusion. It would appear that they were not individually briefed. They were of an excellent physical type and ardent members of the Hitler Youth.

With this characterisation in mind there remains one truly bizarre postscript to the *K-Verbände* operations in Holland. German naval documents reveal that on the night of 27 April at least thirty volunteers from unspecified *K-Verbände* units were to be heavily armed and flown to Berlin where they would act as a personal bodyguard for their *Führer* Adolf Hitler. They apparently got as far as assembling at the aerodrome at Rerick and preparing to board three Ju52 transport aircraft before their mission was abandoned – the sole reason for this cancellation appearing to be the expected inability to land men in the besieged German capital.

On 6 May 1945 the Royal Canadian Hastings and Prince Edward Regiments of the 1st Canadian Division took the surrender of German forces in Ijmuiden. Among the battered remnants of many *Wehrmacht* formations, the *K-Verbände* men marched into captivity with their commander K.z.S. Albrecht Brandi.

> There we, 3,000 comrades of Brandi's *K-Verbände*, were taken into custody. Since he, 'Diamonds-Brandi', had a huge reputation with our enemies, even more so than with the German public, the Canadian General and his men passed on this reputation to us . . . After we had cleaned our weapons and had them inspected one last time, we transferred them all complete with ammunition to a detail of trucks. Then in good disciplined order we marched as 'Marine Division Brandi' into a camp of tents, equipped with a special food supply. The next Allied order was that no military honour with the Swastika on it could be worn, so we deployed close to the town square. Then Brandi spoke to

the assembled troops. 'Our decorations are bestowed by our highest commanders, and if we are not able to wear them in the form given to us, then we will lay them down!' Then he took off his Knight's Cross with Oak Leaves, Swords and Diamonds, along with 3,000 comrades that did likewise. We marched silently back into the camp.[113]

CHAPTER TWELVE

To East and West

K-Verbände *river attacks*

As well as the bitter fighting in which MEK raiders were involved in the Adriatic, the beginning of 1945 saw no let-up in frogman activity on the Eastern or Western Fronts either. Requests continued to be received by Heye for men to operate against bridgeheads over the Oder, Danube and Rhine and special sabotage groups appeared and disappeared with some regularity among captured German records. Often their exact composition remains a mystery, more often than not the results of whatever task they attempted also lost within the bureaucracy of the German military.

On 25 February men of Lehrkommando 700 formed *Kampsch-wimmergruppe Ost*, led by *Leutnant* Frederick Keller. Within days it had transferred to the Eastern Front and was engaged in what became a futile attempt to blow up the Russian-held bridge over the Oder at Vogelsang. Linsens finally brought the bridge down weeks later, though it did little to stem the Soviet advance. On 11 March the ninety men of MEK85 had been transferred to the east, the fully motorised unit ready for missions on the Oder River as well.

In the west K.z.S. Musenberg of *Kommando Stab* Holland enquired of OKW whether, in view of their offensive through the Ardennes, the Nijmegen Bridge was still to be considered as a necessary target. The reply was affirmative and so Musenberg ordered fresh attempts made to destroy the prized crossing. The British had since bolstered its defences by stringing nets across the Waal and MEK40 men were tasked with their elimination. On the night of 12 January they released fifty-four floating mines in three waves in an attempt to destroy the nets. The mines were slipped from rafts that had been towed into position by tugs, the current pushing the charges downstream where they would hook the nets, timer fuses detonating the explosives and breaking the barrier. One raft carrying nineteen mines was destroyed by

Allied artillery, but the MEK men persevered until the remaining thirty-five mines had been despatched.

Seventeen Bibers that had been held in reserve specifically for this mission handled the second part of the assault. The periscopes had been disguised with small camouflage thickets in order to avoid enemy attention, the Bibers armed with torpedoes with which to attack the bridge pylons. They were towed part of the way towards their target, and eight of them successfully slipped only 1km from the first nets, though seven others became stuck fast in the thick mud of the river bed. Two of the successful Bibers were lost after fouling a submerged wreck and two others blew up, probably after being targeted by Allied artillery fire. The remainder returned, dejectedly reporting the mission's failure.

Nijmegen's importance was soon overshadowed on 7 March 1945 when the last great natural barrier that protected Germany's western territories was breached. American troops of the 9th Armored Division operating with the kind of dash and vigour that had once been the hallmark of Germany's *blitzkrieg* seized the intact Ludendorff railway bridge over the Rhine at Remagen. Ironically, the bridge had been constructed during the First World War on the urging of General Ludendorff so that men and material could be shipped to the Western Front with greater ease. As the leading American troops had crested the ridge that lay west of the small town they had been stunned to see the bridge still standing, the Germans having scheduled it for demolition at 16.00hrs that day. A motorised platoon raced through the town, still crowded with straggling German troops retreating over this last available crossing, reaching the waterfront at 15.50hrs and charging pell-mell across the bridge. As accompanying engineers cut every demolition cable in sight, infantry charged forward until the bridge suddenly shuddered as a small detonation was triggered. Another explosion followed, though the main charge strung by the German defenders failed to ignite. The span trembled slightly, but obstinately refused to fall and the attacking Americans hurled themselves across, throwing every available man onto the far side of the Rhine. Within 24 hours, 8,000 American troops were on the Rhine's eastern bank and the bridgehead was secure.

The piercing of the natural defensive line offered by the wide and fast-flowing Rhine River was a psychological blow to Germany as well as being strategically disastrous and Hitler ordered all available means to be used in destroying the bridge. There followed hundreds of abortive air attacks by the *Luftwaffe*, using aircraft as diverse as their arsenal allowed, including Junkers Ju87 'Stukas', Focke-Wulf Fw190s,

Messerschmitt Me109s and the jet aircraft Messerschmitt Me262 and Arado Ar134, but all to no avail. The Americans had quickly deployed a ring of fearsome anti-aircraft defences that were almost impossible to penetrate. German artillery fire fared no better, leaving attack from the river itself as the final option.

The climate within Hitler's immediate entourage at this point of time was wrought with tension as the volatile dictator sought scapegoats for the fall of the bridge, accusing dereliction of duty and defeatism for the military setback. At Hitler's daily situation conference on 8 March, Helmut Sündermann (Hitler's Deputy Press Chief) noted in his diary:

> The *Führer* also plans to send in flying courts-martial to stamp out these signs of dissolution. I have noted down two of his angry outbursts: 'Only Russian methods can help us now,' and 'If we lose the war the Germans will be exterminated anyway – so it's a good thing to exterminate some of these creatures now.'[114]

At least four officers were subsequently tried and executed in the Westerwald Forest for the Remagen catastrophe. Within this highly-charged atmosphere the instinct for self-preservation got the better of some officers and they sought to shift the blame away from themselves. Admiral Heye was dragged into this volatile situation almost immediately when during the same military briefing *Generaloberst* Alfred Jodl, Chief of Operations at OKW, stated that:

> . . . two Navy demolition teams were assigned to destroy the Rhine bridge at Remagen . . . An inquiry with the Commanding Admiral, Small Battle Units, showed that nothing was known there of such an assignment. An investigation has been ordered.[115]

Heye had rapidly – and correctly – denied the accusation that he had already been assigned the task and achieved nothing, which could have exposed him to Hitler's wrath and instead threw himself into the task of carrying out the proposed attack as the following day's conference notes show.

> March 9 . . . 17.00hrs: . . . C-in-C Navy reports to the *Führer* that two detachments have been chosen for blowing up the Rhine bridge at Remagen and that they are being sent there as soon as possible. They are to attempt to blow each of the piers with two torpedo mines (TMC) attached to one another. It is not possible at this time to predict when the preparations will be completed; everything is being done to speed them up.[116]

217

Coincidentally, the idea of using frogmen to destroy the bridge had already occurred to the British as well, or at least the men responsible for the *Atlantiksender* and *Soldatensender* radio propaganda broadcasts. Denis Sefton Delmer, a journalist by profession, had hatched the idea of broadcasting from Wavendon Towers in England to the Continent, posing as a regular German radio station. By the use of subtle innuendo and misinformation the two radio stations – *Soldatensender* aimed at *Luftwaffe* and Army men, *Atlantiksender* at the U-boat crews – were valuable tools in Britain's propaganda arsenal. Delmer remembered the event in his memoirs:

> 'Of course the real people to have a go at the bridge should be the Navy with their frogmen', said Donald as much in jest as anything. I immediately turned to Frankie Lynder.
>
> 'Where are the nearest frogmen units?' I asked.
>
> 'I think Admiral Heye's K-force has some at Nijmegen. We could easily move them upstream and have them make an underwater attack against the bridge with those special torpedo mines, the TMC, you know, sir.'
>
> Frankie had never lost his admirable habit of saying 'Sir' to his superior officers which had won him three stripes in the Pioneer Corps.
>
> 'Oh, I don't think we want to report an actual attack, Sergeant. We'll just say that the *Führer* had the brilliant idea of an underwater attack and that Admiral Heye, eager to add diamonds to his oak leaves, or whatever else it is he covets in the way of decorations, has graciously consented to sacrifice frogmen on "Operation Lorelei". I think you should make a great play of some chap arguing that the whole scheme is impossible rubbish owing to the incalculable underwater currents of the Rhine.'
>
> It was just a routine 'black' story like hundreds of others we had thought up. But what a commotion it caused in Hitler's headquarters in the underground shelter at the Reich chancellery in Berlin, when we put it on the air on March 11th! For, unknown to us at the time, the *Führer* had in fact ordered . . . Dönitz to lay on an underwater operation by naval frogmen against the bridge. . . . Then on 11 March, the *Soldatensender* and its twin brother the short-wave *Atlantiksender* made our announcement.[117]

It was indeed a crushing blow to the morale of those men involved to realise that it appeared that the British were aware of their every move. Hitler was furious, though Dönitz attempted to placate his increasingly paranoid chief by carrying the plan through to fruition in the possibility that the British were indeed bluffing. For Heye the difficulties in launching the attack were more prosaic – he was rapidly running out of available units. A *K-Verbände* memorandum dated 11 March shows that with special units already deployed on the Oder, Drau and Danube the increasing demand for them in the west was difficult to meet. Twelve frogmen and four TMC mines were to be used at Remagen; elsewhere two groups of Linsens with 100 spherical and eight TMB mines preparing for operations in the Wesel–Arnhem area and 1,200kg of mines being readied for use at the bridge at Lohmannsheide. All of these *K-Verbände* commando units forming in the west – collectively codenamed '*Lederstrumpf*' – were placed under the control of K.z.S. Düwel's freshly raised *Kommandostb zbV* responsible for operations within Allied-held German waterways. Local command was passed over to K.K. Bartels, beneath whom there existed at least two further code-named sections – *Puma* and *Sioux*.

The twelve men that were earmarked for the Remagen assault – commanded by Oblt.z.S. Erich Dörpinghaus and designated 'Puma' – had been headed elsewhere on 7 March, but were rapidly diverted after the OKW meeting on 8 March. They reached Remagen that day after losing two of their mines in an air attack along the choked roads during the previous day. The attempt on the bridge was initially fixed for 9 March though the withdrawal of the Pioneer Regiment that were needed as operational support forced a postponement. Meanwhile K.K. Bartels had arrived at Army Group B headquarters from Rotterdam on 10 March with six more mines, the attack planned again for the following day. As the operation was being prepared, Bartels received fresh instructions from Jodl at OKW to await reinforcement: the SS frogmen of Skorzeny's *Jagdverbände*, controlled directly by the RSHA, were to augment the attacking force.

An aircraft carrying *Untersturmführer* Walter Schreiber, commander of one of Skorzeny's units in the East, SS *Jagdverbände Donau*, and eleven SS frogmen of the same unit arrived at Frankfurt from Vienna and the combined group of SS and 'Puma' *K-Verbände* men prepared for an attack on 12 March. The defences they faced were formidable. As well as the Allied units that were pouring across the Ludendorff Bridge, American Military Police of 9th MP Company were stationed at intervals along both sides of the bridge and along the river banks acting as snipers to specifically prevent any such attack using frogmen. To protect the bridge during the hours of darkness a number of obsolete M3 Lee tanks of the 738th Tank Battalion had had their 75mm hull-mounted guns removed and a searchlight mounted in its place. These so-called CDL (Canal Defence Light) tanks had been developed by the British and were deployed along the riverbanks upstream of the bridge, all manner of weapons using the combined effect of thirteen-million candlepower CDLs and searchlights to fire at anything unusual floating down the river.

It was a forlorn hope and even Skorzeny himself doubted their ability to destroy the bridge.

> The water temperature of the Rhine was sometimes only 6° or 8° Celsius and the American bridgehead had expanded at least 10 kilometres upstream. I therefore explained to them that I could see only a very small chance for success. I decided that I would bring my best men to the area and there they could decide for themselves whether they would undertake this operation.[118]

As the German frogmen donned their cumbersome equipment and prepared to enter the swiftly moving river they came under heavy and accurate artillery fire, preventing their deployment and the operation was temporarily broken off. The situation had rapidly deteriorated to the point that the proposed attack was virtually futile. Two pontoon bridges had since been established both upstream and downstream of the Ludendorff Bridge; a 25-ton reinforced heavy pontoon bridge about five miles south (upstream) of the Ludendorff Bridge at Linz and a treadway span on floats some 137m north (downstream) of it. Both spans were fully operational by 11 March and the rate of reinforcement within the American bridgehead correspondingly escalated.

Bartels, seeing the probable sacrifice of his men as no longer justified, opted to attempt other methods of destroying the bridges, floating explosive charges down the river though they failed to have any real effect. The German group armed with Italian chariots – *Maiale Gruppe Lehmann* – had even been earmarked for an attack against the bridge though this idea amounted to nothing as they finally arrived on 17 March; the day that the SS frogmen launched a near-suicidal operation and the day that the bridge finally collapsed. The newly-established rocket battery *SS Werfer Abteilung 500* based at Hellendoorn, Holland fired eleven V2s at the bridge as the *Maiale* were being unloaded. Though the huge rockets also missed their target, the battered bridge finally buckled and crashed into the Rhine. Dönitz claimed triumph for his men, insisting to Hitler that the various explosive attacks launched had cumulatively deteriorated the span's condition to the point that it failed. Hitler in turn congratulated the SS V2 unit for their destruction of the Ludendorff Bridge. In truth it was of no real consequence as the Rhine crossing was firmly secured and supplied by the pontoon bridges.

Nonetheless seven SS frogmen led by Schreiber persevered and entered the water in late afternoon on 17 March, this time their target the pontoon bridge at Linz and thus the final span capable of carrying vehicles. Each diver was armed with four plastic explosive charges though none made it as far as their intended target, coming under intense defensive fire almost as soon as they entered the water. The distance to the pontoon bridge was 17 kilometres in water that was only 7°C and by early the following morning four of them had been killed – two by the cold itself – and the Americans had managed to capture the remainder, including Schreiber.

Remagen remains only one part of the final slide towards utter German defeat. In mid-April Russian forces broke out of their Oder bridgehead and exploded across eastern Germany, headed for the prize of Berlin. Linsens had been used against Russian targets but to little real effect. *Maschinenobergefreiter* Norbert Keller, a veteran of 211 K-Flotilla, was among the Linsen crewmen that prepared for battle against the Red Army.

In the middle of December 1944 we had returned to Plön and in January 217 K-Flotilla was formed. The target for this flotilla was to be service in the Danube in Hungary. During the retreat of the German Army in the Budapest area the Danube bridges had fallen intact into enemy hands . . . We travelled by rail with our equipment from Plön to Gänserndorf near Vienna. There we spent two weeks in the village school before travelling by road to Balatonalmádi [on the northern fringe of Hungary's Lake Balaton – Author's Note]. There we stayed approximately a week – servicing the equipment. But careful! The eastern bank was already hostile. Then we travelled by truck through Székesfehérvár to Komárom at the 'knee of the Danube'. After several attempts we found no chance of success and we broke off and returned to Gänserndorf.

On 1 April 1943 we moved for the last time by train from Gänserndorf through Prague and Berlin to Plön. The journey took two and a half weeks. In the goods wagons we took many women and girls who were very frightened as it was only moments before the Russian Army would arrive in Gänserndorf. But these poor people were then found by German military police at a stop in Czechoslovakia and made to leave the train.[119]

The *K-Verbände Marine Einsatz Kommandos* were also active in destroying several Russian bridges, though the juggernaut that was the Red Army rolled on remorselessly. Defeat was inevitable, yet the men of the *K-Verbände* continued to sell their lives dearly with their commando raids against their triumphant foe. By 29 April some twenty units were controlled by MEK60/*Lederstumpf* – no longer strictly divided between east and west in the final confusion – the headquarters established 7km west of Hagenow, though preparing to retreat to the north in the event of the inevitable enemy breakthrough of thin German lines. Operations were recorded at the end of April in the west and east, against bridges in Bremen and the Lauenburg bridgehead as well as reconnaissance of Russian positions between Werbellin and Altwarp by MEK85. Eventually the units that were formed and then disbanded on an almost daily *ad hoc* basis on all fronts lost the grinding war of attrition, whatever remains they left behind becoming amalgamated in the bewildering array of makeshift units thrown together to hold the line. The *K-Verbände Marine Einsatz Kommandos* undoubtedly continued to show the same flair and daring that they had displayed since their inception in 1944, though the triumphs achieved have largely been lost in the tragedy of a crushed nation in its death throes.

CHAPTER THIRTEEN

Norway, the Final Citadel
The K-Verbände *in Scandinavia*

While real enemies assailed German-held Europe from east, west and south, Hitler remained obsessed with the phantom threat to the Scandinavian sector of his Thousand-Year Reich throughout the course of the Second World War. The conquest of Norway and Denmark had secured the Reich's northern flank and, of more immediate importance, the vital Norwegian port of Narvik. Set amidst the natural splendour of Norway's northern reaches, the isolated Arctic town was strategically unremarkable apart from the dock through which tons of iron-ore were shipped to Germany and its war machine from the Swedish Gallivore mines.

The European gateway to Norway was Denmark, the first of the Scandinavian countries to have been conquered by Germany in 1940. In August 1944 365 K-Flotilla, equipped with Negers, was transferred to the country, though their tenure was brief, relieved by the reformed 361 K-Flotilla at the month's end and returned to Suhrendorf for Marder training. The newly equipped 361 K-Flotilla arrived at Skaw on 1 September, moving onwards to Asaa 40km south of Frederikshaven ten days later. Bibers of 263 K-Flotilla were the first midgets to arrive in Norway, thirty of them landed at Kristiansand South from Travemünde on 9 October.

Over the next few weeks several *K-Verbände* units arrived in Denmark and Norway as well as German possessions in the North Sea. By 2 November the disposition of *K-Verbände* units within Scandinavia as approved by Dönitz was as follows: in northern Norway there were approximately sixty Bibers and sixty Marders in the area between Westfjord and the Lofoten Islands; sixty Molchs and thirty Bibers were based in southern Norway, mainly around Oslo and Kristiansand South (the Bibers were planned to move toward Narvik though Dönitz blocked the move); in Denmark, sixty Bibers at Aarhus and Oesterhurup were headed to the west coast of Jutland, sixty Marders and twelve Hechts were stationed at Asaa. Within German held North Sea territory there were thirty Molchs in Heligoland, thirty more at Borkum and thirty Bibers within the Ems estuary at Norden and sixty Linsens at Fedderwardsiel.

To control the far-flung *K-Verbände* units within Scandinavia K.z.S. Friedrich Böhme initially assumed command of units in Denmark and Norway in an almost 'caretaker' position, the post soon divided between K.z.S. Düwel in Aarhus, Denmark (*Kommando Stab Skagerrak*) and K.z.S. Beck (*Kommando Stab Nord*) in Oslo, Norway, while Böhme headed south to the Mediterranean. Beck and his staff surveyed the coastline that they had been charged to defend, estimating that they would require at least forty flotillas to effectively ward off an Allied attack on the labyrinthine waterways.

The deteriorating situation in Holland during December 1944 meant that the Molchs from Heligoland, Bibers from Norden and Linsens from Fedderwardsiel were all transferred for use in the Scheldt, depleting the *K-Verbände* presence in the northern theatre. Further losses were made when, after the threatened shortage of volunteers to man the *K-Verbände* weapons during January 1945, the dozen Hechts at Asaa were withdrawn to Germany and their crews transferred to the Seehund training unit before posted to Holland as part of Brandi's 5 K-Division.

During February 1945 Düwel and his adjutant Wenzel were detached from *Kommando Stab Skagerrak* for duty with the *Kommando Stab zbV* which would soon be responsible for operations within German waterways that had been taken by Allied forces. Specifically, Düwel was asked to study operational employment of *K-Verbände* forces in the Danube, Drau and Oder. Control of his Scandinavian region was meanwhile passed directly to Heye's General Operations branch.

The Scandinavian elements of the *K-Verbände* spent the rest of the war in what transpired to be needless reshuffling of units and redeployment to different defensive areas. The men were involved in constant training and equipment maintenance in preparation for the expected final battle. The tactics that the *K-Verbände* evolved for Norway were relatively simple. The Biber and Molch midget submarines were largely held at central depots ashore. In the case of reported invasion, they were to be brought forward to previously-prepared launching sites and put to sea to predetermined areas of operation. The Bibers and Molchs were assigned the protection of fjord and harbour entrances. Once

224

established in a defensive line across the waterway they would await the oncoming enemy and then launch their attacks. By that stage the enemy should have suffered casualties, and so the place of the midgets would then taken by the Linsen flotillas who would compound the attack with their explosive motorboats. Should any Allied ships break through; the last line of defence was the human torpedo, Marder flotillas operating within the shallow waters of the harbours themselves. Alongside the centrally-stored Bibers there is evidence to suggest that some craft were 'farmed out' to outlying areas aboard *Marinefahrpramm* and also using the U-boat depot-ship ss *Black Watch* as temporary base and repair station, until the latter's sinking on 4 May 1945 by British carrier-borne Avenger and Wildcat aircraft.

Coupled with the *K-Verbände* flotillas in Norway were also several *Marine Einsatz Kommando* units that were attached to the K-divisions, operating as loosely organised mobile commandos along the Norwegian coastline, often in conjunction with the Security Police (*Sicherheitspolizei*, or SiPo) again hinting at a stronger bond with the SS organisation than otherwise noted.

By the end of hostilities in May 1945 eight flotillas, organised into four divisions and comprising approximately eighty-five officers and 2,500 men had been deployed in Norway. The command structure and stationing at the end of hostilities was thus:

1 K-Division (Kplt Woerdeman in Narvik)
K-Flot.1/265 Engeløy Island (Oblt.z.S. Ploger with 120 men and thirteen Bibers). This unit was in the process of transferring to Oslofjord when the war ended.
K-Flot.2/265 Engeløy (Oblt.z.S. Doose with eighty men and eleven Bibers, at Lødingen two Bibers were also surrendered aboard the vessel *MFP233*).
K-Flot.1/215 Ullvik (L.z.S. Hein with 100 men and thirty Linsens).
K-Flot.1/362 Brenvik (L.z.S. Gotthard with seventy men and twenty Marders).
MEK35 Harstad (Kaptlt. Breusch and sixty men).

2 K-Division (Oblt.z.S. Schuirmann in Trondheim)
K-Flot.1/216 Selvenes (Oblt.z.S. Krause with 100 men and thirty-six Linsens).
K-Flot.2/216 Namsos (Oblt.z.S. Thum with eighty men and twenty-four Linsens).

K-Flot.1/267 Kristiansand (Oblt.z.S. Sengbiel with ninety men and fifteen Bibers).

K-Flot.2/267 Molde (Kaptlt. Sommer with ninety men and fifteen Bibers).

(Two Bibers were also surrendered aboard *MFP224* and two more aboard *MFP241*).

MEK30 Molde (Kaptlt. Gegner with eighty men).

3 K-Division (K.K. Silex in Bergen)

K-Flot.1/362 Herdla (Oblt.z.S. Koch with seventy men and twenty Marders).

K-Flot.2/362 Krokeidet (seventy men and twenty Marders).

K-Flot.2/215 Flatöy (Oblt.z.S. Schadlich with 100 men and thirty Linsens).

K-Flot 415 Sola (Oblt.z.S. Breckvoldt with 200 men and thirty Molchs).

K-Flot 1/263 Höllen/Tangvall (Oblt.z.S. Erdmann with ninety men and fifteen Bibers).

K-Flot 2/263 Tangen (Oblt.z.S. Thieme with ninety men and fifteen Bibers).

4 K-Division (Kplt Velguth in Oslo)

K-Flot 1/366 Stavern (Oblt.z.S. Lehmann with sixty men and fifteen Marders).

K-Flot 2/366 Maagerö (Oblt.z.S. Heinsium with forty-five men and fifteen Marders).

Ultimately the bulk of the German forces in Norway remained unused and those *K-Verbände* units still in Scandinavia on 8 May 1945 surrendered without seeing action. While many of the weapons were scuttled before the arrival of British or Norwegian troops, the vast majority were handed over to the victors at their holding depots for later scrapping.

There remains little evidence of the *K-Verbände* presence in Scandinavia, though occasionally the skeletal remains of a Molch or Biber are discovered either at sea in the frigid fjord waters or buried on land after their dismantling in 1945. In Narvik itself rests the remains of a Marder within the maritime museum. Only the nose and the Plexiglas dome remain largely intact – that portion of the scrapped human torpedo 'commandeered' by a Norwegian woman who wanted to use it to plant flowers in!

Elsewhere the remains of the *K-Verbände* were likewise being handed over to the victorious Allies. Many craft were scuttled, including the three Seehunds at Dunkirk though these were swiftly salvaged and later repaired and recommissioned into the French Navy for extensive trials. Curiously a Seehund also now rests off Key West in United States waters. Taken as a war prize by the US Navy it was tested and crewed by its two original complement being held as POWs before being sunk in gunnery trials in the balmy Floridian waters.

The Allies soon discovered several prototype vehicles in development for use by the *K-Verbände*. These included many varieties of improved *Sturmboot* and explosive motorboats, one even propelled by a V1 flying-bomb's propulsion unit, as well as several varieties of midget submarine. There were fresh designs such as the Delphin (Dolphin), Schwertwal (Killer Whale) and large tracked Seeteufel (Sea Devil) as well as improved versions of the Biber and Seehund types. The Hai (Shark) human torpedo was found at AG Weser's shipyard in Bremen, a huge elongated version of the Marder that stretched to 12.7m in length with increased batteries allowing a projected combat radius of 90 nautical miles. None had progressed beyond the prototype testing stage and remain historical curiosities.

Heye's men were ushered into captivity alongside their comrades from all of Germany's defeated services, the history of the *K-Verbände* soon relegated to little more than historical footnotes in works that recount Germany's naval war between 1939 and 1945. This must be due largely to the lack of success enjoyed by the *K-Verbände*. While British, Italian and even Japanese midget submarine operations are often deservedly recounted for their indisputably heroic achievements, the German effort provokes far less recognition. Likewise of their explosive motorboats, human torpedoes and frogmen, the latter who enjoyed comparatively greater success than their service colleagues.

So why did Germany's *K-Verbände* not achieve greater triumph? It certainly was not through a lack of fighting spirit or ardour amongst its largely volunteer members. Nor, arguably, can it solely be put down to the often-primitive machinery with which they were expected to take the fight to the enemy. The weapons made available to the *K-Verbände* ranged from the stopgap measure of the Neger human torpedo to the sophisticated design of the Seehund, a full range of craft spanning the gap between the two. Perhaps the real flaw lies in their commitment to action. While the Italian and Allied Second World War pioneers in the use of midget delivery vehicles utilised them for special

227

actions, more akin to commando operations than conventional naval war, the *Kriegsmarine* quickly gravitated to the use of their *K-Verbände* as another weapon in the arsenal of a conventional navy, pitting the human torpedo against all that the Allies could muster. The German High Command perceived them as a *defensive* weapon as opposed to the specialised *offensive* weapons employed by the other nations. Indeed the Seehunds were deployed in the same role as conventional coastal U-boats and in fact could have had similar success if given the time to iron out design and training flaws and to allow the requisite numbers to be employed. Arguably the sole weapon within the KvB arsenal that could really have caused problems for the Allies seems to have been the Seehund. Though lacking in range, it carried the same weapon load as the Type XXIII U-boat yet only took two men to man and a fraction of the construction time. They were extremely difficult to detect using sonar and also difficult to destroy with conventional depth charges, though the crew no doubt suffered more than their boat under such attacks. If German planners had begun work a year ahead of time on the designs that would eventually lead to the Seehund they could have been deployed against the massed shipping of the D-Day invasion fleet for what could conceivably been devastating results. However, such was not the case and remains in the 'what if' category of alternative history. There also continues to be great misunderstanding about the nature of the men that crewed the weapons of the *K-Verbände*. This is probably not helped by books such as Jack Higgins' wonderful – though fictional – *The Eagle Has Landed* that has men sentenced to death operating the human torpedoes from the British Channel Islands. This image of criminality has continued to dog the men of the *K-Verbände*, though it has a grain of fact to it. While it is possible to state that most men enlisted into the *K-Verbände* were either volunteers or ordinary conscripts, there remain anecdotes of some under military court sentence used in the human torpedoes, such as several of Skorzeny's SS men. Thus the subject is not crystal clear, though the use of criminals in the *K-Verbände* ranks does not appear to have been deliberate policy.

There also remains the label of 'suicide squads' so often used in relation to the *K-Verbände*. To take the most obvious example, between April 1944 and April 1945 the Neger and Marder human torpedoes had mounted twelve operational sorties. Of the 264 machines involved 162 were lost, taking at least 150 pilots to their graves. Clearly, through what we have learned of the *K-Verbände*, they were not originally intended as suicide weapons or missions as is so often claimed. However, though perhaps not envisaged as such, they nonetheless were lethal to a majority of their volunteer operators. Moreover, to additionally confuse the issue, the following extract (also quoted elsewhere in this book) from a conference between Hitler and Dönitz further muddies the waters:

18 January – 16.00: An unexpected storm interfered with the success of the first operation by Seehund midget submarines. However, valuable experience was gained and the boats continue to operate. Because of the long distances involved, other small battle weapons *can be used only as suicide weapons*, and then only if the weather is suitable, as they would otherwise not even reach the area of operations. Despite these limitations, all efforts will be continued to interfere with enemy supply traffic to Antwerp.[120]

Indeed Padfield notes in his book *War Beneath the Sea* that during Eberhard Godt's interrogation (Dönitz's subordinate and Chief Of Operations for the U-boat service) he imparted the view that the midgets were seen as 'expendable' – militarily cheap to produce and man.[121]

Ultimately it could be said that if German naval strategic planning had allowed for the kind of development of midget weapon ideas and techniques necessary before the stimulus of a 'backs to the wall' defensive fight forced there hand, then many things could have been different for the *Kriegsmarine* and particularly the *K-Verbände*. However, the rigidity of thought and conservative nature that marked the *Kriegsmarine* ensured that there was no fostering of such 'out of the box' thinking, the results of which in Britain had allowed the creation of such weapons as the 'bouncing bomb', the Leigh-Light and numerous 'funnies' employed by the Armoured Corps. Germany by no means lacked such individual thinkers that could have developed special naval weapons, but history shows that, bereft of official support from military leaders, any such advances for the German *K-Verbände* remain purely conjectural.

Appendix

K-Verbände Flotillas & Organisation of the **K-Verbände** Staff
Admiral der *K-Verbände*: V.A. Hellmuth Heye

Chef des Stabes: F.K. Fritz Frauenheim

Führungsstab (General Operations)
This central General Operations branch exercised control over five K-Verbände Staffs (Kommandostäbe) or operational headquarters that were located in or near the theatre of operations.

Admiralstabsoffiziere (F1): Kaptlt. Klaus Thomsen 7/44–5/45
F1a: Kaptlt. Wache 8/44–5/45 (representing all MEKs)
Sdf.Kaptlt. Michael Opladen 4/44–5/45 (Foreign Political Advisor)
Kaptlt. Friedrich-Wilhelm Schmidt
F3: Kaptlt. Erich Habelt (Signals)
F4: Kaptlt. Mohrstedt 5/44–4/45 (Intelligence)
Kaptlt. Johann Krieg 8/44–5/45 (Consultant for weaponry and
    midget operations)
Oblt. Hans Gregor
Oblt. Wolf Gericke
Oblt. Friedrich Wendel
Oblt. Kurt Scheifhacken
Oblt. Onaas 8/44–5/45 (Consultant for surface weaponry, S-boats)

Engineering Chief of Staff: Kaptlt. Rüdiger Burkhards 7/44–5/45
Lt (Ing.) Horst Haug
Lt (Ing.) Otto Wolf

Care & Welfare Officer: Kaptlt. Hans-Konrad Perkuhn
National Socialist Ideological Officer: K.K. Friedrich von Holzhusen
Signals Officer: Oblt. Felix Leffin

Press Officer: Oblt. Dr. Wolfgang Frank

Message Officer (*Kurieroffizier*): Oblt. Ilibert von Du fresne von Hohenesche

Quartiermeisterstab
Responsible for the provision of supplies, weapons and reinforcements for the Lehrkommandos and the MEKs. Also responsible for their administration and technical development of their weaponry.
Quartiermeister: F.K. Dahle 2/45–5/45
Administration: K.K. Wicke 1/45–5/45
– Ordnance: Kaptlt. (Ing.) Kattau 7/44–5/45
– Sanitätsoffizier: MStArzt. Dr. Hans-Joachim Richert 4/44–5/45
– Sperrwaffenoffizier (Mines): Kaptlt. Moosmann 6/44–5/45
Torpedoes: Oblt. Scheifhake
– Verwaltungsoffizier: K.K. Lüdke 5/44–1/45
Intendant: MObStInt. Bleese 4/44–5/45
MObStInt. Dr von Harling 1/45–5/45
Technische Abteilung (Research) – K.K. Herbert Burckhardt 4/44–5/45
– Kaptlt. (Ing.) von Rakowski 8/44–5/45
Personnel Office: Oblt. M A Tegtmeyer 2/44–5/45
Gericht des Admirals der K-Verbände: MobStRichter Wiegand

Primary Headquarters & Training Establishments
K-Verbände Headquarters – Hotel in Timmendorferstrand (*Strandkoppel*)
HQ K-Regt (Mot) – Lübeck (*Steinkoppel*)
Personnel distribution centre – Bad Sülze/Rostock (*Schwarzkoppel*)
Map Section (*Kosmos*) – Schöneberg (*Raumkoppel*)
Lehrkommando 200 – Priesterbeck/Waren-Müritz (*Grünkoppel*)
Lehrkommando 200 – Plön (*Netzkoppel*)
Lehrkommando 250 – Lübeck/Schlutup (*Blaukoppel*)
Biber concentration area – Cuxhaven/Oxstedt (*Fischkoppel*)
Biber concentration area – Wilhelmshaven (*Graukoppel*)
Lehrkommando 300 – Neustadt (*Neukoppel*)
Lehrkommandos 350 and 400 – Suhrendorf/Eckernförde (*Dorfkoppel*)
Lehrkommando 600 and 700 – List (*Weisskoppel*)
MEK zbV – Monmark, Denmark (*Gelbkoppel*)

Regional *K-Verbände* Staffs and *K-Verbände* Divisions

Kommando Stab West
(Sengwarden)
K.z.S. Friedrich Böhme 6/44–10/44
Operations Officer: Oblt. Hilliger

Kommando Stab South
Formed August 1944.
(Levico, Italy)
(later 6 *K-Verbände* Division – Pola)
K.z.S. Werner Hartmann 8/44–10/44
K.z.S. Friedrich Böhme 10/44–5/45
MVO: K.K. Hugo Gerdts
(G-Ops) Kaptlt. Günther Thiersch
(Signals) Oblt. Günther Hering
(Interpreter) Lt Ritter Emil von Thierry
Supply Officer: *Oberfähnrich* Wilhelm Gehrke
(Commanded Lehrkommando 600 & 700, *Maiale Gruppe Lehmann*, 213, 411, 363 and 611 K-Flotillas, MEK80. Later additional units 612, 364, 613 K-Flotillas and MEK71 and Gruppe Dexling)

Kommando Stab Holland
Formed in September 1944 and responsible for all K-Verbände *operations west of the Elbe.*
(Rotterdam, depots in Groningen and Utrecht)
(later 5 *K-Verbände* Division Ijmuiden):
K.z.S. Werner Musenberg 8/44–3/45
F1: K.K. Josefi.
(Commanded Seehunds, one Molch Flotilla, 211 and 214 K-Flotillas and MEK60)

Kommando Stab North
Formed November 1944 in purely defensive role against possible Allied attack on Norway.
(Kristiansand)
Main headquarters Kristiansand, subsidiary in Narvik.
K.z.S. Wilhelm Beck 10/44–5/45
(later 1 *K-Verbände* Division – Narvik)
Einsatzleiter Kaptlt. Graf Victor von Reventlow-Crimine
Leader K Stützpunkt Stavanger: Kaptlt. Bosümer
Leader Sengwarden Branch: Kaptlt. Wilfried Kartsen

(Originally formed as 3. *Marinekraftwageneinsatzabteilung* in Fontainbleau in August 1942 under control of Naval High Command Paris – *H.K.Mar.* Transferred to *K-Verbände* in October 1944)
5. Kraftwageneinsatzabteilung: F.K. (Ing.) Sandel 7/44–10/44
In October 1944 these were reorganised into the Motorised K-Regt, comprising four subunits and tasked with supplying all *K-Verbände* units with vehicles and drivers. The reorganised Regiment (its headquarters located at *Steinkoppel* in Lübeck) comprised originally of four battalions; 1 and 2 Btns. at Bad Schwartau; 3 and 4 Btns. at Flensburg. By March 1945 5 and 6 Btns. were forming in Wilhelmshaven. Each complete battalion comprised about 100 vehicles each, divided into three companies – light, medium and heavy – and equipped with Opel-Blitz 3-ton trucks, Saurer 5-ton trucks and tractors and 12-ton trailers respectively. Each company formed a completely self-sufficient unit with HQ Staff, orderly room, kitchen, workshops and wireless trucks. Upon attachment to an active *K-Verbände* Flotilla the companies were operationally combined with the unit in question, though administrative control rested with the Regiment.
K-Regt (Mot):
Commander: F.K. (Ing.) Heinrich Illert 10/44–5/45
Staff Officers: K.K. (Ing.) Helmut Eddicks
K.K. (Ing.) Triestech

Unit commands:
K.K.(Ing.) Dipl. Ing. Bräkow
K.K.(Ing.) Helmut Eddicks
K.K.(Ing.) Grathoff
K.K.(Ing.) Heinrich Hartwig
K.K.(Ing.) Liebing
K.K.(Ing.) Friedrich-Karl Schwarz
In March 1945 4. Kraftwageneinsatzabteilung was subordinated to the Kommando der *K-Verbände*. This unit was renamed Marinekraftfahrabteilung z.b.V.OKM in May 1945.
Kraftwageneinsatzabteilung: F.K.(Ing.) Banditt – 11/44–4/45
Marinekraftfahrabteilung z.b.V.OKM: F.K.(Ing.) Banditt 5/45

Training commands and K-Verbände Flotillas

Lehrkommando	Kaptlt. Ulrich Kolbe	7/44	
200	Kaptlt. Helmut	7/44–	Priesterbeck/
	Bastian	5/45	Waren/Plön

This unit developed from the former Brandenburg Regiment's *Küstenjäger Abteilung* commanded by *Rittmeister* von Seydlitz. The *Kriegsmarine* took at least a major portion of this specialist raiding unit, part of its training staff and at least a dozen Linsen explosive boats.

The initial cadre of Lehrkommando 200 was established in June 1944 on the south bank of the River Trave between Lübeck and Travemünde, named Blaukoppel. Kaptlt. Kolbe commanded the training unit for the prospective Linsen pilots and crew. Among the fifty permanent staff of the Lehrkommando (at least twenty of them Brandenburgers) was Oblt. Taddey, a wireless expert, who also joined Kolbe, his experience crucial for the operation of the remote-controlled explosive Linsen. A small ancillary Linsen training centre was also established on Lake Müritz, named *Grünkoppel* and comprising around 100 men and six Linsens.

In June 1944 Kolbe accompanied 211 K-Flotilla to the mouth of the River Orne. The 250 men and thirty-two Linsens were committed to action, though they achieved nothing for the loss of all but eight of their boats.

In August of that year Lehrkommando 200 moved to Plön (*Seekoppel*) where Kaptlt. Bastian took charge, Kolbe concentrating on the technical development of the Linsen, until his transfer to K-Verbände Süd as director of operations for 213 K-Flotilla.

During the period August to November 1944 Lehrkommando 200 received a monthly supply of 300 explosive and control Linsens, allowing the quick formation of other flotillas to follow 211 into battle.

The final change to command of the training unit occurred in January 1945 when Bastain was transferred to Holland to direct operations, his place taken on the ground by Kaptlt. Witte of SKL though Bastian appears to have remained the nominated Senior Officer.

211 K-Flotilla	Oblt. Helmut Plikat	4/44	Linsen
212 K-Flotilla	Kaptlt. Helmut Hinte	7/44–5/45	Linsen
213 K-Flotilla	Kaptlt. Dr Ernst Rosefeldt	7/44–5/45	Linsen
214 K-Flotilla	Kaptlt. Ludwig Vellguth	11/44	Linsen
215 K-Flotilla	Kaptlt. Vellguth	11/44–5/45	Linsen
216 K-Flotilla	Oblt. Erich Doerpinghaus		Linsen
217 K-Flotilla	Oblt. Dr Ulrich Müller-Voss		Linsen

218 K-Flotilla	Kaptlt. Christoph Schiekel	11/44– 5/45	Linsen
219 K-Flotilla	Kaptlt. Kiehn	1/45– 5/45	Linsen
220 K-Flotilla	Oblt.z.S. Seipold		Linsen
221 K-Flotilla	Oblt.z.S. Ekkehard Martinssen		Linsen
Lehrkommando 250	K.K. Hans Bartels	8/44– 5/45	Lübeck – Schlutup

Trainers: OL.z.S. Dieter Erdmann 8/44–9/44

Evolving from the Biber school at *Blaukoppel* which was officially taken over after Lehrkommando 200's move to Plön in August 1944, this training command was headed by the redoubtable Bartels. An original strength of thirty men and two Bibers soon grew to nearly 300 men with between forty and fifty Bibers

261 K-Flotilla	Kaptlt. Friedmar Wolters (relieving Bartels who was the flotilla's founder/ commander)	8/44– 5/45	Biber
	Kaptlt. Schmidt	1/45	Biber
262 K-Flotilla	Kaptlt. Richard Sommer	1/45– 4/45	Biber
263 K-Flotilla	Oblt.z.S. Dieter Erdmann	9/44– 5/45	Biber
264 K-Flotilla	Kaptlt. Siegfried Timper	9/44– 5/45	Biber
	Oblt.z.S. Walter Fahje	10/44– 2/45	Biber
265 K-Flotilla	Oblt. Plöger	2/45– 5/45	
266 K-Flotilla	Oblt.z.S. Udo Heckmann	10/44– 3/45	Biber
	Kaptlt. Herbert Wagner	12/44– 4/45	Biber
267 K-Flotilla	Kaptlt. Richard Sommer	4/45– 5/45	Biber

268 K-Flotilla	Kaptlt. Joachim Steltzer	?/45– 5/45	Biber
269 K-Flotilla	Kaptlt. Kurt Halledt-Holzkapfel	1945	
270 K-Flotilla	Unknown		
Lehrkommando 300	Lt Kiep	6/44	
	Kaptlt. Hermann Rasch	7/44– 2/45	Neustadt (*Neukoppel*)
	F.K. Albrecht Brandi	2/45– 5/45	

Instructors: Kaptlt. Klaus Ohling 12/44–5/45
This Kommando dealt with the training of Seehund crew, using the unsuccessful Hecht design as a model with which to begin work. Formed at Neustadt (*Neukoppel*) in September 1944.

	Flotilla Engineer: K.K.(Ing.) Erhardt (later CO *Graukoppel*)	
311 K-Flotilla	Oblt.z.S. Felix Schaefer	Hechte
312 K-Flotilla	Oblt. Jürgen Kiep	Seehund
313 K-Flotilla	Kaptlt. Borm	Seehund
314 K-Flotilla	Unknown	Seehund
Lehrkommando 350	Kaptlt. Heinz Franke	7/44– 3/45	Suhrendorf
	Kaptlt. Horst Kessler	3/45– 5/45	

Commanded by the Neger veteran Oblt.z.S. Johann Krieg, this training unit handled the Neger and Marder human torpedoes. It grew from the former independent training school that shared *Blaukoppel* with Lehrkommando 200's Linsens, and was formally identified as a separate kommando in August 1944, after which Kaptlt. Franke took charge.

361 K-Flotilla	Oblt.z.S. Johann Krieg	3/44– 7/44	
	Oblt.z.S. Heinrich Frank	7/44– 5/45	Neger

362 K-Flotilla	Oblt.z.S. Leopold Koch	4/44–4/45	Neger
363 K-Flotilla	Oblt.z.S. Siegfried Wetterich	9/44–5/45	Neger
364 K-Flotilla	Oblt.z.S. Peter Berger	7/44–5/45	Marder
365 K-Flotilla	Oblt.z.S. Hans-Georg Barop	7/44–5/45	Marder
366 K-Flotilla	Oblt.z.S. Paul Heinsius	12/44–5/45	Marder
Lehrkommando 400	Kaptlt. Heinz Franke	9/44–3/45	Suhrendorf
	Kaptlt. Horst Kessler	3/45–5/45	

Formed from Lehrkommando 350 in September 1944, this training establishment was set up as an independent school for the Molch pilots at Suhrendorf under Kaptlt. Franke.

411 K-Flotilla	Oblt. Heinrich Hille	7/44	Molch
412 K-Flotilla	Oblt.z.S. Kuno Arens	8/44–11/44	Molch
412/1 K-Flotilla	Oblt.z.S. Kuno Arens	11/44–4/45	Molch
	Kaptlt. Wolfgang Martin	4/45–5/45	Molch
412/2 K-Flotilla	Oblt.z.S. Wolfgang Martin	11/44–4/45	Molch
413 K-Flotilla	Oblt.z.S. Lothar Vieth	7/44–5/45	Molch
414 K-Flotilla	Kaptlt. Fritz Heinz		Molch
	Kaptlt. Graf Reventlow-Criminie	7/44–9/44	Molch
415 K-Flotilla	Oblt.z.S. Pülschen	9/44–5/45	Molch
416 K-Flotilla	Oblt.z.S. Friedrich Breckwoldt	11/44–5/45	Molch

417 K-Flotilla	Oblt.z.S. Wilhelm ter Glane	4/45– 5/45	Molch
Lehrkommando 600	Kaptlt. Heinz Schomburg	4/44– 9/44	
	Kaptlt. Ernst Wilhelm Witt	9/44– 10/44	
	Kaptlt. Heinz Schomburg	11/44– 5/45	

This unit was formed in April 1944 at the *Decima Mas* school at Sesto Calende. Prior to its official recognition by the *K-Verbände* a number of Germans had been trained by Italian instructors at the establishment, about thirty members of the *K-Verbände* graduating between March and April 1944. Upon their passing out the trained *Kriegsmarine* men were segregated from the Italian personnel of the base, quartered in separate billets in the seaplane base.

This segregation became more pronounced after the Lehrkommando's official formation in April. The Italians continued using the Sesto Calende school, though kept strictly apart from the German cadre, while Lehrkommando 600 expanded its size and opened a further training centre in Stresa during May 1944 for their exclusive use. It was this new centre's opening that ratified the training Kommando's official creation, the schools given subsidiary numbers to the umbrella command: that at Sesto Calende recognised as Lehrkommando 601, that at Stresa as Lehrkommando 602.

Lt Bloomenkamp was appointed OC and Chief Instructor of Lehrkommando 601 under the command of Kaptlt. Schomburg, though Bloomenkamp was moved to the same position in Lehrkommando 602 in May, his previous post taken by Oblt. Frenzemeyer transferred from Germany.

In October 1944 Lehrkommando 600 was transferred to List (*Weisskoppel*) on the German North Sea island of Sylt due to the rapidly deteriorating military situation, both subsidiary branches – 601 and 602 – absorbed into the parent body. Only a small *Abnahmekommando* remained in Sesto Calende, which later formed part of the supplies section of the newly formed Kommando-Stab Süd, responsible for taking delivery of new SMA and MTM boats supplied by Siai Marchetti and Cabi.

611 K-Flotilla 'Hitlerjugend'	Kaptlt. Wilhelm Ullrich	7/44– 4/45	Sturmboot

	Oblt.z.S. Frenzemeyer	4/45–5/45	
612 K-Flotilla	Kaptlt. Ernst Wilhelm Witt	11/44–5/45	Sturmboot
613 K-Flotilla	Oblt. Wilhelm Gerhardt	2/45–5/45	Sturmboot
614 K-Flotilla	Unknown		Sturmboot
615 K-Flotilla	Oblt.z.S. Friedrich Böttcher	3/45–5/45	Sturmboot
Lehrkommando 700	MStArzt. Dr. Wandel	6/44–1/45	*Kampf-schwimmer*
	K.K. Hermann Lüdke	1/45–5/45	*Kampf-schwimmer*

This unit provides the most complicated training structure to be seen within the *K-Verbände*, combining several different services within the German armed forces and intelligence apparatus. It was established at the end of March 1944, based at the swimming baths at Valdagno which the Italian *Decima Mas* used for the same purpose.

Kaptlt. Heinz Schomburg attempted to gain control of the baths for 'Einsatz und Ausbildung Süd' but encountered obstructions almost immediately as both the *Abwehr* and SS were also interested in the same project. By previous agreement between Kaptlt. Heinz Schomburg and the Italian Flotilla trainers, thirty Germans of the *K-Verbände* were already undergoing training at Valdagno, having begun in January 1944. In addition to these men and the Italians, there were fifteen members of the *Abwehr* and ten SS men as well who were training alongside the *Kriegsmarine* personnel.

The Italian Chief Instructor, Ten di V. Wolk, was in actuality eliciting such German interest in order to obtain a greater recognition and source of supply for his school which was largely ignored by the *Decima Mas* hierarchy.

Prior to April 1944, Von Wolk and *Oberfähnrich* Wurzian of the *Abwehr* trained the Germans of all three services. Wurzian resigned his *Abwehr* post immediately upon the formation of Lehrkommando 700. In turn Von Wolk trained the Italian swimmers separately, again the two nationalities kept segregated.

Valdagno covered the initial training of the recruits, another centre opened in May 1944 on the island of San Giorgio in Venice Lagoon and the headquarters for Lehrkommando 700 transferring to Venice also. The subsidiary centres were renumbered: Valdagno as Lehrkommando 704 and San Giorgio Lehrkommando 701. A further training centre at Bad Tölz in the swimming baths at the SS *Junkerschule* was named Lehrkommando 702.

The Venice units relocated to Sylt on 21 October 1944, Lehrkommando 704 following shortly afterward.

Lehrgangslager 701	Oblt. (MA) Strenge	6/44– 8/44	
St-Giorgio/ Venedig	Lt (MA) Gerhardt Kummer	9/44– 11/44	*Kampf- schwimmer*
Lehrgangslager 702 Bad Tölz	Oblt.z.S. Küsgen	7/44– 9/44	*Kampf- schwimmer*
Lehrgangslager 703 List	Unknown	12/44– 5/45	*Kampf- schwimmer*
Lehrgangslager 704 Valdagno	Oblt. (MA) Herbert Völsch	6/44– 11/44	*Kampf- schwimmer*

Lehrkommando 800 – For ground units

Marine Einsatz Kommandos
Inside the organisational structure of the *Abwehr* there lay the foundation of the *K-Verbände* MEKs. With the establishment of the *K-Verbände*, the MEKs that were passed over to Heye's control included the example used by the Hamburg *Abwehr*, the MAREI and MARKO, and in time other MEKs were formed using these as models.

MEK Ausb.Abt: KKMA Hermann Buschkämper 4/45–5/45

MEK MAREI (*Abwehr*)
Sdf KaptltdR. Michael Opladen

MEK Black Sea (*Abwehr*): K.K. Dr Armin Roth (ex leader of *Abwehr* unit Bergen) 6/41–7/43

MEK MARKO (*Abwehr* – renamed MEK20 in April 1944):
Sdf KaptltdR. Michael Opladen
Oblt.MA Broecker

MEK20: Oblt.MA Broecker 4/44–5/45

MEK30: KaptltMA Wilhelm Gegner 44–5/45

MEK35: Kaptlt Breusch 11/44–3/45
Kaptlt. Wolfgang Woerdemann 3/45–5/45

MEK40: KaptltMA Hermann Buschkämper 8/44–3/45
Oblt.MA Schulz 3/45–5/45

MEK60: Oblt.MAdR Hans-Friedrich Prinzhorn 3/44–5/45

MEK65: Oblt.z.S.dR Karl-Ernst Richert 5/44–5/45

MEK71: Oblt.MAdR Horst Walters

MEK80: KaptltMA Dr Waldemar Krumhaar 3/44–5/45

MEK85 Oblt.MA Ernst Wadenpfuhl 1/45–5/45

MEK90 Oblt.MAdR Heinz-Joachim Wilke ?–5/45

MEK z.b.V. K.z.S. Duwel 11 45–5/45
(See also **Kommando Stab zbV**)

Knight's Cross Winners of the *K-Verbände*

6/7/44 Walter Gerhold, *Schreiberobergefreiter*, Neger pilot 361 K-
  Flotilla.
8/7/44 Johann Krieg, Oblt.z.S., Chief 361 K-Flotilla.
5/8/44 Herbert Berrer, *Oberfernschreibmeister*, Neger pilot 361 K-
  Flotilla.
12/8/44 Alfred Vetter, Ltn (V) Group leader, 211 K-Flotilla.
26/8/44 K.z.S. Friedrich Böhme, *K-Verbände* Leader in France.
19/10/44 *Hauptmann* Friedrich Hummel, sometime frogman,
  Lehrkommando 700.
3/11/44 Kaptlt. Helmut Bastian, *Führer der Sprengbootflottille.*

Endnotes

1. *Capitano di Vascello* (Captain) Muriano had commanded the Italian midget service in 1940, Borghese, ex-commander of the submarine *Scire*, taking control later.
2. Cajus Bekker, *K-Men* (translated from . . . *und liebten doch das Leben*) (William Kimber: 1955), p. 18.
3. Ibid.
4. The Floating Dock was eventually destroyed by an X-Craft attack in 1944.
5. Quoted from Admiral Heye, in Bekker, *K-Men*, pp. 18–19.
6. Eberhard Rossler, *The U-Boat* (Arms & Armour Press: 1981), p. 285.
7. Bekker, *K-Men*, p. 29.
8. A lynchpin of the Gustav Line was Monte Cassino, now famous for the ferocious battle waged over it during 1944.
9. Wandel, a U-boat veteran, served as Medical Officer for the *Kleinkampfverbände* (*Verbandsarzt des Kleinkampverbändes*) and would later command its frogman arm.
10. Later, Seehund crew were given just Pervitin (amphetamines) and after several days of use hallucinations were common. Most crews opted to stop using this drug. The use of stimulants in the Second World War was not at all limited to the German Navy, or in fact the German armed services in general.
11. Ten of the trained pilots were persuaded by Krieg to remain in Germany as instructors for those recruits that would follow.
12. *Detailed Interrogation Report on Eight German Officer POW of Kommando Stab Süd, KdK*, ADM 204/12809, UK National Archives.
13. He made no sinkings in either of his U-boats and was killed on 20 April 1945.
14. *Preliminary report on the attack by German S.P.S. on Anzio anchorage – 21st April 1944*, ADM 199/873, UK National Archives.
15. Ibid.
16. Ibid.
17. Kuschke was later given the POW number N2466, listed by Allied Naval Intelligence as having crewed 'Human Torpedo 96'. Interestingly, the destroyer USS *Frederick C Davis* was committed off Anzio because she was equipped with special equipment in order to jam the control frequency of the German radio-directed glider bombs.

18. Unfortunately for Borghese's reputation and subsequent place in history, he had not only opted to continue fighting alongside German forces, but also began converting the *Decima Mas* into a largely land-based infantry formation. This was soon embroiled in the state of civil war that had erupted in Northern Italy, embarking on several bloody anti-partisan operations. Eventually, at the end of the conflict, with imprisonment looming despite his Gold Medal for Valour received years before, Borghese confined himself to Spain in self-imposed exile, which lasted until his death.

19. Cajus Bekker, *Swastika At Sea* (William Kimber: 1955), p. 133.

20. Brandenburger units that had originally been controlled by Canaris' *Abwehr* had been expanded during November 1942 into the Panzer Grenadier Division 'Brandenburg', after 1943 becoming little more than a regular *Wehrmacht* unit. However, in October 1944 the 'special combat educated' troops of PzGrenDiv Brandenburg were transferred to the newly formed SS-Jagdverbände 502 (Commando unit), and were from then on controlled by the RSHA.

21. ADM 204/12809, UK National Archives.

22. *United States Naval Administrative History of World War II #147-E*, Historical Section, COMNAVEU. 'Administrative History of U.S. Naval Forces in Europe, 1940–1946.' vol. 5. (London, 1946).

23. Interview with Walter Gerhold on record at the Explosion! Museum of Naval Firepower, Gosport, England.

24. Bekker, *K-Men*, pp. 48–9.

25. Ibid., p. 50.

26. Werner Schulz, *Im Kleinst U-Boot* (Der Deutsche Bibliothek: 1995), p. 24.

27. Recollection of Ken Davies (D/JX, 420469) from website regarding war memorials in Portsmouth, England: http://www.memorials.inportsmouth.co.uk/churches/cathedral/isis.htm.

28. *Seekriegsleitung Kriegstagebuch* (SKL KTB – Naval War Staff War Diary), Part A, Naval HQ, Berlin 1939 to 1945. NARA Microfilm T1022. 3/8/44, Author's records.

29. Ibid.

30. Ibid.

31. 'A Sacrifice Never Forgotten . . .', *Navy News* (27 August 2004), recollection of survivor AB Christopher Yorston.

32. Recollections of Norman Ackroyd. Taken from combined personal emails to the author and an account published on www.uboat.net.

33. Letters from Funk Haupt.Gefr. Helmut Deppmeier, Linsen pilot 211 K-Flotilla, dated 17/4/99 and 26/4/99. Courtesy of Maurice Laarman.

34. *Vestal* was repaired and later served in the Far East where she was sunk by kamikaze attack on 26 July 1945 off Phuket. It was the first such Japanese raid in the Indian Ocean and she was the last British warship loss of the Second World War.

35. *Newcastle Evening Chronicle*, 31 May 2004.

36. SKL KTB 16/8/44.

37. Apparently these Marders were non-submersible according to POW report in *Biber, Seehund, Marder – Interrogation Of Survivors Captured Between August 1944 and January 1945*, N.I.D. 1/PW/REP/15/45. While possibly they

were simply Neger torpedoes, there is also the possibility that they carried the improved breathing apparatus of the Marder and thus its designation.

38. Heinz Hubeler was the guest of a British television company at the restoration to working condition of the Biber '105' currently at Gosport's Royal Navy Submarine Museum. Parts of his story were later retold by his son Gerhard Hubeler.

39. Biber deliveries for 1944 were: May – 3; June – 6; July – 19; August – 50; September – 117; October – 73; November – 56; totalling 324 Bibers completed.

40. http://www.war-experience.org/collections/sea/alliedbrit/dalzel-job/

41. ADM 223/609, UK National Archives.

42. Bekker, *K-Men*, p. 77.

43. See Michael Jung, 'Sabotage unter Wasser – Die deutsche Kampfschwimmer im Zweitern Weltkrieg', *Militär & Geschichte*, Nr 20 (April/May 2005), p. 106.

44. Syskowitz was posthumously awarded the Knight's Cross for his actions and promoted to *Kapitän zur See*.

45. Cajus Bekker, . . . *Und liebten doch das Leben* (Wilhelm Heyne Verlag: 1973), p. 109.

46. Ibid., pp. 111–12.

47. Jak Mallmann Showell (ed.), *Führer Conferences On Naval Affairs* (Chatham Publishing: 2005), p. 421.

48. Molch production was as follows: June 1944 – 3; July – 38; August – 125; September – 110; October – 57; December – 28; January 1945 – 32; totalling 393 boats.

49. US National Archives (NARA) Ref: 12 page report, titled 'MOLCH' – ONE-MAN U-BOAT. INTERROGATION OF SURVIVORS.' 'N.I.D.I/ PW/REP/11/44'

50. SKL KTB 14/9/44.

51. DesRon 7 comprised USS *Plunkett*, DD 431, Flagship, Destroyer Division 13: USS *Benson, Mayo, Gleaves, Niblack* (Flagship), and Destroyer Division 14: USS *Madison, Lansdale, Hilary P. Jones*, and *Charles F. Hughes* (Flagship).

52. The notable exceptions would be Hecht and Seehund training, the former used as introduction to the latter. In addition, men who had served in human torpedoes were later reported as part of the commando MEK units.

53. Manfred Lau, 'Torpeoreiter – Ein kaum bekannte K-Verbändes-Ausbildung', *Schiff & Zeit/Panorama Maritime* Vol 50 (1999), pp. 48–52.

54. SKL KTB 11 October 1944.

55. *First Detailed Interrogation of Hoffmann, Wolfgang*; Admiralty Report, ADM 223/6019. UK National Archives.

56. The remainder of 363 Flotilla saw no more action, remaining with its transport unit in the concentration area until April 1945; Adm 204/12809, UK National Archives.

57. Recollection of Harald Sander, publishing on the Internet at http://www.memory2000.net/. Interviewed by Franjo Hülck.

58. Actual deliveries of the Hecht were as follows: 2 in May 1944, 1 in June, 7 in July and 43 in August.

59. Three Seehunds were constructed at Howaldt-Kiel, 136 at Schichau and 146 at Germaniawerft, totalling 285. The deliveries were as follows: 3 in September 1944, 35 in October, 61 in November, 70 in December, 35 in January 1945, 27 in February, 46 in March and 8 in April.

60. *Biber, Seehund, Marder – Interrogation Of Survivors Captured Between August 1944 and January 1945*, N.I.D. 1/PW/REP/15/45, UK National Archives.

61. Harald Sander, http://www.memory2000.net/.

62. Personal interview with Eugen Herold, Munich, December 2004.

63. Schulz, *Im Kleinst-U-boote*, p. 43.

64. Ibid., pp. 54–6.

65. Harald Sander, http://www.memory2000.net/.

66. SKL KTB, 6 October 1944.

67. SKL KTB, 9 October 1944.

68. While commander of this boat he had transferred Indian nationalist Subhas Chandra Bose to Japanese submarine *I-29* in the middle of the Ocean.

69. AIR15/272 'Small Battle Units (Kleinkampfverbände) – N.I.D. U.C. Report No.553.', UK National Archives.

70. USN interrogations, personal collection. The wreck was later surveyed and removed as a hazard to shipping in 2003. The salvagers were apparently surprised at the amount of ammunition aboard the ship.

71. 'Awards of Mention in Despatches to 6 officers and men of HM MLs 153 and 1402 for sinking German midget submarines in the North Sea Aug 1944–Aug 1945', ADM 1/30521, National Archives, Kew, England.

72. *Biber, Seehund, Marder – Interrogation Of Survivors Captured Between August 1944 and January 1945*, N.I.D. 1/PW/REP/15/45. UK National Archives.

73. 'Report on the sinking of two German Midget Submarines by BYMS 2213, 2141 and 2221' – Lt RNVR L S Hardy *BYMS2213*, ADM20/0/1286, UK National Archives.

74. 'Report on sinking of midget submarine', Lt RNR J Jobson, *BYMS2141*. ADM 20/0/1286, UK National Archives.

75. 'Nore Covering Minute – HMS *Curzon* Attacks On Midget Submarines On 26th December 1944', UK National Archives.

76. *Obersteuermannmaat* Hans August Witt, Matr.Hpt.Gefr. Friedrich Bursy, Matr.Ob.Gef. Adam, Ballin and Mertens were killed.

77. Bekker, *Swastika At Sea*, pp. 145–6.

78. ADM 1/24295 '*Recovery of German Midget Submarine And Torpedo. Dover. January 1945*' Report to Director of Torpedoes and Mining, UK National Archives.

79. *Recovery of German Midget Submarine And Torpedo*, UK National Archives.

80. Letter from Captain (S/M) Twelfth Submarine Flotilla to C-in-C Western Approaches, 19 April 1945, Subject – German Midget Submarine Biber Type – Trials. UK National Archives.

81. Ibid.

82. Showell (ed.), *Führer Conferences On Naval Affairs*, p. 423.

83. See Winston S Churchill, *The Second World War*: Vol V *Closing the Ring* (Cassell & Co.: 1954), pp. 354–8.

84. According to Jürgen Rohwer, *Axis Submarine Successes of World War Two* (Greenhill Books: 1999), it is unlikely the battleship was hit and the second explosion against the destroyer was more likely a depth charge dropped by the *Zharkij*. Also see Friedrich Ruge, *The Soviets As Naval Opponents* (USNI: 1979), p. 177.

85. C Rumpf, 'Les Castors Dans L'Arctique', *Navires & Histoire*, Vol 2 (March 2000), p. 77.

86. Hans Georg Hess, *Die Männer von U995* (Hess Press [self-published]: 1999), p. 16.

87. C Rumpf, 'Les Castors Dans L'Arctique', p. 79. Taken from 1980 letter from Zetzsche.

88. Anthony Martienssen, *Hitler And His Admirals* (E P Dutton & Co.: 1949), pp. 224–5.

89. *Biber, Seehund, Marder – Interrogation Of Survivors Captured Between August 1944 and January 1945*, N.I.D. 1/PW/REP/15/45.pp. 30–31, UK National Archives.

90. Schulz, *Im Kleinst U-Boot*, p. 79.

91. Ibid., p. 84.

92. Showell (ed.), *Führer Conferences On Naval Affairs*, p. 426.

93. Harald Sander, http://www.memory2000.net/.

94. Listed as German Radio Intercept – 'B-Meldung 1425a'.

95. One of the successful missions – to land four agents during mid-April south of Livorno – was retrospectively deemed a failure after it was discovered that they had actually been dropped behind German lines.

96. FDS 65/54 *German Small Battle Unit Operations*, UK National Archives.

97. 'Festung Pola' was commanded by KA Georg Waue, former Chief of Staff of the *Kriegsmarine*'s Aegean Command.

98. Klaus Mattes, *Die Seehunde – Klein U-Boote* (Verlag E.S. Mittler & Sohn: 1995), pp. 112, 113.

99. ObMasch Paul Vogel was later killed in an air-raid while on leave in Germany on 18 March 1945.

100. Bekker, . . . *und liebten doch das Leben*, pp. 150–1.

101. Harald Sander, http://www.memory2000.net/

102. 119 Squadron Logbook, AIR 27/910, UK National Archives.

103. ADM 1/30324, UK National Archives.

104. 254 Squadron Logbook, AIR27/1516, UK National Archives.

105. ADM 1/30324, UK National Archives.

106. Harald Sander, http://www.memory2000.net/

107. Horton was recommended to be mentioned in despatches, as were two other crewmen in relation to the two Seehund hunts.

108. AIR 27/1516 PRO, 254 Squadron, UK National Archives.

109. Rohwer, *Axis Submarine Successes*, p. 193n.

110. Mattes, *Die Seehunde*, p. 136.

111. ADM201/11 810 Sqdrn FAA Log, UK National Archives.

112. AIR27/910, UK National Archives.

113. Recollection of Ernst Etel, Linsen pilot of 211 K-Flotilla. Courtesy of Maurice Laarman.

114. Quoted in David Irving, *Hitler's War* (Avon Books: 1990), p. 781.

115. Showell (ed.), *Führer Conferences on Naval Affairs*, p. 459.
116. Ibid.
117. Sefton, Delmer, *Black Boomerang*, available online as *Black Propaganda – The World War Two Top Secret British Psychological Warfare Operation* at: http://www.seftondelmer.co.uk
118. Otto Skorzeny, *Wir Kämpften – wir verloren* (1962), p. 196. Quoted in Jung, 'Sabotage Unter Wasser, p. 130.
119. Letter from Norbert Keller to Maurice Laarman of 30 March 1987. Courtesy of Maurice Laarman.
120. Showell (ed.), *Führer Conferences On Naval Affairs*, p. 426.
121. Peter Padfield, *War Beneath The Sea* (Pimlico: 1995), p. 456, taken from interrogation of Adm Godt, 12/5/45, PRO ADM 1 17617.

Select Bibliography

Primary Sources

Biber, Seehund, Marder – Interrogation Of Survivors Captured Between August 1944 and January 1945, N.I.D. 1/PW/REP/15/45.

Biber, Seehund, Molch – Interrogation Of Survivors Captured Between August 1944 and January 1945, N.I.D. 1/PW/REP/15/45.

Detailed Interrogation Report on Eight German Officer POW of Kommando Stab Süd, KdK, ADM 204/12809, National Archives.

German Small Battle Unit Operations 1943–1945, FDS65/54, Foreign Documents Section, Naval Historical Branch, MOD, Whitehall (Revised August 1968).

German Torpedoes and Development of German Torpedo Control (Technical Staff Monographs) Underwater Weapons Department, Admiralty, U.W.O. 5314/50. 1951.

Seekriegsleitung Kriegstagebuch (SKL KTB – Naval War Staff), Part A, Naval HQ, Berlin 1939 to 1945. Nara Microfilm T1022.

United States Naval Administrative History of World War II #147-E, Historical Section, COMNAVEU, Administrative History of U.S. Naval Forces in Europe, 1940–1946. Vol. 5 (London, 1946)

Articles & Periodicals

Jung, Michael, 'Sabotage unter Wasser – Die deutsche Kampfschwimmer im Zweitern Weltkrieg', *Militär & Geschichte*, Nr 20 (April/May 2005).

Korten, H J, 'Die Brücken von Nimwegen', *Der Landser*, Volume 1760 (December 1991).

Lau, Manfred, 'Torpeoreiter – Ein kaum bekannte K-Verbändes-Ausbildung', *Schiff & Zeit/Panorama maritime* Vol 50 (1999).

Rumpf, C, 'Les Castors Dans L'Arctique', *Navires & Histoire*, Volume 2 (March 2000).

Selected Books

Bartels, Hans, *Tigerflagge heiss vor* (Deutscher Heimatverlag: 1941).

Bekker, C.D, *K-Men*, (translated from . . . *und liebten doch das Leben*) (William Kimber: 1955).

——, *Swastika at Sea* (William Kimber: 1953).

Bekker, C.D, *Und liebten doch das Leben* (paperback copy) (Wilhelm Heyne Verlag: 1973).

Blocksdorf, Helmut, *Das Kommando der K-Verbände der Kriegsmarine* (Motorbuch Verlag: 2003).

Delmer, Sefton, *Black Boomerang* (Secker & Warburg: 1962).

Dönitz, Karl, *Memoirs: Ten Years And Twenty Days* (Greenhill Books: 1990).

Fock, Harald, *Marine Kleinkampf-Mittel* (Koehlers Verlagsgesellschaft mbH: 1996).

Grabatsch, Martin, *Torpedoreiter – Sturmschwimmer, Sprengbootfahrer* (Verlag Welsermühl: 1979).

Hess, Hans-Georg, *Die Männer von U-995* (Hess-Press [self-published]: 1999).

Heye, Helmuth, *Marine-Kleinkampfmittel* (Wehrkunde: 1959).

Irving, David, *Hitler's War* (Avon Books: 1990).

Jung, Michael, *Sabotage Unter Wasser* (E.S. Mittler & Sohn: 2004).

Kurowski, Franz, *Deutsche Komandotrupps 1939–1945, Band I & II* (Motorbuch Verlag: 2003).

Lau, Manfred, *Schiffssterben vor Algier* (Motorbuch Verlag: 2001).

Lucas, James, *Kommando* (Arms & Armour Press: 1985).

Martienssen, Anthony, *Hitler And His Admirals* (E. P. Dutton & Co.: 1949).

Mattes, Klaus, *Die Seehunde – Klein U-Boote* (Verlag E.S. Mittler & Sohn: 1995).

Padfield, Peter, *War Beneath The Sea* (Pimlico: 1995).

Rohwer, Jürgen, *Axis Submarine Successes of World War Two* (Greenhill Books: 1999).

Rossler, Eberhard, *The U-Boat* (Arms & Armour Press: 1981).

Ruge, Friedrich, *The Soviets As Naval Opponents* (USNI: 1979).

Schulz, Werner, *Im Kleinst U-Boot* (Der Deutsche Bibliothek: 1995).

Showell, Jak Mallmann (ed.), *Führer Conferences On Naval Affairs* (Chatham Publishing: 2004).

Tarrant, V E, *Last Year of The Kriegsmarine* (Arms & Armour Press: 1994).

Suggested Websites

The U-Boat War (http://www.uboatwar.net)
U-Boat History (http://www.ubootwaffe.net)
U-Boat Operations (http://www.uboat.net)
Submarine Art Gallery (http://www.subart.net)
German Armed Forces History (http://www.feldgrau.com)
Japanese Submarine Operations (http://www.combinedfleet.com/sensuikan.htm)

Index